Dedication

Joe Frank Jones III died in January 2015. He was a fine academic who embraced a spirit of adventure for life that followed his adventures in philosophy. He was a dedicated teacher who will be missed by many students. He was also a great friend. This book is dedicated to his memory.

PJ & SB

Acknowledgements

I want to first thank my mother and father for their love and support. They served as my first view of what being an ethical human being is. I want to thank my loving wife, Amanda, and my sons Dillon and Clayton. They have taught me the true meaning of love and compassion. I also want to thank Kristi Haggard for her love and support. Growing up was a lot easier having you in my life. Glad to see the successes you have achieved including your beautiful family. I am proud to call you my sister. I want to thank my colleagues at the University of North Texas.

I want to thank my graduate assistants Nicole Boatman and Michelle Hassell. Thank you for all your hard work on this project.

SB

Each time I write a book or a research paper the patience, understanding and interest shown by Christine and Maxime surprises and delights. Thank you.

PJ

Contents

Chapter 10—Ethical Issues in Probation and Parole   111

Chapter 11—Ethical Issues and the Juvenile Justice System   121

Chapter 12—Racial Discrimination in the Criminal Justice System   141

Preface

Writing a book is both a pleasure and a pain. It causes the authors to embrace many emotions: intellectual stimulation, physical endurance, mental anxiety. It tests relationships: professional and personal. The result is that you are never the same person once the work is complete. Any book once finally published causes the authors to reflect; is it the best it could be, might we have put something differently, was an idea expressed quite how we meant it to be? Many of these challenges are of course what ethics and morals address, personal decision making within the context of the society in which we exist. So the preface to a book about ethics and morals is of itself something to cause an inward search. In this case, since our book is an edited volume that has drawn upon a number of voices, we, the editors, as authors and as editors, are stretched further by the challenges of reasoning out our own contributions and by those of the invited authors; our fallibility is exposed twofold. Fortunately we are all philosophers, including you the reader of this text. You can both empathize with us and criticize. We hope you do.

What follows from this preface is an exploration of ideas and information in and around ethical decision making. The vehicle for this discussion is criminal justice—because we want students and practitioners of criminal justice to be ethical, moral, and reasonable when they make decisions. We want this of all professions, but ours is the field of criminal justice and upper division criminal justice students are the primary audience for this text. We hope many others will be attracted to the discussion also and find the contents of this book stimulating and informative; the contributing authors have certainly provided a varied and challenging palette of offerings from pure philosophy to common sense practical professional advice. We, the editors, have shamelessly attempted to lure you into a fascinating discussion, not to curb your criticism of us but to alert you to the need for criminal justice practitioners to make informed, ethical judgments. In one part of this book the authors state, "Ethics is a matter that should be taken seriously. Working in the criminal justice system entails interacting with the American public and the community daily. Philosophically, ethics asks questions that pertain to how an individual comes to the conclusions of right and wrong. Individual beliefs vary; therefore, people must arrive at a satisfactory medium that allows civility and conformity within society. It is the duty of the criminal justice system to ensure that law and order is maintained and delivered based upon fairness and equity. Ethical behavior is expressed by an ethos that drives the rationality behind ethical decision making." The raison d'être for this book.

In the many years that we have been in the classroom it has become clear to us that our audience has reduced the volume of reading they consider necessary for mastery of a topic. The somewhat dated idea that students will read for the pleasure of gaining knowledge has required considerable personal modification over time. With this in mind we decided to attempt to write a book that would be practical and interesting. A book that students would continue to read beyond the required and specified quota. A book that students (might) enjoy. A book that would stimulate students to continue the dialog outside of the classroom. This book is not about absolutes; it is about further questions. It has to be because the subject matter itself is about formulating more questions based upon the questions you have already asked. We hope you enjoy the journey.

References have been included within the body of the text and also as notes. If we have missed a source or misquoted you, it is entirely unintentional and please accept the apology you deserve. In compiling this book our respect for the individuals working in the field of criminal justice has increased enormously. Our admiration for our contributing authors has intensified. We really did not always know you knew so much. This has been more fun than we anticipated. Please accept our gratitude.

SB & PJ
Denton, 2014

Contributing Authors

Scott H. Belshaw, Ph.D.

Dr. Scott Belshaw holds a Ph.D. in Juvenile Justice from Prairie View A&M University, a member of the Texas A&M University System. He earned his Bachelor of Science in Social Sciences and Psychology from the University of Houston – Downtown. He also holds both a Master of Liberal Arts from Houston Baptist University and a Master of Arts in Criminology from the University of Houston – Clear Lake. Dr. Belshaw's Ph.D. dissertation examined sexually abused females in the juvenile justice system. His dissertation research has been cited and used by numerous advocacy groups and organizations. He also served as a counselor and probation officer at Harris County, Texas' boot camp program. Dr. Belshaw was also the creator of the county's "Prison For a Day" program. This program was similar to the "Scared Straight" program in New Jersey. Dr. Belshaw has served as a probation officer and sentencing advisor to the judges of Harris County. Dr. Belshaw has published research in numerous academic journals such as *Criminal Justice Review*, *Criminal Justice Policy Review*, *Journal of Criminal Justice Education*, *American Journal of Criminal Justice*, *International Journal of Punishment and Sentencing*, *Southwestern Journal of Criminal Justice*, and numerous other educational and criminal justice related journals. Dr. Belshaw is also a veteran of the U.S. Navy and Naval Reserve and served during Operation Desert Storm.

Peter Johnstone, Ph.D.

Dr. Peter Johnstone is Professor of Criminal Justice at the University of North Texas and Scholar-in-Residence at the Caruth Police Institute, Dallas. He holds a doctorate in law, an L.L.M. in international criminal law, and an M.A. in history. Peter has worked in universities in the United Kingdom and the United States as a professor and senior administrator. He has published numerous articles and is author of twelve books.

Joe Jones, Ph.D.

Dr. Joe Jones is Professor and Chair of the Department of Philosophy and Religious Studies at Radford University. Joe was an Air Force brat. His father took the family to the Philippines for two tours, 5 1/2 years, and one tour in Germany, three years, and did an unaccompanied year tour in Korea when Joe was 6. When Joe was 17, he went to college at Clemson University, majored in beer, and flunked out. In late 1968, at 19 1/2 and with a 1-A draft classification prior to the lottery, he enlisted for 4 years in the Air Force. Between 1970 and 1972, he spent twenty-one months in Thailand, Vietnam, Cambodia, and Laos. When he was discharged early, just turned 23, he had spent about ten years abroad, which has affected his view of the world. This view is not so centered on the United States as the views of some folk. Better motivated, Joe tried college again, discovered it comfortable, and became a lifelong student. After 11 years, Florida State University said there were no more degrees he could get and threw him out with a Ph.D. in ancient Greek philosophy and mathematics, the history of science, logic, ethics, and a thing called metaphysics. He is still learning and appreciates the chance to speak with students concerning philosophical issues, which he sometimes considers ongoing therapy for himself. He wishes for students to also benefit from the conversations.

Charles Scheer, Ph.D.

Dr. Charlie Scheer is an Assistant Professor in the School of Criminal Justice at The University of Southern Mississippi. He has research specializations in police workforce management, police training, and organizational development. He received his Ph.D. from Michigan State University (2013). He also holds a master's degree in criminal justice from the University of South Carolina (2007) and a master's degree in history from Wake Forest University (1993). A former sheriff's deputy prior to his academic career, Dr. Scheer has publications on police recruitment and retention strategies, police civil liability, and a national assessment of police training capacities. His current work involves a multi-site training evaluation and case comparison study of internal sergeant and first-line supervisor training programs and curricula. His course teaching involves criminal justice ethics and police leadership.

Jaya Davis, Ph.D.

Dr. Jaya Davis is an Assistant Professor in the Department of Criminology and Criminal Justice at the University of Texas at Arlington. Her primary areas of research include juvenile justice and disproportionate minority contact, victimization, and criminal justice education. She holds a Ph.D. in juvenile justice from Prairie View A&M University (2011). She obtained a master's degree in criminology and a bachelor's degree in psychology, both from the University of Houston – Clear Lake, after serving six years in the United States Navy. Dr. Davis teaches a number of courses at the undergraduate and graduate levels including courses on ethics, juvenile justice and delinquency, institutional corrections, policy, and women and crime.

Julian L. Scott, III, Ph.D.

Dr. Julian Scott received a bachelor's degree in criminal justice from Fort Valley State University, and a Master of Science in Criminal Justice from Valdosta State University. He then received his Ph.D. in Juvenile Justice from Prairie View A&M University. Dr. Scott is passionate about teaching and research. He has been on the faculties of Texas Southern University, Wiley College, and currently Prairie View A&M University. Dr. Scott's area of interests are related but not restricted to criminological theory, race and crime, and education. Dr. Scott has published articles and chapters in various criminal justice journals and scholarly books.

Brooke Miller, Ph.D.

Dr. Brooke Miller is a lecturer in the Department of Criminal Justice at the University of North Texas. She received her Ph.D. in criminology from The University of Texas at Dallas. Her research interests include criminological theory, cybercrime and victimization, and community corrections.

Amanda Belshaw

Amanda Belshaw is a master's candidate in criminal justice and history at the University of North Texas. She has previously presented at conferences of the Academy of Criminal Justice Sciences, Phi Alpha Theta National History Honor Society, and the Texas Medieval Association. Her current research addresses witchcraft prosecution in England and Scotland, the development of Common Law in the United Kingdom and its application in the American Colonies, and capital punishment in the early Jamestown colony, all with a focus on connections to current legal and criminal procedure in the United Kingdom and the United States. Amanda is a former private investigator and has co-authored a book chapter on Allan Pinkerton, the father of modern private investigations. A native of Texas City, Texas, Amanda also has researched the history of organized crime and international connections in Galveston County.

Maria Eirini Papadouka

Maria Eirini Papadouka is a Ph.D. student and Teaching Fellow in the Department of Sociology of the University of North Texas, working on collaborating sociological and criminological perspectives especially in the area of organized crime, human trafficking, globalization, and media representations. She received her B.Sc. degree in Sociology from Panteion University of Social and Political Sciences in Athens, Greece in 2008 and her M.Sc. in Criminology, Criminal Justice and Social Research from University of Surrey, United Kingdom in 2009. In her spare time, she really enjoys travelling.

Phil Grant, J.D.

Phil Grant is currently the First Assistant District Attorney for Montgomery County, Texas. He received his undergraduate degree in Economics from the Virginia Military Institute. He received his law degree from the University of Texas at Austin. During his eight years as a prosecutor in Harris County, Texas he specialized in child sexual abuse and public integrity cases. He moved to Williamson County where he served as a chief felony prosecutor in the 26th and 368th District Courts while handling civil litigation matters including asset forfeitures for the local District Attorney's office. He was named Child Abuse Prosecutor of the Year in 2007 by the Williamson County Children's Advocacy Center and Child Protective Team.

Donley Jack

Mr. Jack is currently the Course Leader and a senior lecturer in the Criminology department at the University of West London in the United Kingdom. Mr. Jack received a BA Sociology (University of Greenwich), Pg.Cert Research (University of West London), MA Criminology (Middlesex University), M.Cert Critical Criminology and Criminal Justice (Universitat Des Saarlandes). He belongs to London Gangs Forum at the House of Commons. Mr. Jack also facilitates a study abroad program at the University of West London bringing criminology students to the United States to understand the legal and criminal justice system around the world.

Introduction to Ethical Theory and Practice

CHAPTER 1

"A person may cause evil to others not only by his actions but by his inaction, and in either case he is justly accountable to them for the injury."

—*John Stuart Mill, On Liberty*

"A man without ethics is a wild beast loosed upon this world."

—*Albert Camus*

"Bad people . . . are in conflict with themselves; they desire one thing and will another, like the incontinent who choose harmful pleasures instead of what they themselves believe to be good."

—*Aristotle, Nicomachean Ethics*

As a student sitting in a criminal justice class you might be asking yourself, "Why do I have to take this class?" You might also be saying to yourself, "How is this class going to help me—learning about what a bunch of old men in Ancient Greece were talking about over a thousand years ago?" Not to sound cliché, but we can learn from our past. We can learn from the experiences of others. Learning philosophy is about questioning what has been thought in the past and applying it to the present day. You will find that these old philosophers had a lot to say, and all of it was very relevant to the study of ethics. As one of my former philosophy professors would say, this book will serve as an intense (but we hope enjoyable) "ethical boot camp," investigating the ways that ethics are pertinent to professionals working in the criminal justice system. Let us begin our journey there.

What comes to mind when someone asks you, "What does being ethical mean to you?" Some people might think about the Bible and the Golden Rule ("Do unto others as you would have them do unto you"); others might think about a code of professional conduct such as the Hippocratic oath ("First of all, do no harm"). This is the oath that thousands of medical school graduates take each year before entering the medical profession. Others might think of the religious creeds such as the Ten Commandants. Either way you look at it, ethics is a part of our everyday lives no matter what profession we go into. As Resnik (2011) stated, "Most people learn ethical norms at home, at school, in church, or in other social settings. Although most people acquire their sense of right and wrong during childhood, moral development occurs throughout life and human beings pass through different stages of growth as they mature."[1]

Let us look at an example of an ethical conflict in our everyday lives. "You have worked as a bank teller for several months when one of the other tellers who has become a good friend tells you that her daughter is extremely ill and that she must have an operation to survive. She also tells you that she has no insurance and the operation will cost $10,000. Sometime later you ask her about her daughter and she tells you she is just fine now. She then confides in you that she took $10,000.00 from a dormant account at the bank to pay for the operation. She assures you that she has already started paying it back and will continue to do so until it is all returned."[2] What do you do? Do you notify the bank? Do you not say a word? Ethics and ethical dilemmas are constantly apart of our everyday lives.

Think about this from a criminal justice perspective for a moment. You are a police officer patrolling an area of town that you know to be drug infested. As you are driving, you see a car being driven very erratically. You observe the car weaving in and out of other vehicles, and then it almost hits a pedestrian. You clearly know that the driver must be intoxicated or under the influence of a controlled substance. This person meets all the standard signs and you have probable cause to pull him or her over. You pull the car over and cautiously approach the vehicle. You can smell a very strong odor of alcohol and marijuana as you approach the vehicle. You notice two young girls in the car. As you walk to the window you notice that the intoxicated driver is your sister. What would you do in this instance? Would you arrest her and her friend? Would you let them go?

Now, consider this scenario. You are working as an intern for a District Attorney's office. As the intern your role is to dig up background information from the internet on cases that are currently pending. The senior assistant district attorney asks you to pull up Facebook photos on the Internet of the defendant whose case is going to trial in a few weeks. You look at the defendant's Facebook page and you find pictures of the defendant smoking marijuana. In another picture you see the defendant using drugs but in the background you see a face that looks familiar. This face is of one of the other district attorneys in the office. Clearly, this has some serious legal implications. You're just an intern. What do you do?

The above scenarios give great examples why a student must study ethics not only in criminal justice but business, medicine and research, as well. The criminal justice field is about taking away someone's freedom and clearly making decisions in the lives of others. We all have to make some hard decisions in our lives. Wouldn't it help to have some roadmap of how to make the right decisions? It has been said that ethics is really about making the right decision when nobody is looking. As a criminal justice professional, whether in the police, the courts, or corrections, hard decisions are often made. Professionals working in the criminal justice system must ask themselves whether they are making the right decisions. Sometimes we must ask ourselves if making a decision is legal.

We often see this in the political arena. Legislators often make laws that define how a person must live and act. This is a tremendous amount of power to set guidelines on how a person must conduct himself. What is the right way to live? What is defined as moral? Another example of how moral decisions affect the criminal justice system is in the court system. Prosecutors have to decide if charges are to be pursued. Prosecutors also decide if the case will continue. Prosecutors have an ethical obligation to pursue justice rather than getting a conviction; however, as we have seen in the news, this issue is not always black and white.

"Philosophy or Not to Philosophy?" Understanding Ethics

Throughout the study of ethics you should be asking yourself numerous questions. This is a healthy part of coming to the right answer. You might spend most of your class asking more questions than getting answers. That is perfectly all right. What is the right thing to do? Are my actions moral? What are ethics? Am I an ethical person? What is morality? How can one behave in a moral manner? It is normal to ask these questions. It is also normal not to know the answers to them. Philosophy is not just learning about what other people have thought. The student must become an active inquirer, thinker, and solver of various problems. Studying philosophy is not about memorizing various ideas and regurgitating them on paper. Studying and learning philosophy is all about critical analysis.

This is the major goal of all academic institutions of higher learning—to develop critical analysis skills in their students.

When studying philosophy or ethics it is all right to be confused about the material that is given to you. Numerous times I have told my class that if you walk out of my class more confused than when you entered, that is a good thing. For college and university students, confusion is not a bad place to be. It shows that you are thinking about the issues. We do not all know the answers to the proverbial questions of life. Philosophers were trying to answer these questions 600 years ago and the closest they got is that the answer is different to all of us.

Working in the criminal justice system as a police officer, a probation officer, or as an attorney is one of the noblest professions that one can have. These people do not work for the money, glory, or fame. They work for the satisfaction that one day they might make a difference in a person's life. They also work in these fields to have an impact on society. This is unlike any job that most people can have.

Utilizing the above scenarios, it shows that decisions that professionals in the criminal justice system make might not be easy. To come to grips with this is one of the hardest things to do. Consider a police officer who is called to a scene of domestic violence. He observes the male figure pull out a gun and point it at a fellow officer or bystander. The officer must make a quick decision that could alter the suspect's life forever. Likely, the officer will shoot the individual and he will succumb to the wounds. The officer must carry this burden around his entire life—knowing that he took a person's life. The idea that the person was trying to take his life makes the burden a little bearable. However, guilty feelings will still linger. What if that person was going to hand him the weapon and give up? The officer perceived that the subject was going to shoot and kill him, but maybe that was not the suspect's intentions. Either way, we had an officer that had to make a quick decision. The officer must now explain his actions to his supervisors and administrators. He must also be able to explain his actions to a grand jury. Whatever happens, that officer will live with that split-second decision (right or wrong) for the rest of his life.

Having an understanding of ethics and ethical decision making can serve as a moral compass that helps one make the right decision in critical times. An understanding of ethics is equally important for individuals with great influence and in positions of power and prominence. Professionals in all aspects of criminal justice make critical decisions every day and their choices have a profound effect on our lives and the lives of the people in custody. It is very important that a person working in the policing field, the courts, or the correctional side of the justice system be free to make informed decisions that are unimpeded with bias and prejudice.

Understanding Ethics in Our Professional and Everyday Lives

How do we know what the right thing to do is? Where did we learn the difference between right and wrong? Some say that we learned from our families. Some might say that we learn right and wrong from our friends, and others might say that religion is a source where we learn it. More specifically, our mothers and fathers taught us to do the right thing. However, the definition of ethics and morality can be different from person to person. According to the Merriam-Webster Dictionary, "ethics" is defined as (1) "a discipline dealing with good and evil and with moral duty" or (2) "moral principles or practice." For the purposes of this discussion, we are examining morality and ethics as one and the same. Ethics is a term that is often tossed around with different meanings and connotations. The ancient philosophers such as Aristotle, Plato, and Socrates often debated what was ethical and moral. Some have defined ethics as a set of moral principles that guides human behavior (Braswell, 2008).

The word ethics comes from the Greek word *ethos*, meaning "character" or "belief," while the Latin word *moralis* means "character."[3] According to David Perry the words "ethics" and "morality" have Greek and Latin origins, respectively. Traditionally they referred to customary values and rules of conduct (as in "cultural ethos" and "social mores"), as well as insights about what counts as human excellence and flourishing. "Ethics" and "morality" are often used interchangeably today. But ethics also refers to moral philosophy, i.e., a discipline of critical analysis of the meaning and justification of moral beliefs.[4] As citizens of a community we often follow the laws of that jurisdiction. If a citizen breaks these laws, then the government has a duty to bring an action against the citizen for violating these rules. This action is often a criminal complaint. This complaint is based on the jurisdiction's penal code that the citizen violated. If the citizen has been found to break the law the person is punished in accordance with the law. The question we must ask ourselves is, is breaking the law a moral issue? Are there moral and ethical rules that we must follow that are not laws of the state? These are difficult questions because the answer is "sort of." Is murder an ethical violation? It is clearly a violation of the law, but what if a burglar breaks into your house with a gun and threatens you? Is it ethical to kill that burglar? The obvious answer is "yes." That person is threatening you and your family. However, it is still murder. So the moral to understanding what ethics and morality truly are is defined differently by each of us and depends on the "Zeitgeist"[5] or the spirit of the times. Morality can change over a particular period of history and over time. Essentially, what was illegal 40 years ago might be legal today or vice versa. For example gambling and prostitution are illegal in pretty much every state in the United States except Nevada. Prostitution is illegal in a few jurisdictions outside the major cities in Nevada. So what is legal in Nevada is a violation of the law when you travel into another state. The law that you break could send you to prison for some time. Think of the study of ethics as an ever-changing idea, with one minor caveat. There is a foundation that one builds to understand what is right and wrong, no matter what jurisdiction you might be in and what time you might be there. Think of understanding ethics as building that foundation with help from your family, friends, and religious affiliation. This foundation will serve to guide you in making decisions no matter what the situation is. This is why ethics is important. No matter what your role in criminal justice, you will be confronted with countless ethical challenges. Having a moral foundation will serve you in making the right decisions.

Professionals in the criminal justice system are often confronted with various tests of their ethical and moral decision making. For example, a police officer who stops his friend for driving while intoxicated will wrestle with the decision of arresting her or letting her go. In the court system, a prosecutor finds evidence that the defendant whom she is trying for a murder was not the murderer. Should the prosecutor continue with the case or turn over this evidence to the defense? A defense lawyer knows his client is guilty of domestic violence, but decides in the best interest of his client to discredit his wife with personal issues that might not be relevant to the case. And in the correctional system, a corrections officer could help an inmate out by giving him a postage stamp to mail a letter, even though this is a violation of the institution's policy. According to Pollack (2010), there are four common ethical elements that each criminal justice professional encounters:

- *Discretion*: The power to make a decision or act in a manner that the individual feels is right or correct.
- *The duty to enforce the law*: Service to the law is part of every criminal justice career and is expected even if the individual disagrees with the law itself.
- *The duty to uphold constitutional protections*: Fundamental to the Constitution are the concepts of due process and equal protection.
- *They are public servants*: The job of those in criminal justice is to serve the best interest of the citizens and they must hold themselves accountable to the public.

Each one of the above components is integrated into each one of the codes of ethics that police and correctional personnel are sworn to follow. According to Banks (2014), knowledge of ethics enables a person to question and analyze assumptions that are typically not questioned in areas of activity like business and politics. Questioning and challenging the criminal justice system should also be encouraged. This is what makes the system stronger for the persons who work in it or move through it. Banks (2014) also states that this includes raising issues regarding such topics as the relationship between crime and justice, the role of law enforcement, the place of punishment, the limits of punishment, the authority of the state, the proper function of prisons, fairness in the workplace through creating a safe working environment, and equal opportunity.

BOX 1.1

CODE OF ETHICS FOR TEXAS LAW ENFORCEMENT OFFICERS FROM THE TEXAS POLICE ASSOCIATION

AS A LAW ENFORCEMENT OFFICER, my fundamental duty is to serve the community; to safeguard lives and property; to protect the innocent against deception, the weak against oppression or intimidation, and the peaceful against violence or disorder; and to respect the Constitutional rights of all persons to liberty, equality and justice.

I WILL keep my private life unsullied as an example to all, and will conduct myself in a manner that does not bring discredit to me or to my agency. I will maintain courageous calm in the face of danger, scorn or ridicule; develop self-restraint; and be constantly mindful of the welfare of others. Honest in thought and deed in both my personal and official life, I will be exemplary in obeying the laws of the land and the regulations of my department. Whatever I see or hear of a confidential nature or that is confided to me in my official capacity will be kept ever secret unless revelation is necessary in the performance of my duty.

I WILL never act officiously or permit personal feelings, prejudices, political beliefs, aspirations, animosities or friendships to influence my decisions. With no compromise for crime and with relentless prosecution of criminals, I will enforce the law courteously and appropriately without fear or favor, malice or ill will, never employing unnecessary force or violence and never accepting gratuities.

I RECOGNIZE the badge of my office as a symbol of public faith and I accept it as a public trust to be held so long as I am true to the ethics of the police service. I will never engage in acts of corruption or bribery, nor will I condone such acts by other police officers. I will cooperate with all legally authorized agencies and their representatives in the pursuit of justice.

I KNOW that I alone am responsible for my own standard of professional performance and will take every reasonable opportunity to enhance and improve my level of knowledge and competence.

I WILL constantly strive to achieve these objectives and ideals, dedicating myself before God to my chosen profession . . . LAW ENFORCEMENT.

Source: Copyright © by Texas Police Association. Reprinted by permission.

Why Do We Study Ethics in Criminal Justice?

We nearly universally grant the public servants of our criminal justice system one important power in order to accomplish their day-to-day tasks. Discretionary power is the one commonality among all members of the criminal justice system. From the street level to the management level, we allow those public servants to make decisions based on their individual assessments of particular situations.[6] Certainly, public sector employees are bound by rule sets; however, these rules cannot define all possible situations that a public sector employee might encounter. Indeed, even if they could, we could not expect any one person to have adequately studied them all. Utilizing discretion in the everyday operation of the criminal justice system allows the system to adapt to nearly any situation it might encounter. It becomes necessary in many situations in which action might have to be taken immediately, prompting the need for crucial decisions to be made in a matter of seconds. Discretionary power is also mandatory for any unique situation in which there are no rules and regulations to act as a guide.

As expected, this power can be taken too far or the wrong decision could be made, requiring subsequent damage control. Being such an abstract concept, discretion can be hard to manage. However, the study of ethics can provide the criminal justice system with the tools necessary to train their personnel in quickly assessing a situation and making the most appropriate decision that they can. First, however, it is important to acknowledge that a decision can be made without any ethical standards.[7] Human nature provides us with inherent abilities to make decisions. These abilities include natural feelings such as emotional reaction or immediate instinct. Certainly, there are proponents of the "gut instinct" and those who support this concept suggest that following the decision you made in the first few seconds of analyzing a situation is likely the most correct decision.[8] Take, for instance, the person who is attempting to make a decision between which two items they should purchase. This person might finally depend on a coin toss to leave it up to random chance; however, supporters of the gut instinct would suggest that the person will know which item they want while the coin is up in the air regardless of whatever side the coin lands on. A further example would be an expert art appraiser recognizing a fake piece in the first few seconds he or she lays eyes on it and, without any sort of evidence, reporting to the museum that it had purchased a fake.[9] Of course, experts in their fields may be able to make monumental decisions in a matter of seconds, but not without basis for their decisions.

Ethics provides the groundwork for one of these bases. The study of ethics provides a unique and crucial framework for the moral decision making that will likely occur on the job; this is especially true as discretionary powers granted to criminal justice professionals are an integral and vital part of the criminal justice system. Ethical frameworks create a sense of what is morally right and morally wrong; in other words, without the study of ethics we cannot have an understanding or a working definition of what is unethical or morally incorrect behavior.[10] Certainly we could not have a universal understanding of what could be considered bad behavior. More importantly, having a working knowledge of ethics provides the grounds for analytical thinking and development.[11] By providing this groundwork, we are giving criminal justice professionals the ability to create their own understandings of right and wrong, thereby providing them with the tools they need to make the most morally correct decision. Banks (2014) also states that the study of ethics increases sensitivity to issues of right and wrong and the right way to conduct oneself, and aids in identifying acts that have a moral content. Banks (2014) indicates that only through studying ethics is it possible to define unethical behavior. A full understanding of ethical behavior demonstrates that it includes not only "bad" or "evil" acts, but also inaction that allows "bad" or "evil" to occur.

In a profession that requires discretionary judgment, it is imperative that individuals have an understanding of the ethical criteria and implications of their actions. Through this understanding, the criminal justice professional will be able to apply discretionary judgment in a responsible manner.[12] It will also increase the criminal justice professional's understanding that there are consequences that are attached to actions. An understanding of ethical reasoning will allow the professional to make decisions that will lead to the least dangerous of consequences. These professionals have a moral obligation to utilize their discretionary power in such a manner that denotes both responsibility to and the safety of the general public.[13] When confronted with decisions about matters such as the use of potentially deadly force, we need our criminal justice professionals to be able to make a morally correct decision in a matter of seconds. This concept is even more integral when taking into consideration that many professionals, especially in policing or corrections, are quick to dismiss an ethical framework. Many believe that it is a hindrance to their work and do not want to accept that at times what they believe is correct behavior is not always what is considered morally ethical behavior.[14] An anecdotal example of this might include improper interrogation techniques used to obtain confessions from suspects, such as actual acts of violence or threats of greater consequences that are perceived as true by those being questioned. These actions can lead to improper or false confessions.[15]

The argument can be made that many things that criminal justice professionals do or do not do are not necessarily illegal. Following the previous example of improper interrogations, lying to a subject to convince him or her to confess is not necessarily illegal; however, the argument could be made that lying is morally incorrect behavior.[16] What is law and what is ethics can be two completely different concepts. To understand this simply, laws are not, by definition, required to necessarily match ethical standards or requirements; however, ethical criteria can be occasionally reflected in the law.[17] Therefore we cannot consider what is law to be a standard for an ethical code of conduct.[18] Another factor to consider is that laws typically define what is explicitly illegal or regulate a specific type of conduct. Anything not defined in the law might be a perfectly legal action, but this is not a guarantee that it is a morally correct action. The study of ethics, then, provides a basis for criminal justice professionals to analyze a situation in which the law does not define their actions, and from that analysis make the most morally correct decision. The validity of ethical reasoning and understanding is, by the same rationality, not necessarily dependent on the law.[19]

Ethics, then, provides a means to police the discretionary powers that criminal justice professionals enjoy. Where laws and regulation do not define specific protocol, it becomes a free choice for the criminal justice professional to decide the manner in which he will handle a situation. As discussed previously, free choice is not necessarily regulated by any moral standpoint as it is humanly possible to make choices without analyzing or considering a situation. Training criminal justice professionals in ethics provides them with reasoning and analytical skills that will allow them to make ethical choices that will benefit not only the general public they serve, but also the organization in which they work. Ideally, an understanding of ethics might also allay issues of arbitrariness in the criminal justice professional's use of discretion. Understanding when and how to employ a use of force in a correctional facility or in the efforts of an arrest can be trained by understanding ethical analysis and reasoning. It is also important for police to know how to handle situations in which they must make a decision on whether or not it is appropriate or morally correct for them to enforce the law.[20] Certainly, it is vital for the criminal justice system to provide a means for their professionals to be able to make these decisions successfully.

Understanding ethical reasoning also provides professionals with a basis to understand when powers within the organization they work for are being abused. They will also be able to better recognize when the conditions placed around their work are immoral. Further, especially in policing, there is not only a sense of duty required to perform their job—it is expected to the point of requirement for an officer to have loyalty. This is true not only in regards to the citizens they protect, but also the people with whom they work. Indeed, the conditions placed upon this loyalty might make the professional believe that she should not act when she sees her fellow officers do something legally or morally incorrect.[21] An example of this might be a police officer who sees his partner taking bribes. Loyalty to their police bond of brotherhood might make that officer hesitate to report his partner. The question of whether or not whistleblowing is ethical does not only affect police officers; it also can be a part of other forms of public service. Table 1.1 indicates that police misconduct can come in various forms. It can range from using excessive force to being arrested on an alcohol-related offense. The criminal justice system is not unique when talking about the actions of others. Criminal justice practitioners are consistently scrutinized for their behavior. This scrutiny can consist of behavior at work and outside of their official duties. Police departments are even going as far as asking potential recruits to turn over their passwords to social media accounts. This will allow the agency to examine the potential officer's pictures and interactions on social media to determine if the officer will make good decisions while on the job. Do you think this is right? Should an agency that is sworn to protect the public be that intrusive in examining a person's background?

Without a comprehension of ethics, we cannot even begin to answer the question of whether whistleblowing is right or wrong; however, with an understanding of ethics it is possible to come to a consensus on what the morally correct behavior might be in situations such as the one in the example. Further, this is also applicable to situations of possible corruption or questionable conduct, especially in cases such as entrapment, undercover police work, the use of deadly force, or, in the case of corrections, when the use of significant or brutal force is necessary or appropriate.[22]

TABLE 1.1 2010 National Police Misconduct Statistics and Reporting Project (NPMSRP) Police Misconduct in the United States by Misconduct Type[25]

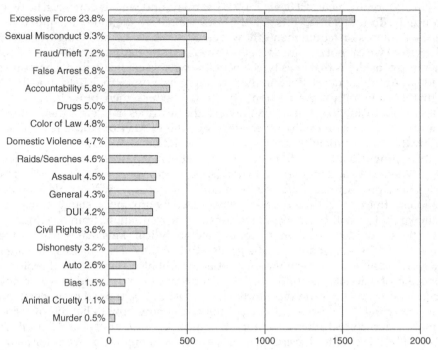

Source: Copyright © 2011 by The CATO INSTITUTE. Reprinted by permission.

Designing a basis of ethical standards will not only provide street-level employees with the tools they need to make these decisions, but it will also provide managers with a system of reference to review their employees against, thus further providing a method for criminal justice managers to monitor the use of discretionary powers by their employees.

It is not as if these situations that require an understanding of right and wrong as well as a basis for ethical reasoning are few and far between. On the contrary, these situations are quite common and it can be expected that criminal justice professionals will need to make ethically based decisions on a daily basis.[23] There are different levels of ethical dilemmas as well. One might have a personal ethical problem that must be resolved before one can attempt to perform one's duty. It may be difficult for a prison chaplain to sit on a deathwatch before an execution, for example, or a police officer working her beat might have a problem issuing a ticket to a man speeding to meet his wife who is in labor. It is important that individuals recognize these dilemmas and be capable of solving them. Simply, having an ethical issue arise on a personal level means we are human; being capable of solving that issue means we are capable individuals with a moral character. The other type of ethical dilemma is large-scale ethical issues.[24] These types of issues are typically issues involving social policies or laws that might be considered immoral. Laws involving segregation, for example, might be considered unethical or immoral. Again, it is useful to have an understanding of how to approach and manage these individual and large-scale dilemmas. Accomplishing this will provide increased safety and security for not only for the criminal justice professional, but also for the general public and the individuals the criminal justice professional might have to work with in the process of his or her job.

Ethics provides criminal justice professionals with the means to accomplish their jobs better while promoting the safety of the general public and protecting the interests of their departments. Understanding the difference between what is morally correct behavior and what is incorrect behavior is important in the day-to-day efforts of the criminal justice professional. While discretionary power is vital to the operation of the criminal justice system, it is equally vital that the individual know how to utilize their discretion properly. Understanding what moral behavior is will provide the professionals who must make quick decisions with a means to properly analyze their situations and reason their way to the best decision they can make, instead of reacting with an emotional or instinctual response. Knowing the difference between what is morally right and what is morally wrong will provide criminal justice professionals with sufficient guidelines to make good decisions when they are presented with a situation in which there is no regulation or law to guide them. They will also be able to understand that the ends do not always justify the means, especially if the means chosen are immoral. Ultimately, the study of ethics not only creates professionals who are capable of informed decision making, but also provides the means to improve the safety and wellbeing of not only the people they serve, but also the criminal justice professionals themselves.

UNDERSTANDING ETHICAL THEORY AND THE PHILOSOHY OF ETHICS

The first thing that students think when they walk into a criminal justice ethics class is "How much philosophy do I have to know?" They often get very nervous because they feel that they will not understand what is being said in class. That is not an uncommon feeling when walking into an ethics class. The good news is that you really think about these ethical and moral challenges every day. Let me give you an example. This morning you woke up and decided if you were going to come to class. You were lying in bed with an ethical dilemma, a simple dilemma, but nevertheless a dilemma, deciding if you were going to come to class or not. You weighed all the options. You might have said to yourself, "I have been going to class all semester, so I am good" or "I have been missing too much so I might need to go." Another calculus that was being decided was your overall heath. Maybe your throat was sore and you decided to rationalize that you did not want to get anyone sick; therefore, going to class was not a good idea. Do these sound familiar? I am sure they do. Do not worry, before we were crotchety old professors we were students as well. This was a dilemma. Somehow you resolved it: Good or bad.

BOX 1.2

POLICE MISCONDUCT LAWSUITS AND THE DALLAS POLICE DEPARTMENT

- March 2014: The Dallas City Council approves a $1.1 million settlement for Ronald Jones, who was beaten up and jailed on a charge of aggravated assault against a public servant in December 2009. The charge was later dropped, and dash-cam video contradicted much of the officer's account of the incident.

- January 2014: A jury awards Olivia Lord $800,000 after finding that a homicide detective wrongly jailed her on a murder charge. Video of an interrogation shows the detective yelling at her that she was guilty.

- December 2013: The City Council approves $1.15 million for the family of Fred Bradford, who was fatally struck by a squad car while he was apparently trying to elude officers on his bicycle on April 21, 2013. The lawsuit alleged that the officers moved evidence and tried to cover up the incident.

(Continued)

BOX 1.2 (Continued)

- June 2013: The City Council approves a $435,000 settlement for James Gurski. The lawsuit alleged that Gurski was discriminated against after he told supervisors that he had mental disorders that limited his ability to work a patrol rotation. He was placed on leave, and bulletins with his picture were posted all over police buildings saying he was not allowed inside. He also alleged that officers were assigned to monitor him and guard his supervisors.

- June 2012: The City Council approves a $423,000 settlement for Lavell Fairbanks. He alleged that officers beat him repeatedly in the head with a flashlight, which later led to the removal of part of his skull.

- June 2012: The City Council approves a $500,000 settlement for Rodarick Lyles. Dash-cam video showed an officer kicking Lyles in the head and pepper spraying him after he was handcuffed and lying on the ground motionless.

- May 2012: The City Council approves a $500,000 settlement for Andrew Collins. Dash-cam video showed Collins, who was fleeing officers on a motorcycle in September 2010, get clipped by a squad car. The video then showed officers beating him on the ground.

- February 2012: A jury awards Thomas Hannon $169,000. Hannon was arrested in 2007 after police said he was holding a bag with guns and drugs outside a hotel. He spent 10 months in county jail awaiting trial before the charge was dropped. Surveillance video showed he was not the suspect in the case. His attorneys accused officers of hiding the video.

Source: REPRINTED WITH PERMISSION OF *THE DALLAS MORNING NEWS*.

Ethics is a branch of philosophy focused on studying and understanding what is right and what is wrong. Its intention is to design a series of standards of what is ethical and unethical behavior and then apply these standards to ethical dilemmas and controversy. Of course, the study of ethical philosophy and theory is more complicated than that, but this serves as an easy-to-understand definition of the field. Those who study ethics are concerned with defining a system of morally correct behavior that can then be applied to defining appropriate ways to live our everyday lives. On an even more complex level, ethical philosophers are interested in understanding good and evil as well as what causes people to make these good or evil choices.

What is the purpose of studying such an abstract and complex idea? The reason is twofold. First, creating a system of understanding ethically correct or incorrect behavior is useful so that people can make beneficial decisions that will not intentionally harm anyone. This is useful in everyday life decisions from something as simple as deciding whether or not it is appropriate to hit a sibling, to deciding if it is appropriate to steal from someone. Ethical theory is also useful in various professional fields such as criminal justice or business practices. Police officers might have to make the decision of whether or not to use deadly force in the process of an arrest or a business professional might be faced with decisions to use unsafe means in order to generate a product that will produce a profit.

In many of these situations, however, incorrect behavior can be justified by the particular elements of the situation at the time. This is where the second reason for studying ethics comes in. It is useful to create a systematic understanding of what is right and what is wrong that allows for us to have a homogenous concept of correct and incorrect behavior. For example, in Victor Hugo's *Les Miserables*, the character Jean Valjean steals a loaf of bread because his family is starving. Certainly, this is justifiable behavior; he chose to steal to save his family. Ethicists, however, would argue that his behavior was still morally incorrect. In this example, it is quite easy to understand how stealing might be ethically incorrect; however, life presents us with situations in which the lines of what is correct behavior can become much more blurred.

Ethics is obviously a complicated field of study, so ethical philosophers have broken ethics down into three major categories: meta-ethics, normative ethics, and applied ethics. These three categories of ethics allow for ethical philosophers to develop the complex theories of ethics without being limited by how abstract the concept of ethics is.

Meta-Ethics

This area of study is certainly the most abstract of ethical fields. The prefix *meta-* comes from a Greek word meaning after or beyond. When applied to a theory, it typically refers to understanding and developing the methods behind the theory or its language and reasoning. Someone who studies meta-ethics might seek to find the answer behind what the words right and wrong mean. Meta-ethics is in part concerned with answering two major thoughts. The first is whether or not the concept of morality is independent from humans. What this question asks is whether humans created and defined morals and, thus, without humans, morality would not it exist, or if morality is somehow spiritual or divine in nature and that all things must adhere to it. The purpose behind this particular study of ethics is effectively to look at the field from an unbiased third-person perspective. Meta-ethics is also concerned with answering questions such as the meaning of the words good and bad, or what right and wrong might mean. By answering these questions, meta-ethical philosophers intend to establish the language in which normative and applied ethics can base their theories. Ideally, meta-ethics helps prevent human traits or weaknesses, such as emotional reactions, from biasing the field as a whole, allowing for a more proper homogenous ethical understanding to emerge. Meta-ethics is not interested in defining specific ethical standards as much it is in describing the appropriate language and methods of reasoning found in ethical study.

Normative Ethics

This field of study is much less abstract in comparison to meta-ethics, but no less complex. Where meta-ethics focuses on developing an abstract understanding of ethics, normative ethics is concerned with developing methods of ethical reasoning and behavior and developing standards of ethical conduct. Ideally, this form of ethics provides a means to understand and subsequently instill moral decision making into the process of everyday behavior. The actual study of normative ethics is much more concrete than this basic definition. Theorists who study normative ethics believe that there is one set of concrete criteria that makes up ethical behavior. For example, a basic normative ethics theory would be something along the lines of "do unto others as you would have them do unto you." In more relatable terms, you would not want someone to steal your wallet, so you should not steal someone else's wallet. Or perhaps another normative ethics theory might be to "do no harm." This theory might suggest that you should consider all your actions before you perform them so that you do not hurt anyone or anything; if your action does harm, then it should be considered morally incorrect.

Normative ethics can be split into several separate fields of study. Consequentialism is one such field. More on this theory will be discussed in Chapter 4. Consequentialism is the theory that the way you go about accomplishing an action does not matter as long as the action is for the greater good; consequences justify a person's actions. In a more colloquial turn-of-phrase: the ends justify the means. Basically consequentialism is concerned with something called the greater good. If your actions serve the greater good they can be considered ethically correct. Perhaps an example of this might be an action movie hero who has to redirect a nuclear missile in such a way that it destroys a small inhabited island in order to save a giant metropolis. Consequentialism would say that the hero's actions were morally correct because the end result of saving a million people is better than the action of killing a few hundred.

The response to consequentialism is a theory called deontology. This theory focuses on the understanding that as human beings we have certain imperative duties that we must accomplish in life. For example we have an obligation not to commit murder or parents have a duty to care for their children. Deontology is less concerned with the greater good and more concerned with an individual's considerations for his or her own actions; in other words, the means cannot be justified by the end result. Philosopher Immanuel Kant is one such deontologist; his theory focused on what he called the categorical imperative. Kant's imperative suggested that ethical behavior is black and white. One cannot justify one's actions by the result they achieved, the action is either right or it is wrong. In our wallet example, Kant would say stealing someone's wallet is wrong because then you are using that person via his or her wallet to achieve your own happiness. When you choose to commit to an action, you must not consider the most favorable end result, but instead focus on choosing the most moral individual action. Kant would argue that our action hero committed an unethical act when he chose to direct the missile into the inhabited island, despite the fact that the act saved a million people.

Applied Ethics

Discussing ethical issues is probably the most common use of ethical theory and philosophy. Topics such as animal rights, the death penalty, or abortion might be controversial ethical subjects that can enter into everyday conversation. Applied ethics is a branch of ethics in which social scientists analyze controversial ethical issues and attempt to resolve them through the use of applied ethical standards. Typically, controversial topics in which there is no clear moral answer are the subject of applied ethical study. It is important to remember, however, that just because a topic might contain a controversial or sensitive subject does not always make it a moral issue. Gay marriage is a modern controversial example: certainly it is the subject of much media coverage and public opinion; however, marriage in general is a social policy not a moral one. Conversely, an ethical controversy does not have to be a social policy issue. For example, teenage promiscuity and pregnancy might be an ethical issue; however, this issue does not necessarily mean that social policy involving teenage promiscuity needs to arise from the debate.

BOX 1.3

AMERICAN CORRECTIONS ASSOCIATION
CODE OF ETHICS

Preamble

The American correctional Association expects of its members unfailing honesty, respect for the dignity and individuality of human beings and a commitment to professional and compassionate service. To this end, we subscribe to the following principles.

- Members shall respect and protect the civil and legal rights of all individuals.
- Members shall treat every professional situation with concern for the welfare of the individuals involved and with no intent to personal gain.
- Members shall maintain relationships with colleagues to promote mutual respect within the profession and improve the quality of service.
- Members shall make public criticism of their colleagues or their agencies only when warranted, verifiable, and constructive.
- Members shall respect the importance of all disciplines within the criminal justice system and work to improve cooperation with each segment.

- Members shall honor the public's right to information and share information with the public to the extent permitted by law subject to individuals' right to privacy.
- Members shall respect and protect the right of the public to be safeguarded from criminal activity.
- Members shall refrain from using their positions to secure personal privileges or advantages.
- Members shall refrain from allowing personal interest to impair objectivity in the performance of duty while acting in an official capacity.
- Members shall refrain from entering into any formal or informal activity or agreement which presents a conflict of interest or is inconsistent with the conscientious performance of duties.
- Members shall refrain from accepting any gifts, services, or favors that is or appears to be improper or implies an obligation inconsistent with the free and objective exercise of professional duties.
- Members shall clearly differentiate between personal views/statements and views/statements/positions made on behalf of the agency or Association.
- Members shall report to appropriate authorities any corrupt or unethical behaviors in which there is sufficient evidence to justify review.
- Members shall refrain from discriminating against any individual because of race, gender, creed, national origin, religious affiliation, age, disability, or any other type of prohibited discrimination.
- Members shall preserve the integrity of private information; they shall refrain from seeking information on individuals beyond that which is necessary to implement responsibilities and perform their duties; members shall refrain from revealing nonpublic information unless expressly authorized to do so.
- Members shall make all appointments, promotions, and dismissals in accordance with established civil service rules, applicable contract agreements, and individual merit, rather than furtherance of personal interests.
- Members shall respect, promote, and contribute to a work place that is safe, healthy, and free of harassment in any form.

Source: TO COME

Applied ethics is based upon the very simple concept that, if you take the standards of ethics developed through normative ethics and you apply them directly to the controversy at hand, you will find the answer to your moral conflict. In practice, this concept is a lot more complex. The standards built in normative ethics often do not agree with each other. Take consequentialism and deontology, at their core they are two completely different ethical principles—consequentialism is concerned with the end result and less with the means while deontology insists that the means are more important than the end result. However, normative ethical theory is much more expansive than these two topics—issues such as a person's rights, or what justice is, or social and personal benefits are at the heart of normative ethics.

Let us take, for instance, a pregnant woman who has just been informed by her doctor that if she carries her pregnancy to term there is a great chance she will die. The baby will likely be born with extreme physical defects and the doctor cannot guarantee that the baby will survive, but it just might. The ethical dilemma here is clear: do the parents choose to abort the child to save the mother, or do they choose to allow the child to be carried to term at the risk of the mother with the chance that the baby could live a long life? Someone who studies in ethical theory might say that the parents are justified in aborting the child since the end result would be the guaranteed survival of the mother. Other theorists might argue that the act of aborting the child is wrong and the parents are duty bound to carry the child to term and care for its survival.

The result of this complication is that those who study applied ethics attempt to weigh the evidence of the ethical dilemma against the normative standard and come up with the most desirable solution that they can.

Ethical Relativism

Ethical relativists theorize that morality is relative to a particular culture or social group. In this theory, standards of ethics cannot be applied universally because they will vary by country or culture. These relativists do not believe that we cannot judge a culture on their moral beliefs, but it is necessary to accept that they have different moral beliefs. However, if one accepts ethical relativism is correct then the concept of finding a standard of ethics and applying it universally cannot be correct. This would contradict many of the standards of both normative ethics and applied ethics. For this reason, many ethical theorists disagree with ethical relativism. An ethical realist might argue that because there is no proven absolute ethical standard that can be applied universally, the possibility of an ethical standard does not exist. This is called an *ad ignorantiam* argument, which is an argument in which a premise is considered true simply because it has not been proven false or that a premise is considered false simply because it has not been proven true.

Ethical relativism has provided a beneficial point of view to the study of ethics, however, in that it raises the point that different cultures and social groups have different beliefs of what is ethical and unethical behavior. Relativism gives a way to study the reasons why these different groups think the way that they do.

Ethics is a complex and abstract field of study. Many different ideas must be understood and established in order to generate a foundation upon which ethical reasoning can be developed. It is necessary, for example, to study the field of meta-ethics in order to begin developing the basis for normative ethics.

In general, ethics is an important field of study with many applications. Business education, for example, will often include a class on ethics to give students and idea of what business practically are ethically correct or incorrect. More importantly, ethical study provides us with the means to work through ethical dilemmas that might occur in everyday life. Ideally, establishing a universal understanding of ethical standards will provide a method for determining exactly what is good behavior and what is bad behavior. Ethical theorists have not designed a universal standard of ethical behavior, but they have established an understanding of how to decide what action to take in the face of difficult moral questions. Ethical standards are especially useful any time a profession provides for discretionary powers – in which one can make their own decisions on how to approach a situation when there are no rules or regulations on how to guide them. Ethical dilemmas might not always be as dramatic as an action hero who has to redirect a nuclear missile, but the circumstances behind a real life ethical dilemma might be just as difficult and have just as devastating consequences. Deciding when it is appropriate to see military retaliation, for example, or on a smaller scale, deciding whether or not to apply the use of force in the course of an arrest.

Ethics is broken into three primary fields of study: meta-ethics, normative ethics, and applied ethics. Each field is an important building block for the design of ethical philosophy and theory. They help create the framework to design concrete standards that are useful to everyone out of abstract concepts.

Meta-ethics is the most abstract of the ethical fields of study. Philosophers who study in this field are concerned with establishing the language and the reasoning methods behind understanding ethics. Meta-ethical philosophers attempt to answer questions such as what the terms good and evil really mean. They are also interested in establishing an understanding of whether or not ethics is a human creation bound only to humans or if ethics belongs to something greater and humans are simply defining it for themselves. Meta-ethics is concerned primarily with developing a solid basis for the other two ethical fields to build upon.

Normative ethics is interested in establishing ethical standards to follow. Theorists who study normative ethics believe that there is one universal standard of ethics. Consequentialists, for example, believe that the ends justify the means. As long as the consequence of an action is favorable to the action itself, the action is ethical. Deontologists, on the other hand, believe that everyone has certain duties and obligations to which they must adhere. They do not believe that the consequences of an action can justify the action itself. Despite conflicting views, these different standards of ethics provide a framework through which ethics can be applied.

Applied ethics is the practical application of ethics to everyday dilemmas. If you take the standards of ethics developed through normative ethics and apply them to the moral dilemma at hand, you will be able to solve your moral dilemma. Typically applied ethics is used to discuss controversial ethical dilemmas such as animal rights or abortion. Those who study applied ethics often try to weigh the evidence of the dilemma against a normative standard and attempt to come up with the most favorable solution to the dilemma.

Ethical study is clearly useful for establishing criteria to understand and reason through various ethical dilemmas. Ethics can be applied to individual problems or applied to large-scale issues to come up with favorable outcomes to various dilemmas. Developing a standard of ethics can provide an ethical framework with which appropriate decisions can be made in many difficult situations, such as the discretionary issues that criminal justice professionals face every day.

ENDNOTES

1. What is Ethics in Research & Why is it Important? by David B. Resnik, J.D., Ph.D. Article can be found at http://www.niehs.nih.gov/research/resources/bioethics/whatis/

2. Ethical dilemma taken from http://www.differencemakers.com/swapshop/pdf/dilemma_examples.pdf

3. Charlton T. Lewis & Charles Short, *A Latin Dictionary*, Oxford: Clarendon Press, 1879.

4. Ethics in Public Service. By Dr. David L. Perry. *Adapted from a workshop conducted for Leadership Santa Clara on 8 June 2000. http://www.scu.edu/ethics/publications/submitted/Perry/service.html*

5. *Oxford Dictionary* (2014) defines Zeitgeist as "The defining spirit or mood of a particular period of history as shown by the ideas and beliefs of the time."

6. Lipsky, M. (2010). *Street-Level Bureaucracy: Dilemmas of the Individual in Public Services*. Russell Sage Foundation: Lipsky's work further explains why discretion is necessary in the day-to-day operations of all public service systems. He attributes this not only to the fact that it would be impossible to contain all possibilities within a set of rules and regulations, but also to the human element involved in public works. Street-level bureaucrats, as Lipsky calls them, have the most direct interaction with the public and therefore the public's individualized needs. The tasks that these employees encounter also tend to be "complex and human intervention is considered necessary for effective service."

7. Banks, C. (2013). *Criminal Justice Ethics* (3rd ed.). Banks, C. *Criminal Justice Ethics: Theory and Practice*: without an ethical basis, emotional or instinctual decisions lack moral qualifiers to justify behavior. In other words, a person without an understanding of what is right and what is wrong is as likely to make an immoral decision as to make a moral one. However, the argument for ethics is that we cannot leave such important decisions to chance.

8. Gladwell, M. (2005). *Blink: The Power of Thinking Without Thinking*. Back Bay Books.

9. In the introduction to *Blink*, Gladwell describes an anecdote in which the J. Paul Getty Museum in California was approached by an art dealer who had a marble statue dated from the 6th century B.C.E. After conducting many tests on the statue, the museum could not find any evidence

that the statue was a fake. Before purchasing it, they asked several experts to come look at the statue. Within seconds of looking at the statue, the experts informed the museum that they believed the statue was a fake. Further testing and research was ordered, and once completed it was clear that the statue had indeed been faked.

10. See Banks, Chapter 1.

11. Banks ibid.

12. Felkenes, G. T. (1987). Ethics in Graduate Criminal Justice Curriculum. *Teaching Philosophy*, 23–36.

13. Felkenes ibid.

14. ibid.

15. Further anecdotal examples of these interrogation techniques that lead to false confessions in particular can be found in the Anthology *True Stories of False Confessions*. The anthology is separated into several primary segments of what could be considered morally incorrect police behavior in interrogations such as taking advantage of mental fragility, verbally abusive techniques to obtain confessions from juveniles, and techniques that include brute force. Drizin, S. A., Warden, R. (2009). *True Stories of False Confessions*. Northwestern University Press.

16. As Felkenes suggests in his curriculum article, many police interrogators would disagree with this sentiment. They might believe their behavior is right because it achieves a result. They might also not believe that their behavior should come under moral or ethical fire. This might be a result of the fact that their behavior might not be necessarily illegal, or that they consider their behavior as a means to an end.

17. See Banks.

18. In her text, Banks provides the example of laws on slavery in the United States or more recently the Apartheid laws in South Africa. We can recognize, especially in this modern era, that these laws are immoral. Nevertheless when these laws existed they were expected to be obeyed and enforced.

19. Ibid Banks.

20. These are questions suggested by Felkenes in his graduate curriculum paper. See note 8 for reference.

21. Ibid Felkenes.

22. ibid.

23. See Banks.

24. Ibid Banks.

25. Of the 6,613 law enforcement officers involved in reported allegations of misconduct that met NPMSRP criteria for tracking purposes, 1,575 were involved in excessive force reports, which were the most prominent type of report at 23.8% of all reports. This was followed by sexual misconduct complaints at 9.3% of officers reported, then theft/fraud/robbery allegations involving 7.2% of all officers reported. The following chart displays the breakdown of misconduct types by percentage of reports and the number of reports each by type.

The Importance of Ethics in Criminal Justice

"I count him braver who overcomes his desires than him who conquers his enemies, for the hardest victory is over self."

—*Aristotle*

The criminal justice system is arguably one of our most important public service systems. Certainly, it is one of the systems the public is likely to interact with on a daily basis. Often, those employed by the criminal justice system are forced into situations in which they must make individualized and quick decisions—decisions that could have detrimental or even fatal outcomes. Without proper training or proper analytical or reasoning skills, law enforcement, legal professionals, or corrections officers could find themselves forced to recover from the fallout of poor decision making. As a public works system that is tasked with protecting and defending the public from crime and the dangers crime presents, the criminal justice system has an obligation to have and maintain all of the tool sets it might need to be capable of handling these situations to the absolute best of its ability. The study of ethics presents an opportunity for the criminal justice system to give its members such an abstract tool set.

Ethics, at its simplest, is philosophy that is interested in the study of questioning what is right and what is wrong. The study of ethics presents a more complicated understanding of the philosophy, but it still stands as a basic building block with which the criminal justice system can ensure, to the best of its ability, that its public servants have a method of determining what is right and what is wrong. Of course, from an academic perspective, further understanding of ethics is necessary to fully develop a curriculum to teach the public servants of the criminal justice system. First, however, it is necessary to establish why ethics is vital.

Consider this example . . .

You have just completed training at the police academy and you are on a ride along in a suburban neighborhood with your FTO (Field Training Officer), Officer Jones. The day is rather quiet and a fellow officer going in the opposite direction stops to exchange casual conversation about the day while you attentively observe the people and surroundings. A car stops to allow two children riding their bikes to cross the street, then continues after the children safely cross the street. Your FTO does not realize that there is not a stop sign because the car commands attention—it is quite flashy, with new rims and dark tint on the windows. The FTO views the vehicle as suspicious because he knows the neighborhood and has not seen this car before. He stops the car and you observe as the FTO walks to the passenger side of the vehicle. The driver is an African American male with his son they are going home from the neighborhood convenience store.

You notice that your FTO's tone is abrasive as he asks the age of the driver's son. The other officer casually pulls behind the squad car driven by the FTO and smirks as your FTO takes a seemingly aggressive posture towards the driver and his son. Afterwards, he runs the license and insurance of the driver. Everything is valid. The driver's wife, going by in her car, sees what is happening and pulls over to ask what is going on. Your FTO sharply instructs her mind her business and stay in her vehicle. The driver and his wife adamantly explain to the officer that there is not a stop sign and he stopped to yield the right of way to the children riding their bikes in the neighborhood. The driver and his wife explain that they just bought a home in the quiet suburb and are both employed by the nearby college. Your FTO proceeds to write the driver a ticket for failure to stop at a stop sign. The driver grudgingly accepts the ticket, and he and his wife drive away in their cars. Your FTO remarks, "You can never be too careful about those types of people." You are caught off guard by the FTO's comment, yet quietly feel bad because of his actions. Your FTO then goes to explain, "It's citation time and a little slip here or there won't hurt anyone. Welcome to the team, rookie—it's okay to cut a few corners." Remember, you are a rookie and you do not want to ruffle any feathers within the precinct—especially not on your first day on the job. *First of all, were the FTO's actions ethical? Second, whether the actions were or were not ethical, what do you do?*

IMPORTANCE OF ETHICS AND ETHICAL DECISIONS IN CRIMINAL JUSTICE

The criminal justice system maintains its own system of values that is distinct from other fields and occupations. Additionally, the criminal justice system in many aspects can be referred to as a *subculture* that maintains a distinct set of rules and regulations, codes, and symbols (i.e., firearms, uniforms, badges) with rules that differ from those in mainstream society. Coser (1974) expounds the notion of the criminal justice profession by comparing it to a "greedy institution," meaning that the institution itself does not literally intend to incarcerate every individual, but it seeks the unmitigated commitment to the profession while navigating through a wider social context. Additionally, it demands total allegiance to the institution yet mentally severs its members' ties from institutions that are in conflict with its function (i.e., family and community). The criminal justice institutions must establish specific guidelines and must reinforce a myriad of ideas that directly impact the legitimacy of the law enforcement apparatus in an ever-changing society. Specific rules, regulations, and sanctions must be adhered to in order to maintain structure and order among and between individuals whom the law enforcement community must govern. Individuals who work within the legal community, especially law enforcement, are not far displaced from the average individual. Humans by nature are imperfect. Possibly, then, great value must be placed upon a strong ethical foundation to carry out the mission of law enforcement. Philosophers such as Plato have made the argument that ethical behavior is a set of ideas that cannot be taught but rather it is an essential element that is taught throughout an individual's upbringing. Even the most ethical person might argue that ethical behavior would be difficult to measure because ethical decision making varies by the individual; in fact, each person maintains a different set of values that they bring to their occupation. Moral reasoning is a key element that is fundamental to understanding ethics.

The Value of Ethics to Maintain Civility

Rokeach (1973) and Zho, He, & Lovrich (1998) would agree that a society would not maintain order if a sense of utility was absent. Behaviors vary amongst individuals as well as cultures, therefore members of society must agree upon what is best for the entire group to establish structure and order to achieve a desirable means to an end. The achievement of a positive outcome gives society what is called *terminal value*. Criminal justice agencies and practitioners must reinforce the values that society has already agreed upon. Moreover, it is vital that the criminal justice community be highly committed to ethical standards that surpass those of an ordinary citizen. Philosophers like Plato realized that the concept of ethics might require an individual to evaluate his or her decision making from a broad perspective. In theory, *ethics* could be considered as the postulates that are solely based on the study of the right conduct and the good life (Sahkian & Sahkian, 1966: 31). Most important, when the good life is achieved, the end result or *end state* results from the realization that good is a counter reaction to immoral behavior.

Ethics can be considered to be judgments that involve the application of what an individual would consider to be moral. Philosophically, ethical values can be based upon an interpersonal belief of what is considered to be moral or immoral behavior based upon the observation of a variety of societal forces in action. Ethics can be considered those guidelines or a moral compass that determine whether a society lives harmoniously or thrusts itself into utter chaos. Most importantly, the criminal justice system acts as enforcers of the laws created based upon consensus and our own interpretation and insight coupled with the interpersonal beliefs of what is considered ethical behavior. Ethical behavior is based upon an *ethos*, or what one would call a particular set of values, that would either rationally support or conflict with a particular set of values that directly or indirectly affect an individual's actions. For example, Whisendhand (2006) clarifies ethics by examining the following set of values as a means to distinguish the moral character and guided beliefs of an individual or group. Does your ethos support or conflict with your ethics?

- Compassion
- Respect
- Discretion
- Accountability
- Integrity
- Respect for others
- Honor
- Loyalty

Let us make the assumption that we possess these values. Now, does your ethos agree? Most importantly, are your actions reflective of these values? Additionally, knowing what's right, being committed to it, and doing it are vital to performing the duties of a criminal justice practitioner.

THE PLATONIC CAVE

Ethical socialization within the criminal justice organization derives from interpersonal ideology and training. Criminal justice is broken down into two broad categories: law enforcement and corrections. Ethics, however, is construed simplistically as those moral choices between right and wrong behavior. Professionals who work within the criminal justice field are faced with moral dilemmas on a daily basis. Training on ethics in criminal justice must often highlight the dilemmas that are faced in this particular occupation. Plato eloquently explains such moral dilemmas in the dialogue between Socrates and Cephalus when Socrates says, "But what about this thing you mentioned, *doing right?* Shall we say it is, without qualification, truthfulness and giving back anything that one has borrowed from someone? Or might the performance of precisely these actions sometimes be right but sometimes wrong? This is the kind of thing that I mean. I'm sure everyone would agree that if I borrowed weapons from a friend who was perfectly sane, but he went insane and asked for the weapons back, and if you give them back you wouldn't be doing the right, and neither would someone who was ready to tell the whole truth to someone like that" (Plato, 1993: 8). The dialogue between Socrates and Cephalus shifts our attention to why moral choices are made with regard to absolute terms. Consequently, the absolute terms can and will result in individuals contradicting themselves when making ethical decisions.

The Platonic caves are those instances where moral choices may be considered right, yet the dilemma may contradict the proposed action. Plato ironically views the cave as a place that is dark and inferior yet when we remove our minds from that darkness, we view things in a different manner. There may be times that we are overcome by the shadows of the consequences of decisions that have been made, but once we have left the caves that consume normative thinking, realities of the decisions that are made begin to sink in. For example, a police officer notices a car slightly swerving and proceeds to stop it. The driver happens to be a sergeant in the same precinct. The sergeant is noticeably intoxicated, but he lives around the corner from the initial stop. The officer looks at "Sarge" and says: "Go home, sir, and sober up. See you at roll call." This example is considered to be a Platonic cave. The sergeant is one of "you," so you let him go. Would the officer's reaction be the same if the intoxicated driver were a different individual who lived in the neighborhood? Of course the answers would vary, but nonetheless a decision was made that the officer perceived to be in the best interest for those involved. On the other hand, Plato's analysis is based upon a moral premise that would otherwise consider the officer's actions detrimental. Why? What if the sergeant had hit a tree or, worse, swerved across the line into oncoming traffic and killed himself or someone else? Platonic caves are part of the decision-making process whether the result is right or wrong. A Platonic cave is literally based on an individual's judgment and discretion. Literally, the detriment of this line of thinking allows an individual to makes concessions for a particular individual or group and does not do the same for others.

ETHICAL DECISIONS AND CORE ORGANIZATIONAL VALUES

Throughout the chapter it has been clarified that interpersonal accounts of what is either right or wrong are an important catalyst of what drives one's desire to be ethical. Since the criminal justice system can be considered an organization, we can direct our attention to the hows and whys of the decision-making process. Kohlberg (1969) developed an insightful schematic that might provide important insight into the aspects of cognition as it relates to ethical decision making in organizations (Table 2.1). Since criminal justice is an organization, it is important that one indulges in asking pertinent questions that may address a myriad of complex issues revolving around ethical dilemmas. Furthermore, it would be wise to illustrate the central features that provide a succinct yet lucid look into one specific criminal justice organization—the police force.

Conti & Norman (2005) examined the organizational efficacy and ethics taught to recruits in a police academy. A recruit's life can be based on one specific feature that he or she may be subjected to, and that is adherence to a single authority. It is this authority in which recruits are constantly under surveillance, and the moral imperative of the individual is shaped to carry out the function and the mission of a centralized administration. Often, police recruits are reminded that they cannot live like ordinary people and their behavior is held to a higher standard. A moral imperative is thrust upon recruits almost immediately. Recruits must insulate themselves from the judgmental attitudes of the general public that requires their assistance and the criminals who seek to test an officer's standard of moral turpitude. Second, the recruit begins to become socialized into the organizational setting by being placed with other individuals of the same social position doing the same things in unison.

Lastly, all activities are scheduled around a higher authority that follows a predetermined structure. Most notably, the institution has designed a plan that compels the individuals involved to become what the institution wants them to become. One cannot assume that the example used is reflective as to whether it produces good or bad criminal justice practitioners, yet the steps that are taken are significant with the intention to transform an individual into an effective criminal justice practitioner in sequential stages. Of course, this process is rather antithetical because it differs from an individual's natural and organic course.

TABLE 2.1   Kohlberg's Stages of Cognitive Moral Development

Stage	What is considered to be right
LEVEL ONE – PRECONVENTIONAL	
Stage One – Obedience and punishment orientation	Sticking to rules to avoid physical punishment. Obedience for its own sake.
Stage Two – Instrumental purpose for exchange	Following rules only when it is in one's immediate interest. Right is an equal exchange, a fair deal.
LEVEL TWO – CONVENTIONAL	
Stage Three – Interpersonal accord, conformity, mutual expectations	Stereotypical "good" behavior. Living up to what is expected by the people close to you.
LEVEL THREE – PRINCIPLED	
Stage Five – Social contract and individual rights	Being aware that people hold a variety of rules that are relative to the group. Upholding rules because they are the social contract. Upholding nonrelative values and rights regardless of majority opinion.
Stage Six – Universal ethical principles	Following self-chosen ethical principles, act in accord with principles.

Adapted from Kohlberg, L. (1969) Moral stages and moralization: The cognitive-developmental approach. In T. Lickona (Ed.), *Moral development and behavior: Theory, research, and social issues* (pp.34–39) Holt, Rinehart, & Winston.

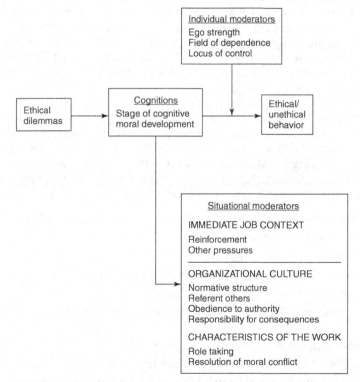

FIGURE 2.1   Interactionist model of ethical decisions in organizations

Source: Trevino, Linda Klebe. Ethical Decision Making in Organizations: A Person-Situation Interactionist Model. *The Academy of Management Review, (11) 3,* 1986 Jul.

ETHICAL DECISION MAKING WHILE NO ONE IS WATCHING

Let us suppose a group of police officers is involved in a major drug raid and found $400,000 in cash and $250,000 in illicit narcotics at the scene of the crime. These officers immediately realize that they may be alone for up to an hour and wonder who is going to know the specifics with regard to the size of the cache of drugs and money. Until this point, the officers had no trouble abiding by the rules and regulations of the department and are known amongst colleagues to be "stand up" officers of sound moral character. However, the allure of the drugs and the cash could possibly entice the officers to make an erroneous decision based upon self-deception. Any individual, let alone a police officer, could see this as hitting the "lottery." Possibly, then, one might rationalize the taking the loot: a payment to secure my child's college education, retirement, the house my wife always wanted, etc. Self-deception with regards to this type of dilemma can create a dangerous situation for the officers. Consequently, human nature may force the officers to behave unethically while they neutralize the negative consequences by rationalizing the good that would come from taking some of the drugs and money, while making the bad choice to steal the seized items.

Corruption within criminal justice organizations is not a new phenomenon. Within the police culture, to be specific, it has been noted that there is an unwritten rule called the "Code of Silence." The code perpetuates itself via an "us vs. them" mentality. This code may create detrimental consequences for a unit or, in the worst-case scenario, an entire department. For example, the Rampart Division of the Los Angeles Police Department made major headlines in most newspapers and media outlets by engaging in illicit drug sales. It was alleged that the officers within the narcotics division had used street-level dealers and informants to sell confiscated drugs, while the officers acted as protection by tipping specific drug dealers off that they were being observed by fellow narcotics officers. The corrupt officers received substantial financial benefits and some were so boastful that they sold drugs out of the department. The scandal gave the LAPD a bad reputation that proved difficult to recover from (Renford, 2003). Afterwards, the LAPD became proactive in creating a culture that demanded integrity from the top to the bottom.

The more we consider the potential impact of every little decision that an organization must make for every situation, the more likely we are to make better ethical decisions. Individuals who are practitioners within the criminal justice field must realize that decisions may create a chain reaction. The outcomes of the reaction are based upon the ethics surrounding the decision. Additionally, we should ask the following questions when faced with an ethical dilemma, then internalize them to determine the ethical premises that are either of high priority or of low priority according to the persona that criminal justice organizations require:

1. Will the decision that I make violate the dignity and humanity of others?
2. Will my decision making affect my reputation?
3. Am I confident with the decisions that I make?
4. Do I have a personal agenda behind the decisions that I make?
5. Are my decisions done at someone else's expense?
6. How would I react to a decision if it were made for me—would my reaction be positive or negative?
7. What are the principles that govern my actions?
8. If I cannot make a concrete decision, who can I rely on to do so?
9. Will my decisions impact the trust that I have built with others?
10. Will my decisions affect my credibility within my profession?

Individuals who are professionals within the criminal justice community seek to do the right things. Yet the decisions that are made sometimes create conundrums that conflict with the individuals' moral nature and structure. One would imply that more training could equate to the likelihood of better ethical decision making. However, it is difficult to recondition the ideals of what is right and what is wrong because the world is not a utopia, nor does everyone analyze problems similarly. Who we are ethically has been already ingrained within the soul of each individual. Moreover, we must disagree to agree yet hope that what is agreed upon allows us the confidence to realize that we have made the right decisions based upon the pillars upon which the criminal justice community so heavily relies, not only to make communities safe, but also to maintain peace of mind and confidence in those who uphold the laws of the land.

ETHICAL DECISION MAKING AND RACIAL PROFILING

BOX 2.1

QUESTIONS SURROUND SHOOTING OF BASEBALLER'S SON

Robbie Tolan, son of a famous baseball player, was shot by a police officer while he stood in his own driveway. Tolan's attorney, David Berg, alleged that it was a classic case of racial profiling that led the police officer to shoot Tolan. The officers confronted Tolan and his cousin, Anthony Cooper, in the early morning hours of Dec. 31, suspecting that they had stolen the car they were driving. Berg said that if they had been white, this incident never would have occurred. The Bellaire, Texas neighborhood where Tolan was shot is an affluent suburb in southwest Houston and its residents are mostly white.

Source: Adapted from cnn.com at http://www.cnn.com/2009/CRIME/01/08/baseballer.shot/

BOX 2.2

ONE MAN'S EXPERIENCE WITH DISCRIMINATION

I was preparing to board a shuttle bus from the train en route to Houston to see my wife and child. At the train station, we received specific instructions to stand away from the bus before loading. As I waited to board the bus, a man approached me and started asking me questions. I ignored him and wanted him to move away from me. Suddenly he displayed his badge and said, "I am with the Smithfield* Police Department Narcotics Division, "May I check your bags?" I was instantly surrounded by three officers who began to drill me with questions as to why I was going to Houston, who I was going to see, when I was returning, and why I was carrying a garment bag. They searched my belongings to the point that it was humiliating. I presented my identification and my employment I.D. fell to the ground from my wallet. The officers grabbed it and saw that my university I.D. read, "Julian Scott, PhD, Faculty, Criminal Justice Department." The officers' attitudes immediately changed from aggressive to worried. They tried softening the situation by attempting to exchange humorous chatter such as, "Wow, you have a PhD." I was finally released and allowed to continue my journey.

(Continued)

BOX 2.2 (Continued)

As I boarded the bus, I recognized that it comprised a variety people who differed in age, gender, and ethnicity. I peered out the window and began to observe the officers and the passengers they searched, African American or Hispanic males between the approximate ages of 18 and 35. I have never traveled on that train line again. However, the incident allowed me to examine my academic training immediately, then ask myself an important yet logical question: "Does a criminal or would-be criminal come from a distinct group of people, or are criminals indistinguishable regardless of race?"

Throughout the United States there has been a growing concern about racial profiling. Advocates would assert that profiling is essential to good police work. The term "profiling" refers to the police practice of viewing certain human characteristics as indicators of criminal behavior. Unfortunately, some law enforcement organizations have taken profiling to a higher level. Officers have unwittingly used factors as age, dress, time of day, geography, and race and ethnicity to separate what they believe to be a good person from a bad person. Being racially profiled is nothing new to many people who are professionals and law-abiding citizens.

There have been instances in poor urban areas where African American boys have been profiled as potential gang members, when it was later discovered that these boys were actually good kids. Subsequently, police departments in large cities have tried to resolve such issues by establishing programs that encourage mentorships with the youth through community policing. Many of the programs have been discontinued because the "good" kids have occasionally become victims of profiling practices and they have ultimately lost all confidence in the police or in the possibility of being treated fairly.

The killing of Trayvon Martin in Florida by George Zimmerman brought out many questions with regard to the autonomy of African American boys who live in integrated neighborhoods. The commentaries were mixed, but African Americans living in the area with sons have talked of losing trust in the decision-making practices of the police. In fact, some parents claimed to be just as afraid of the police as their children were. As young precocious children we have been taught that police officers are our "pals," but in some communities they would rather see the police going than coming due to acts which the community has observed to be unethical practices by law enforcement.

In 1997 Charles and Etta Carter, an elderly African American couple, were stopped by the Maryland State Police on their 40th wedding anniversary. The State Police requested that a K-9 dog be used as supplementary assistance for this particular traffic stop. The couple's belongings were rummaged through and, while the K-9 units found nothing, the dogs proceeded to urinate and defecate on the couple's items. In subsequent litigation, the Maryland State Police were found to have acted excessively and decided to settle out of court. Unlike young African American males, the elderly community has a higher respect for law enforcement, yet they are oftentimes mistreated and traumatized by bad decision making. Think, for example, how a White police officer would react if an African American law enforcement officer devalued the dignity and respectfulness of his mother and father during a routine traffic stop. It is unfortunate that racism exists in society, but as moral individuals whose work shall be built by helping others we must look at what not to do while becoming more understanding of the differences among one another.

Research has shown that there is an accumulation of factors that causes an officer to react with suspicion which then leads the officer to racially profile individuals. Often, traffic violations have been cited as a pretext to stop a vehicle with the intention of possibly discovering an additional crime. Many call this phenomenon DWB (Driving While Black). Social scientists unraveled the phenomenon by gathering traffic data from the New Jersey State Police. The findings were rather startling.

Individuals opposed to racial profiling have asserted that the logic based solely on statistics creates faulty tautological reasoning. Statistics or over reliance on them may paint a picture leading to assumptions that African Americans commit a disproportionate amount of crimes than people from other racial demographics. For example, statistics have demonstrated that there is little difference between a White drug trafficker and an African American drug trafficker. Many criminal justice advocacy and action groups complain that criminal justice organizations on the federal, state, and local levels have begun to concentrate more efforts on minorities while ignoring other groups. For example, in the small town of Hearne, Texas minority residents experienced unethical treatment by narcotics task force agents, which eventually garnered the attention of the ACLU. The Roberson County district attorney, John Paschall, allowed multi-jurisdictional drug task forces to conduct drug stings within a specific minority community in the town. The 2000 Census report documented Hearne's racial demographics as comprising 44 percent African American, 27 percent Hispanic, and 27 percent Anglo; however, the arrests by the drug task force sweeps conducted revealed that 39 percent of drug arrests were of African Americans (Census, 2000).

Shockingly, the task force relied upon the use of a shady informant who noted that the district attorney was the mastermind behind the operation. The district attorney supplied the informant with 29 names of individuals whom he wanted arrested for "so-called" drug offenses. The district attorney threatened the informant that he would build a case against him and ensure that every day that he spent in prison he would find another inmate who was willing to rape him on a daily basis in a brutal and sadistic manner. The informant had no choice but to comply with the district attorney's unethical, troubling behavior to keep from suffering abuse at the hands of fellow inmates. Additionally, a special agent showed the informant how to turn crack cocaine into a powdered form to induce buyers and supplied the informant with a tape recorder to record the alleged drug transactions. Task force officers denied the informant's ability to report any misconduct in terms of the informant's testimony being against the officers who were involved.

Subsequently, one of Paschall's daughters testified that she had overheard her father speaking with the task force commander saying: ["It was time to round up the niggers and make all the niggers shit in their pants . . . Hearne would be a decent place if we bomb all the niggers."] Unfortunately, this paints a very troubling picture as to the district attorney's motivations and character. The bogus sting operation cost individuals not only their livelihoods; some of the victims have yet to get their records cleared of the charges (Levy, 2005). The incident in Hearne clearly demonstrates that racial profiling is a serious anomaly. The lack of sensitivity and unethical behavior affected one specific racial group and their community. If an officer only arrested and targeted African Americans more than other groups, the arrest statistics would most certainty skew the statistics in the officer's favor; otherwise, it would justify the right to profile African Americans. Markedly, when someone reads a magazine or newspaper that sensationalizes drug arrests based upon race, the average individual does not break down the numbers or ask questions pertaining to statistics. The casual reader examines the statistics and correlates the numbers by race, then erroneously concludes that certain crimes are specific to a particular ethnic group. Unfortunately, profiling creates negative reactions from minorities, which leads to a severe level of distrust and detachment from the criminal justice system. Additionally, this detachment encourages minorities to withhold information from, or cautiously report criminal activities to, the authorities. Mistrustful feelings against the law enforcement community encourage minorities to vacillate against officers and tenuously make it substantially difficult for the police to solve crimes or gather important information from minority citizens. Advocates for profiling must really ask themselves these ethics-based questions: Is profiling a fundamentally sound practice? Has the criminal justice institution hit an amoral dilemma with regards to the human dignity of others who are different based upon not only the color of their skin but the perceived ethical values based upon their cultural inheritance?

THE CODE OF SILENCE

Police misconduct has been criticized across the country. Highly publicized and intense misconduct cases have created negative views and anxiety among police departments as well as the general public. The primary goal of the criminal justice system is to instill public trust. Moreover, if a code of silence actually exists, it would be plausible to say that the criminal justice system is paradoxically a glass house. Despite perceptions of the public and the media portrayal that can create false perceptions, law enforcement officers do not condone egregious acts by their peers (Ferrell, 2014). An internal affairs investigation from 1992 to 2000 in the Houston Police Department revealed that more than 50% of all complaints were generated internally rather than externally. The complaints ranged from minor infractions to serious felony investigations. Concerns about ethical behavior are not uncommon—in fact, federal legislation has been recently passed to "investigate and initiate civil litigation to eliminate a pattern or practice" of misconduct by law enforcement under the authority of 42 U.S.C 14141 and 42 U.S.C. 3789 (c)(3) (Ferrell, 2014).

The key to regaining public trust can be initiated by departments through proper training, proactive supervision, and open communication with citizens. Ultimately, responsibility lies primarily with the individual officer but supervisors play a monumental role by taking a proactive approach in preventing misconduct. The public's cause for concern is that police agencies are apt to diffuse internal complaints about misconduct. The reason is simple: liability issues. Police agencies do not want to give the perception that they are bashing an officer who has been fired or asked to resign. When the public watches the news about cases that involve police misconduct, it is likely to assume that the entire department is corrupt rather than just the officers who have been accused.

Police agencies must take the initial step by either creating an ethical behavior policy or reviewing the current policies. The rules that guide the agency should be structured in a way that it is lucid, succinct, and precise. Ethical practices are some of the greatest challenges faced by executive leadership within criminal justice agencies, yet what is more challenging is that all supervisors must be proactive in creating an organizational culture that is consistent with the agency. Gaining an officer's acceptance of policy can be reached by explaining the benefits of compliance to the officer. When an officer understands pertinent rules and regulations that are being conveyed, then the officer is more likely to accept the ethical standards set forth by the agency (Papenfaus, 2003). Adherence to ethical standards is everyone's responsibility. The clearer the standards, the better the agency will react to external or internal complaints that revolve around police misconduct.

BOX 2.3

A CASE STUDY IN ETHICS: THE ZIMBARDO PRISON EXPERIMENT

Zimbardo – Stanford Prison Experiment

Aim: To investigate how readily people would conform to the roles of guard and prisoner in a role-playing exercise that simulated prison life.

Zimbardo (1973) was interested in finding out whether the brutality reported among guards in American prisons was due to the sadistic personalities of the guards or had more to do with the physical prison environment.

Procedure: Zimbardo used a lab experiment to study conformity.

To study the roles people play in prison situations, Zimbardo converted a basement of the Stanford University psychology building into a mock prison. He advertised for students to play the roles of prisoners and guards for two weeks. Twenty-one male college students, chosen from 75 volunteers, were screened for psychological normality and paid $15 per day to take part in the experiment.

Participants were randomly assigned to either the role of prisoner or guard in the mock prison environment. The prison simulation was kept as "real life" as possible. Prisoners were arrested at their own homes, without warning, and taken to the local police station.

Guards were also issued khaki uniforms with whistles, handcuffs, and dark glasses—to make direct eye contact with prisoners impossible. No physical violence was permitted. Zimbardo observed the behavior of the prisoners and guards.

The students selected to play prisoners were treated like any other criminal. They were fingerprinted, photographed, and "booked." Then they were blindfolded and driven to the basement of the psychology building, where Zimbardo had had the basement set out as a prison, complete with barred doors and windows, bare walls, and small cells. Here the de-individuation process began.

When the prisoners arrived at the prison they were stripped naked, deloused, had all their personal possessions removed and locked away, and were given prison clothes and bedding. They were issued plain prisoner uniforms and referred to by their numbers only. The prisoners' uniforms consisted of smocks with their numbers written on them, but no underclothes. They also had a tight nylon cap and a chain around one ankle.

On a normal "shift," there were 3 guards to the 9 prisoners, taking shifts of eight hours each (the other guards remained on call)

Findings: Within a very short time both guards and prisoners were settling into their new roles, the guards adopting theirs quickly and easily.

Within hours of beginning the experiment, some guards began to harass prisoners. They behaved in a brutal and sadistic manner, apparently enjoying punishing the inmates. Other guards joined in, and other prisoners were also tormented.

The prisoners were taunted with insults and petty orders, given pointless and boring tasks to accomplish, were generally dehumanized.

The prisoners soon adopted prisoner-like behavior as well. They talked about prison issues a great deal of the time. They "told tales" on each other to the guards. They started taking the prison rules very seriously, as though they were there for the prisoners' benefit and infringement would spell disaster for all of them. Some even began siding with the guards against prisoners who did not conform to the rules.

Over the next few days the relationships between the guards and the prisoners changed, with a change in one leading to a change in the other. Remember that the guards were firmly in control and the prisoners were totally dependent on them.

As the prisoners became more dependent, the guards became more derisive towards them. They held the prisoners in contempt and let the prisoners know it. As the guards' contempt for them grew, the prisoners became more submissive.

As the prisoners became more submissive, the guards in turn became more aggressive and assertive. They demanded more obedience from the prisoners. The prisoners were dependent on the guards for everything and tried to find ways to please the guards, such as telling tales on fellow prisoners.

One prisoner had to be released after 36 hours because of uncontrollable bursts of screaming, crying, and anger. His thinking became disorganized and he appeared to be entering the early stages of a deep depression. Within the next few days, three others also had to leave after showing signs of emotional disorder that could have had lasting consequences. These were people who had been pronounced stable and normal just before beginning the experiment.

(Continued)

BOX 2.3 (Continued)

Zimbardo (1973) had intended that the experiment should run for a fortnight, but on the sixth day he brought things to a halt. There was real danger that someone might be physically or mentally damaged if the study was allowed to continue. After some time for the researchers to gather their data, the subjects were called back for a follow-up debriefing session.

Conclusion: People will readily conform to the social roles they are expected to play, especially if the roles are as strongly stereotyped as those of the prison guards. The "prison" environment was an important factor in creating the guards' brutal behavior; none of the participants who acted as guards showed sadistic tendencies before the study. **The roles that people play can shape their behavior and attitudes.**

After the prison experiment was terminated, Zimbardo interviewed the participants. Here is an excerpt from a participant's interview:

> Most of the participants said they had felt involved and committed. The research had felt 'real' to them. One guard said, 'I was surprised at myself. I made them call each other names and clean the toilets out with their bare hands. I practically considered the prisoners cattle and I kept thinking I had to watch out for them in case they tried something.' Another guard said 'Acting authoritatively can be fun. Power can be a great pleasure.' And another: '. . . during the inspection I went to Cell Two to mess up a bed which a prisoner had just made and he grabbed me, screaming that he had just made it and that he was not going to let me mess it up. He grabbed me by the throat and although he was laughing, I was pretty scared. I lashed out with my stick and hit him on the chin although not very hard, and when I freed myself I became angry.'

Most of the guards found it difficult to believe that they had behaved in the brutalizing ways that they had. Many said they hadn't known this side of them existed or that they were capable of such things. The prisoners, too, couldn't believe that they had responded in the submissive, cowering, dependent ways that they had. Several claimed to be normally assertive people. When asked about the guards, they described the usual three stereotypes that can be found in any prison: some guards were good, some were tough but fair, and some were cruel.

Ethics: The study has received many ethical criticisms, including lack of fully informed consent from participants and the level of humiliation and distress experienced by those who acted as prisoners.

The consent could not be fully informed as Zimbardo himself did not know what would happen in the experiment. Participants playing the role of prisoners were not protected from psychological and physical harm from the guards. For example, one prisoner had to be released after 36 hours because of uncontrollable bursts of screaming, crying and anger.

Source: Haney, C., Banks, W. C., & Zimbardo, P. G. (1973). A study of prisoners and guards in a simulated prison. *Naval Research Review*, 30, 4–17.

Ethics is a matter that should be taken seriously. Working in the criminal justice system entails interacting with the American public and the community daily. Philosophically, ethics asks questions that pertain to how an individual comes to the conclusions of right and wrong. Individual beliefs vary; therefore, people must arrive at a satisfactory medium that allows civility and conformity within society. It is the duty of the criminal justice system to ensure that law and order is maintained and delivered based upon fairness and equity. Ethical behavior is expressed by an ethos that drives the rationality behind ethical decision making.

Individuals must understand that the criminal justice establishment is composed of various individuals of various walks of life and experiences. As individuals choose criminal justice as a career, we must understand that they are reshaped by the organization and must carry out the mission of the agency. Criminal justice relies not only on efficiency but also on effectiveness.

Ethical decision making is difficult. As individuals we must come to the best possible conclusions, although many different conclusions may not be incorrect. Criminal justice practitioners sometimes have to make split-second decisions. Those decisions impact not only the life of the officer but other people. Regardless of the training and the policies set forth by each criminal justice agency, the burden lies on the individual officers and the ideology that they have made a decision that they can live with.

REFERENCES AND FURTHER READING

Conti, Norman & James J. Nolan, III. (2005). Policing the Platonic cave: Ethics and efficacy in police training. *Police and Society*, 13, 87–99. DOI. 10.1080/104394605000071705.

Coser, L.A. (1974). *Greedy Institutions: Patterns of Undivided Commitment*. New York: Free Press.

Ferrell, Craig E. (2012). Ethics and professionalism: No lying, cheating, or stealing. *The Police Chief*, 79 (Nov), 10–11.

Haney, C., W.C. Banks, & P.G. Zimbardo. (1973). A study of prisoners and guards in a simulated prison. *Naval Research Review*, 30, 4–17.

Kohlberg, L. (1969). Stage and sequence: The cognitive developmental approach to socialization. In D.A. Goslin (Ed.), *Handbook of Socialization Theory and Research*. Chicago: RAND, pp 347–480.

Papenfuhs, Steve. (n.d.) Ethical dilemmas cops face daily: The impact of human factors upon individual performance must coincide with timely and fair discipline. *PoliceOne.com, retrieved* 30 June 2014.

Plato. (1993). *The Republic*. Translated by Robin Waterfield. Oxford, UK: Oxford University Press.

Renford, Reese. (1993). The Multiple Causes of the LAPD Rampart Scandal, 2003. Paper Presented at California State Polytechnic University, Pomona, CA.

Sahakain, W.S. & Sahakain, M.L. (1966). *Ideas of the Great Philosophers*. New York: Barnes & Noble.

Trevino, Linda Klebe. (1986). Ethical decision making in organizations: A person situation interactionist model. *The Academy of Management Review,* (11), 601–613.

Weisenhand, Paul. (2007). *Supervising Police Personnel* 6th Edition. Upper Saddle River, NJ: Prentice Hall.

Is Acting on Principle the Answer? Immanuel Kant Said Yes

CHAPTER 3

"Experience without theory is blind, but theory without experience is mere intellectual play"

—*Immanuel Kant*

This chapter, and the next two, concern ethics and morality. As mentioned previously, the word "ethics" comes from the Greek *ethos*, which has no direct, one-word translation into English. Homer and Herodotus both used *ethos* to mean the home or habitual places where a certain kind of animal could be found. Aristotle used *ethos* to mean habit or character, as in the habitual behavior of a group or community. It could refer to an individual, but usually to an individual as a member of a group or community. The word "morality" comes from the Latin *mos*, which is related to the English word "custom," but tends toward a more personal value structure than *ethos*. Some wish to separate these two words, ethics and morality, taking ethics to mean a critical look at morality, while morality is the value structure exhibited by either a culture or an individual. Unless these distinctions make a difference to my meaning, I will use the words interchangeably here, and try to be clear in the surrounding prose what is at issue. It is obvious that certain individuals do not always accept the habits of behavior prescribed by the culture in which they reside. This makes police officers necessary. Law enforcement officers generally defend the habits of behavior valued by the jurisdiction in which they reside, though there are notable exceptions.

If you ask why, a good idea, then the answer is that a jurisdiction's valued habits of behavior, of course, have evolved over time. We usually think of our Western communities as ancient, stemming from the Greeks, or the Romans, or the Jews then Roman Christians, or the German Angles and Saxons. In this particular case, the word "Western" is used as opposed to the word "Eastern," as in Occident and Orient, large historical-cultural terms, not, say, cowboys and Indians. We, you and me, evolved as intelligent creatures no less than fifty thousand years ago. Some argue we as a species evolved anatomically into modern humans two hundred thousand years ago, and adopted modern behavior patterns fifty thousand years ago, while others argue that the physical and behavioral evolution occurred at the same time. That means we as a species have had the time, as creatures equal in intelligence to ourselves, to evolve different civilizations ten times, ending in the latest five thousand year run. Five thousand years is a rough number, associated with the Chinese, not a Western culture, invention of a kind of writing. Writing itself is not a sign of civilization necessarily. Greek culture formed, less than three thousand years ago, as an oral tradition. Athenians, following the

31

Peloponnesian War and the restoration of the democracy in the early fifth century B.C.E., voted to adopt a more standard Greek than was used, for instance, to write down Homer's (eighth century B.C.E.) orally transmitted work. Not all influential Greeks embraced writing, having been educated in an oral tradition, memorizing music and poetry, and engaging in lots of physical training. Socrates is notable in this regard. In any case, the ways, including moral ways, of our cultures and communities are not so ancient as we often think. In anthropological terms, they are relatively recent. And, even within the boundaries of Western culture, there are contradictory sets of metaphysical assumptions that cause some persons, including some law enforcement persons, to get crossways with each other and their own culture.

Not only that, criminal justice in the United States operates with a remarkably paradoxical claim at its center, namely that social and/or moral good follows from punishing those who break the laws of the land. Most folks are quite aware that punishment by imprisonment often results in neither social nor moral good for those punished, and, of course, not for victims of formerly or presently imprisoned persons, except that it may satisfy revenge or, perhaps, deterrence. One of our longest running and most popular TV shows is *Cops*, a documentary/reality legal series, which has run on the Fox TV channel since 1989. With the combination of weird laws[1] and the constant possibility of deadly violence, millions of people are fascinated by police behavior. Most of the street criminals in the cases considered in episodes of *Cops* are shown shirtless, tattooed, and bleeding—and that includes the men. Violence is an escalating threat to law enforcement officers, who are of course trained to use violence, or the threat of violence, to enforce the law. Using violence or the threat of violence against others in the workplace has become common enough in this country for the United States Department of Labor to adopt a strict internal workplace violence policy governing all U.S. government organizations, including the FBI (Department of Labor, n.d.).[2] It seems clear that armed law enforcement agencies would be particularly at risk for internal violence.

Law enforcement officers had placed 6,937,600 offenders "under the supervision of adult correctional systems at yearend 2012," according to the online Bureau of Justice Statistics report.[3] While the prison population has gone down since 2009, it now stands at about the same rate of incarceration exhibited in 1997, 1 in 35 adults. The New York Times reported, in 2008:[4]

> The United States has less than 5 percent of the world's population. But it has almost a quarter of the world's prisoners. Indeed, the United States leads the world in producing prisoners, a reflection of a relatively recent and now entirely distinctive American approach to crime and punishment. Americans are locked up for crimes—from writing bad checks to using drugs— that would rarely produce prison sentences in other countries. And in particular they are kept incarcerated far longer than prisoners in other nations.

The University of London reports that incarceration rates in the United States are the highest in the world at 743 per 100,000 in population, followed by the Russian Federation at 577. Denmark and Norway are both at 71, while Japan is at 59.[5]

Speaking of Criminal Justice in the United States in particular, P. K. Manning has said:[6]

> The idea that a criminal justice system exists by design, and that it is held together by laws, flowcharts, algorithms, dispositions, and outcomes, is a relatively recent conceit. It is yet to be proven what common values and purposes, other than communicating itself,[7] bind together this notional system. Perhaps the subsystems are articulated around negotiations over particular cases, shaped by dramaturgical principles of "looking good" and "maintaining respect," and governed by a self-sustaining wish to produce and reproduce uncertainty in "outposts." These "rules of thumb" reflect expediency, pragmatism, and sensitivity to a local political order. This state of affairs, according to Souryal, can and should be altered if one takes ethical principles seriously.

The following three chapters concerning ethics and criminal justice take no such passionate aim at reform as Souryal did. In fact, the approach to reform put forth by Souryal is criticized here. Students, of course, can use what is said here to do their own work as reformers if they choose. But these chapters are intended to simply describe Immanuel Kant's duty and principle point of view, Jeremy Bentham's and John Stuart Mill's utilitarian-consequentialist point of view, and Aristotle's virtue ethics point of view, as much as possible as they each relate to modern crime and punishment scenarios. To properly understand a point of view, one must be able to criticize it. To hold a point of view means to understand criticisms of it, and be able defend it from those criticisms. The authors of this textbook have chosen a philosopher to write these three chapters on ethics, so expect there to be no position that is invulnerable to criticism.

One other thing worth pointing out before beginning is that thinking ethically requires imagination. There are people who do not, for instance, go to movies because, "it's just a story," or "it didn't really happen." My father was one of them. While I am not any sort of lobbyist for the movie industry, I must point out that *imagining things to be other than they are is an essential skill for ethical reflection*. People who cannot imagine that their unfair, violent childhood might have been different cannot recover from it, because they cannot imaginatively re-parent themselves. Any given situation must be re-thought, re-ordered in your mind, in order for you to apply any ethical point of view to it, and that includes situations to which we will apply the three ethical points of view presented here.

I was accustomed, in my youth, to Marines responding to, "If we go over there, we will have a big fight with ____," with "What do we get if we win?" I don't know whether they were using their imaginations or were just exhibiting machismo. But to change anything, for the better or for the worse, using your imagination is crucial. Without it, things just stay the way they are. If we do not like how things are, and cannot imagine an alternative, we can never change anything. Imagining things otherwise is a necessary pattern of thought for realizing that an action does not fit our values, not to mention changing/challenging that action. If the thought that things need not be as they are is impossible for you, then you are incapable of ethical reflection. That is an undesirable characteristic for an armed officer of the law and I would encourage you to seek other training. Retail, perhaps. With this orientation, let us begin.

KANTIAN ETHICAL PHILOSOPHY

Immanuel Kant (1724–1804) was an extremely influential Prussian thinker who scholars say ushered in the critical period of modern philosophy. These scholars also say he saved Enlightenment philosophy from being derailed by Scottish skepticism, restoring it to the mainstream. Others consider he was too accommodating to the new science as a dominant way of knowing, privileging science in ways still contorting and restricting philosophical thinking.

Whatever Kant's ultimate status will be, ethically he thought that persons would not consistently obey any moral principle they did not freely and autonomously author themselves. He also thought people were rational and would conform to a moral principle if it could be shown to be essential to rational agency. He suggested a moral principle, called "the categorical imperative," which he thought represented the fundamental law of morality that was essential to rational agency. Actually, he called it *"Der kategorische Imperativ,"* because he wrote in German. Moreover, it is the presence of this self-governing reason in each person that Kant thought offered decisive grounds for viewing each person as possessed of equal worth and deserving of equal respect. This last is worth consideration by any officer of the law.

Understanding the Categorical Imperative

There are several formulations of the categorical imperative. The first is: "act only in accordance with that maxim through which you can at the same time will that it become a universal law."[8] The second, "humanity formulation," is: "we should never act in such a way that we treat Humanity, whether in ourselves or in others, as a means only but always as an end in itself." The third, "autonomy," formulation is: "the Idea of the will of every rational being as *a will that legislates universal law*."[9] This can be phrased more like the others as: "always act so that the principle of your action can be willed to be a universal law of nature." The fourth, "kingdom of ends," formulation is "act in accordance with the maxims of a member giving universal laws for a merely possible kingdom of ends."[10] The intuition serving this formulation is that we are only required to act on principles that would be accepted by a "kingdom," or community, composed of fully rational and equally powered legislating agents.

The humanity formulation, "we should never act in such a way that we treat Humanity, whether in ourselves or in others, as a means only but always as an end in itself," is the easiest to explain. Say, you stop in at the Starbucks drive-in window for a Caramel Frappuccino on a hot day. You are not really thinking about the lady handing you the cup as an end in herself. You are using her as a means to an end, namely the end of getting a Caramel Frappuccino. Are you acting immorally? No, because you are not necessarily treating her as *only* a means. There is no opportunity for you to show you are also capable of treating her as an end in herself, but in the normal course of events, you do not have to show that in order to be considered to be acting morally. We use each other as means in any number of ways every day. It is not an issue most of the time.

But consider this. As you reach for your Frappuccino, the lady's hand goes limp as she takes a sniper's bullet to the head. You lunge, catch the drink, mutter, "Whew, that was close," and quickly drive off. Have you now treated the lady as *only* a means to an end, and not also as an end in herself? Yes, you have, and you have done something immoral in Kant's view. Particularly as a police officer, but also as a human being, you should do much more. This is the kind of act Kant meant to condemn as immoral. It is a bit like Inspector Clouseau in a short scene from *The Pink Panther Strikes Again*, https://www.youtube.com/watch?v=-Y8MdcMY2yU. It is really morally wrong, not to mention obnoxious, to treat another human as merely a means to place yourself upright in your chair by pulling their tie and smashing their face into the desk. In this scene, Clouseau seems to care less about the man's face being smashed into the desk, so long as he can sit upright in his chair. This is what it is to treat other human beings as means to some other end only, and not also as an end in themselves. You might think of it as considering another person as a mere thing, or piece of furniture, rather than a real human being with natural, intrinsic value.

Interpreting the Categorical Imperative

Intuitively correct moral insights are captured by Kant's categorical imperative. People should not be treated as things only, but always also as an end in themselves. We are "only required to act on principles that would be accepted by a 'kingdom,' or community composed of fully rational and equally powered legislating agents." Part of this second insight is that we must "get along" with others. The first insight is usually a path to the second.

But I ask that you think critically about these insights. Consider a situation in which "getting along" in a community requires bigoted, unjust patterns of behavior be accepted. Does any community "have to" be that way? No, of course not. But such communities exist. If you lived in one, or worked in one, could you be fair and just in such a community? Plato and Aristotle agreed that you would/could not; such is the pervasive influence of a community *ethos*. Do you agree or disagree?

When there was a draft in the United States, the country was nearly torn apart by an unmanageable conflict between the personal values of many and the requirement of military service. Tim O'Brien described the day after he realized he could not face the embarrassment of stepping over the border into Canada and not going to war as follows:[11]

> The day was cloudy. I passed through towns with familiar names, through the pine forests and down to the prairie, and then to Vietnam, where I was a soldier, and then home again. I survived, but it's not a happy ending. I was a coward. I went to war.

Whether O'Brien was "right" or not, there was an obvious difference between the values he felt internally and those his country externally embraced.

Further, does there exist, or has there ever existed, a community that is composed of fully rational and equally powered legislating agents? I do not live in a community like that, and neither do you. We cannot say what it would be like to live in one without (a) using our imaginations, and (b) basing our utopia on some sort of principles, rational or not. In order to even say, "a community that is composed of fully rational and equally powered legislating agents," we must imagine a community unlike any we have experienced. To do that, we must have in mind some set of value judgments about human behavior. Does that mean ethical principles are not "real" in some sense? What about the principle that we should never treat a person as a means to other ends only, and always as an end in themselves? Did we not just explain that principle in real life, with the Caramel Frappuccino/ sniper example? No, we did not. What we did was interpret a potentially real-life situation imaginatively, and decided one of the actors in that situation acted immorally. The real-world situation was one in which a person clearly cared only about him/herself, and cared not at all about a presumably innocent person being gunned down. We applied the principle that a person should never be treated as a means only, but always also as an end in themselves, to make the judgment that the person who lunged to catch their Caramel Frappuccino and drove off feeling lucky had acted immorally.

So, neither the principle that we should "get along" in a community, nor that we should not treat other people as things only, can be said to be simply true, or "true," as in corresponding to some fact of the world. That is why Kant goes to so much trouble to show that applying his intuitive principles to real-life situations is essential to rational agency. If these principles are part of being rational, and everyone who is human is rational, then we can expect everyone to recognize these principles as the correct ones for making moral judgments. Are human beings rational? Can they be reduced to that single characteristic in order to explain their behavior? Is it the case that human beings often act irrationally and out of passion and/or emotion? You might discuss this and come to a class consensus.

Further, some people consider that rationality requires getting theirs before and/or instead of others getting theirs. The notion of moral realism, or the belief that might makes right, has been around in Western culture since its beginning with the Greeks. See Chapter One of Plato's *Republic*. That there is such a point of view does not make *it* right, but it does make it clear that Kant's notion of rationality is not universally embraced. There are alternative measures of rationality, and alternative foundations with different value results. One might present these alternative measures and/or foundations as supporting a quite different deontological system. Ayn Rand announces selfishness is good, required of a rational person, and proceeds to draw out the consequences of this value in a moral system of selfishness she calls Objectivism. Some legislators, namely Paul Ryan, are trying to make the national budget in the United States reflect Rand's value system. Ignoring the wounded barista as a person would be entirely acceptable on such an understanding of rationality and "principled" values.

All of us have been born and raised in some particular culture, family, faith community, etc., and there are beliefs we hold that are very difficult to defend when they are made clear to us. This section started out with one of these. Why do we uncritically consider that punishing people who violate our law codes will make them better people, or indeed result in any social or moral good, when in fact it seems not to satisfy these desiderata and to satisfy unrelated desiderata, such as our desire for revenge, or to deter people from committing similar acts in the future? So, while there is clearly something wrong with lunging to catch your Frappuccino and driving off without acknowledging in any way the wounded barista, it is extremely difficult to frame that wrongness in terms of a universal principle, "accepted by all."

Souryal's Principled Activism

Sam Souryal thought there were actions that exhibited "self-evident truth," or an "accepted by all" characteristic, in the same way Kant meant. He thought the lesson of such actions was "to abide with the universal rules of moral behavior and to attempt at all times not to delude universal morality by succumbing to the temptation of radical and relativist ethics."[12] An example that he thinks supports his absolutist, deontological claim is that of former president Jimmy Carter's role in negotiating the end of a military coup in Haiti in 1994. The United States Marines were about to invade Haiti to restore the former, democratically elected president to power. A delegation of former president Jimmy Carter, Senator Sam Nunn, and General Colin Powell were dispatched to negotiate a peaceful return of power to the former president.

President Bill Clinton's administration's "charge to the delegation was to secure agreements by which (1) members of the military junta would step down, and (2) they would leave the island into exile."[13] In a week's time, the first was accomplished, but Carter chose not to accomplish the second, arguing it would be "an act of banishment that is unconstitutional in the United States," and violates human rights. Carter also indicated, "if members of the junta were to be accused of criminal acts, he would be willing to charge them and try them in a court of law." This resolution was not challenged, and defused the crisis without military invasion.

Souryal calls this a "denunciation of situational morality," and claimed Carter's "decision was accepted by all concerned as a 'self-evident truth.' Carter did the right thing on the basis of moral authority alone."[14] Souryal's claim concerning the moral status of Carter's decision, if it is true, would have to be based on the general claim that banishment is a violation of human rights, because unconstitutionality is not a general claim, but rather a claim local to the United States. Yes, once again I am asking you to think critically, to use your imagination. Carefully review the next to last sentence and be sure you understand it. Further, the claim that all people involved accepted Carter's proposal, as a general, universal, self-evident truth is not established. Avoiding a costly military invasion while removing the junta from power was already accomplished at the point Carter objected to banishing the junta members. Why would Clinton, or anyone else, quibble over it? And an acceptable alternative was proposed, namely trying those leaders in a court of law. Even if one were NOT convinced AT ALL that human rights are essential to rational agency, as Kant claimed, or that avoiding banishment is a general, universal, self-evident truth, as Souryal claimed, one would still have no practical reason to object to Carter's solution, to certainly include not banishing the junta members. And, of course, many in the world are not convinced that human rights should be distributed equally to all. There are many who consider that women do not deserve equal rights—or gays,—or people of color. In other words, even if a person were not convinced that the notion of universal human rights makes sense, that person would still have no reason to object to Carter's proposal in the Haiti situation as Souryal presented it.

I have no idea why Souryal considers the alternative to absolutist moral decisions based on principle to be "radical and relativistic ethics." Principles are significant. An officer of the law should be aware of the particular principles that play a part in creating the moral/ethical/legal context in which she works. But an absolutist interpretation of an action or event is very difficult to defend. And not defending one does not mean automatically embracing a radical and relativistic ethics.

Indeed, most absolutist claims are subject to this kind of criticism. Far more victories are claimed than can be defended properly. It is, from a philosophical or critical point of view, difficult to defend principles stated as moral absolutes, even though the impulse to do so is also clear. Would it not be nice if there were a clear, unambiguous foundation from which we could derive our moral judgments? That would make life so much easier and less fraught with conflict. Why does everyone not just accept the same framework for living, the same worldview, and the same religion? Of course, once you ask these questions, the answers come directly into view. Children are born to people who are already immersed in different frameworks, worldviews, and religions, in which those children are raised.

Some philosophers consider language itself incapable of expressing moral intuitions that can survive situational criticism. And some consider this more an issue of the shortcomings of language than of human moral intuitions. They point to commonalities between all cultures, worldviews, etc. I shall not try to straighten that issue out here, and likely could not if I tried.

If you think this is an attack on moral principles, or on ethics generally, you could not be more mistaken. Choosing a particular way to articulate moral commitments, especially in a prescriptive manner, invites criticism of that particular way of saying things. All three of the chosen methods of expressing moral values will come in for criticism here. There just is no way to escape personal moral responsibility in real life. Blaming what one does on deontology, consequentialism, virtue ethics, or for that matter on one's religion, does not lift that burden of making, and taking personal responsibility for, decisions that result in actions. A more grounded approach might be that we should never do anything with which we could not live as defining us morally, with no necessary connection to a "universal" reason at all.

The Issue of "Accurate" Language

When you find yourself thinking language can be uttered that has clear and precise meaning regarding human experience, then what sort of situation are you in? Is it one in which you and your community of friends agree? If so, some thoughts about that are in order. If I were to try to describe to you what, say, driving a 1968 Shelby Mustang is like, I could talk for a long time without you understanding at all. If you had, say, a 2008 Shelby Mustang, we might compare notes and perhaps agree on a few things, but without much confidence. The only way to develop any mutual understanding would be for you and me to both drive both cars. Then we could talk, and we would pick out certain words or phrases, like, "rear squirrely under power in a tight turn," and we might develop a vocabulary we both consider clear and accurate. If we strayed into a description like, "much more stable than a stock Mustang," then we would need to add driving stock models from those respective years to our direct experience. We would get to know each other in this process of building a shared vocabulary for describing our experiences. Then, when someone without those experiences comes along, we would just tell them to trust us as experts. Does this mean the words and phrases we have chosen are simply "true," communicate clearly, are universally trustworthy, and will never be misinterpreted? No, of course not. And if you expand this common sense scenario for using and agreeing on the meanings of words and phrases to more difficult to duplicate experiences, such as giving or receiving just treatment, or dying, then the margin of error becomes so great that claiming universally correct descriptions becomes very much less attractive and/or desirable.

Kant's Own Troubles

Kant himself had a frustrating experience trying to defend some of his categorical imperative intuitions. In 1797, Kant published a paper titled, "On a Supposed Right to Lie from Altruistic Motives."[15] It began like this:

> In the Journal *France*, for 1797, Part VI, No. i, page 123, in an article entitled "On Political Reactions" by Benjamin Constant, there appears the following passage:

>> The moral principle, "It is a duty to tell the truth," would make any society impossible if it were taken singly and unconditionally. We have proof of this in the very direct consequences which a German philosopher has drawn from this principle. This philosopher goes so far as to assert that it would be a crime to lie to a murderer who has asked whether our friend who is pursued by him had taken refuge in our house.

> The French philosopher on page 124 refutes this principle in the following manner:

>> It is a duty to tell the truth. The concept of duty is inseparable from the concept of right. A duty is that which in one being corresponds to the rights of another. Where there are no rights, there are no duties. To tell the truth is thus a duty: but it is a duty only in respect to one who has a right to the truth. But no one has a right to a truth which injures others.

Kant immediately challenged the idea that one can have a "right to truth," and suggested such a right would make no sense. In the real world, Kant claims, we do not have any objective "right to truth" in a conversation with another person. If I were inserting swords, long, sharp pieces of steel, into a storage device with slits and asked, "Is there anyone in there?" then it does not follow that the answer I receive is necessarily true, certainly not just because harm would result from a lie, or because I have some "right" to know. That would be a peculiar way to confer truth on a statement. Then Kant said:[16]

> . . . For instance, if by telling a lie you have prevented murder, you have made yourself legally responsible for all the consequences; but if you have held rigorously to the truth, public justice can lay no hand on you, whatever the unforeseen consequences may be. After you have honestly answered the murderer's question as to whether this intended victim is at home,

it may be that he has slipped out so that he does not come in the way of the murderer, and thus that the murder may not be committed. But if you had lied and said he was not at home when he had really gone out without your knowing it, and if the murderer had then met him as he went away and murdered him, you might justly be accused as the cause of his death. For if you had told the truth as far as you knew it, perhaps the murderer might have been apprehended by the neighbors while he searched the house and thus the deed might have been prevented. Therefore, whoever tells a lie, however well intentioned he might be, must answer for the consequences, however unforeseeable they were, and pay the penalty for them even in a civil tribunal. This is because truthfulness is a duty which must be regarded as the ground of all duties based on contract, and the laws of these duties would be rendered uncertain and useless if even the least exception to them were admitted.

To be truthful (honest) in all declarations, therefore, is a sacred and absolutely commanding decree of reason, limited by no expediency.

This passage indeed echoes Kant's comment in *The Metaphysical Principles of Virtue*, in the case of a servant lying to a visitor regarding his master's whereabouts, while the master sneaks out and commits a crime:[17] "Upon whom . . . does the blame fall? To be sure, also upon the servant, who here violated a duty to himself by lying, the consequence of which will now be imputed to him by his own conscience."

So, Kant defends the position that, if a murderer showed up at your door, intent on killing a person who had just entered your dwelling, you should tell the truth. This is not because the potential killer has a right to the truth from you, but because you have a duty to all persons to tell the truth. If you do not tell the truth, then you assume responsibility for the consequences of your lie. You cannot predict the consequences of your lie. If the murder occurs in the context of your lie, you are responsible for it. If you tell the truth, however, you cannot be held accountable for the consequences of doing so. Perhaps you can come to a class consensus regarding whether or not you would be justified lying to the killer at the door.

The passages cited above from Kant's work are usually presented as an absolutist claim against lying, ever, for any reason, *and* as part of Kant's argument against consequentialism, the view that an act should be judged good or bad according to its consequences, which view will be considered in its own right in the next chapter. We have been discussing deontological views. Regarding the second point, Kant's argument against consequentialism is that one can rarely be certain of the consequences of telling a lie, or telling the truth for that matter, so why make moral responsibility dependent upon them? Very well intentioned people do the most awful things to others, well, unintentionally.

Consider that you arose this morning, left your roommate sleeping soundly, and headed for the dorm shower room, leaving your keys in plain sight on your bedside table. You returned twenty minutes later and the door was locked, your roommate nowhere in evidence. After a frantic few minutes in your bath towel, you procured entrance to your room from your dorm supervisor, but it was not in time to prevent you from being late to your philosophy class, in which there was a ten-minute reading quiz at the beginning which could not be made up because discussion of the reading, and answers to the quiz questions, followed. This threatened your grade, of course, and made you look bad in front of your favorite professor. After a later class, you went to lunch at the dining hall and saw your roommate headed for your table. What do you do?

Do you immediately reflect that you dislike this person and want to be rid of her? To do that, what would you have to assume? Stop reading here and think about that. Of course I am going to tell you, but perhaps I am wrong, and in any case you would not be giving your brain a chance to do/learn something if you just read on. Okay, I have no control over you. You would be assuming, if you indulged the display of such a dislike, that her motive that morning had been to inconvenience and sabotage you *on purpose*. In other words, her motives were bad. But, really, how do you know that? You do not, so let us say you are neutral until you can gather more evidence.

If the roommate sits down as if nothing has happened, then perhaps you would say how you had been inconvenienced, mentioning that your keys were in plain sight and she should have known you would be locked out if she left and locked the door. Two very different reactions, at least, are possible. I will describe them.

Let us say, first, the roommate registers horror at your story and apologizes profusely, offering perhaps that she had overslept, did not look at anything in the room, threw on her clothes and left, thinking vaguely that you must already be up and out. She offers to buy a pizza for you both that evening, and to watch a movie you like, seeming genuinely surprised and sorry for her behavior. Well, okay. The relationship may survive.

But that reassuring behavior may not occur. An altogether different reaction might occur. Let us say, second, the roommate narrows her eyes, smiles, and says, "So, the suck-up didn't impress the teacher this morning. Gee, that is too, too bad." And the roommate sits chuckling in a self-satisfied manner. Now are you justified in thinking your relationship with this person should end as soon as possible? Yes, it seems to me you are so justified. Why? What is the difference between these two cases? The behavior that inconvenienced you, and made you look bad, was the same in both cases. Why does the reaction of the roommate make so much difference?

It is because, in the first case, the roommate seems genuinely to wish you well, not to wish you any ill. Instead, she feels shame that she inconvenienced you. This, in fact, is to wish you well. Kant says the only unqualified good is a good will. Everything else, including all behavior, must be qualified. You could even forgive someone who shot you, if it was unintentional. In the second case, the roommate seems genuinely to wish you ill, not to wish you well, and to have intentionally inconvenienced you. While you cannot conceive of a successful relationship with the second-case roommate, the first may represent a person with whom you may indeed enjoy a long-term relationship. Note that the consequences of what the roommate did are the same, bad for you, in both cases. The intuition Kant is trying to get right by rejecting behavioral standards for goodness, or consequentialism, is that a person's motivation is what is morally significant, not the consequences of his/her actions.

If the consequences were different, the moral judgment based on motives, or good or ill will, would not change. Let us say that there is a gas leak in the building in which the philosophy class was held, and half the building was blown away in an explosion, killing everyone in the classroom. You were not there and, so, were left alive. Would it then be clear that your roommate had saved your life and was therefore a good person? No, it would not. Moral judgments would not be changed in the least by this added consequence of the roommate's actions. This would be, for Kant, another instance in which judging based on consequences would lead one to make a wrong judgment of perhaps even moral praise or blame.

But, in spite of this, most people believe at least some consequences can be predicted, and should be taken into account morally. People who speed are given tickets, whether they hurt anyone or not, because they were clearly risking that. If a person places one bullet in a revolver, spins the cylinder, and then points the gun at another person and pulls the trigger, then most people consider that person to be comfortable shooting the other person. This is because a reasonable consequence of that behavior would be for the gun to fire. To say the cylinder-spinning shooter is not necessarily guilty, because the gun stood, say, five chances of not firing and only one of firing, would be unacceptable for most people. Telling a murderer where their intended victim is, or has been recently, would strike most people the same way. And their behavior would likely reflect their reluctance to be truthful, along with any number of other variables, such as whether the murderer threatened them as well. This argument has been around since the eighteenth century at least, and has received a lot of attention.[18] I have not solved it here, but simply use it to illustrate how principled moral thinking has been described in our, Western culture.

Thinking in a morally principled way serves several important moral intuitions. It serves the intuition that people should not be treated as things. It also serves the intuition that people need to get along in community with one another. And it serves the intuition that judging by consequences is often mistaken. These are not trivial intuitions. People regularly risk a lot to defend the application of these intuitions to real life. To choose a movie example, in *Platoon*, Charlie Sheen's character, Chris, risks much to prevent armed soldiers from using Vietnamese young girls as sexual objects.

It does not follow from our ability to criticize moral principles, or criticize the claim that moral principles should govern our behavior, that the intuitions these principles try to express are not real or important. They should be part of any person's thought processes, especially a person who is given authority and can choose to treat people as things, for instance, in everyday routines, as is the case with armed police officers.

Considering Religion as a Principled Ethic

Knowing the standard patterns of reasoning and behavior wherever you are will make you a better police officer, lawyer, judge, or person. You will know better what to expect, how to react to others, and how to achieve peaceful and just resolutions to conflicts. There is no way to think about ethics that will remove from your shoulders the personal responsibility to identify what you consider "just." This includes the most popular way to claim there are standards everyone must accept: religion. In the United States, the most popular religion is Christianity, and sometimes people will articulate a wish to replace the secular government with something like the Ten Commandments, particularly in southern states.

Folks who support politicians who articulate such wishes consider these politicians to be telling the "truth," and refusing to "play politics." Consider a politician who allows her religious worldview to permeate her legislative life. Her political positions can only be understood using the theological lens through which she sees the world. For instance, and the example is not the point, if this politician does not believe humans are the cause of climate change, then you can reasonably conclude that this is not because she pays attention to environmental science and considers, perhaps, we are in a natural, not human-caused, warming period as has happened before in history. Rather, you can reasonably conclude that she believes God, not human beings, causes any change in the climate. If the climate is changing, it is because God is making it happen. Debates over scientific accuracy are irrelevant to the question. If it were empirically proved that the climate is changing, then there is nothing humans could do about it, because the change is God's will and part of God's plan.

Such environmental providentialism is the majority belief in some places, rendering political discussion of what to do about the carbon burden of fossil fuel burning rather difficult, even impossible. The issue between environmental providentialists and those who wish to work politically to reduce the carbon footprint of their community is not science at all, but rather God's role in, and involvement with, the world. Until people can agree concerning why things happen the way they do and what if anything humans can do to change what is happening, then there is no study, argument, or environmental catastrophe that will convince an environmental providentialist that humans should take action concerning the environment. For such providentialists, it is a simple issue of faith. The only effective thing to do for such folks is pray.

Of course, prayers at public, political meetings have been ruled upon many times. The general consensus of the courts is that sectarian prayers are fine, but any policy that discriminates against different faiths is unconstitutional. For some Christians, such rulings, which make clear that inclusion and diversity are positively valued, are anathema, because they prevent the public appeasing of God in the only "right" way, namely their way. When such Christian politicians represent a diverse religious population, which is the case even in the South these days, they often act irresponsibly and fail to represent properly the people they were elected to serve. This irresponsibility is a result of principled ethical thinking, they would likely say. Such thinking should be familiar to a reasonable officer of the law, but, no matter what the personal beliefs of the officer, allowing providential patterns of thinking to trump inclusion and diversity as values is to change the United States into a fundamentally different country by establishing a dominant religion. That is unconstitutional under any interpretation of the Constitution. Both military officers and police officers are sworn to uphold the Constitution. We might say that the Constitutional principles of inclusion and diversity trump other principles, including particularly religious ones, in view of the disestablishmentarianism of that document. All such sources should be familiar to an effective police officer, to facilitate communication and offer strategies for defusing conflict.

REFERENCES AND FURTHER READING

Gensler, H. J., & Spurgin, E. W. (2008). *Historical Dictionary of Ethics.* Rowman & Littlefield Publishers, Inc.

Gensler, H. J., Spurgin, E. W., & Swindal, J. (2004). *Ethics: Contemporary Readings.* Philosphy Press.

Kant, I. (2008). *Critique of Pure Reason.* Penguin Classics.

Kant, I., & Paton, H. J. (2009). *Groundwork of the Metaphysic of Morals.* Harper Perennial Modern Classics.

Paton, H. J. (1971). *The Categorical Imperative: A Study in Kant's Moral Philosophy.* University of Pennsylvania Press.

Portmore, D. W. (2011). *Commonsense Consequentialism: Whereing Morality Meets Rationality.* Oxford University Press.

Scuton, R. (2001). *Kant: A Very Short Introduction.* Oxford University Press.

Waluchow, W. J. (2003). *The Dimensions of Ethics: An Introduction to Ethical Theory.* Broadview Press.

Wood, A. W. (2007). *Kantian Ethics.* Cambridge University Press.

ENDNOTES

1. For instance, in Walnut, California, it is apparently illegal for a man to dress as a woman without permission from the sheriff, http://observationdeck.io9.com/the-complete-list-of-weird-sex-laws-in-the-u-s-a-1485048155, see also city code Section 17-31, http://qcode.us/codes/walnut/

2. http://www.dol.gov/oasam/hrc/policies/dol-workplace-violence-program.htm.

3. http://www.bjs.gov/index.cfm?ty=pbdetail&iid=4843, consulted 4/13/2014.

4. http://www.nytimes.com/2008/04/23/us/23prison.html?pagewanted=all&_r=0, consulted 4/14/2014.

5. http://www.webcitation.org/5xRCN8YmR, consulted 4/14/2014.

6. In his 2010 Forward to Sam S. Souryal's *Ethics in Criminal Justice: In Search of the Truth* (Burlington, MA: Anderson Publishing, 2011), v.

7. Manning here parenthetically cites "Luhmann, 1985." There is no "References" page until following Chapter One in Souryal's book. Luhmann's name does not appear there. The assumed target is Niklas Luhmann, a well-known German sociologist and systems theorist.

8. Immanuel Kant, *The Groundwork of the Metaphysics of Morals*, 4:421.

9. *Ibid.*, 4:432.

10. *Ibid.*, 4:439.

11. Tim O'Brien, *The Things They Carried* (New York, NY: Broadway Books, 1990), 61.

12. Souryal, *ibid.*, 21.

13. *Ibid.*

14. *Ibid.*

15. From Immanuel Kant: *Critique of Practical Reason and Other Writings in Moral Philosophy*, ed. and trans. by Lewis White Beck (Chicago: University of Chicago Press, 1949), 346–50. Reprinted: New York: Garland Publishing Company, 1976.

16. Ibid., 347.

17. Imanuel Kant, *The Metaphysical Principles of Virtue*, in Prussian Academy Volume VI, (1797); James Ellington's translation in *Immanuel Kant: Ethical Philosophy* (Indianapolis: Hackett, 1983).

18. If you interested in the scholarship of this example, you might start with Christine Korsgaard, "The right to lie: Kant on dealing with evil," in *Philosophy and Public Affairs*, Vol. 15, no. 4 (1986): 325–349.

Consequentialism-Mill: Considering the Ethical Consequences

"A person may cause evil to others not only by his action but by his inaction, and in either case he is justly accountable to them for the injury."

—*John Stuart Mill*

John Stuart Mill was born in 1806, two years after Kant died. He was the son of James Mill, a Scotsman who had moved to London to become Chief Examiner of the East India Company, and lead a group of reformers lobbying for Jeremy Bentham's utilitarian approach to legislation. Jeremy Bentham was the son of a wealthy London barrister (attorney), and a child intellectual prodigy. He taught himself to read very early, and began studying Latin at age three. He attended Queen's College, Oxford, and his father thought he would become Lord Chancellor of England. Upon hearing the leading jurist of his day, William Blackstone, speak, Bentham began writing criticism of English law. He continued this the rest of his life, living quietly on his considerable inheritance, never practicing law, and gathering a following. Into his eighties, he produced ten to twenty pages of writing a day. Bentham's view of how government policy decisions should be made, utilitarianism, contended that all law or policy should bring about the greatest good for the greatest number. This way of thinking was also presented as an ethic guiding personal moral decisions. It is the dominant way of thinking ethically in the United States.

JOHN STUART MILL

John Stuart Mill was also an intellectual prodigy. Bentham assisted James Mill in planning John Stuart's education. John Stuart learned Greek at age three. In 1823, James gave John Stuart a junior clerk's position at the East India Company. The younger Mill also rose to the position of Chief Examiner. In 1865, he was elected to Parliament. His positions came to be at odds with his constituency's wishes, and he was defeated in 1868.

Mill's Consequentialist Utilitarianism

John Stuart Mill (hereafter, Mill) argued, in a great many publications, that the moral worth of actions is to be judged in terms of the consequences of those actions. This is, of course, in direct contrast to Kant, or anyone else who appealed to moral intuitions expressed as principles. Mill thought it obvious that moral intuitions conflict, and that intuition itself cannot arbitrate between conflicting intuitions. Mill attracted opponents, such as William Whewell and T. H. Green, who argued that there were objective ways to arbitrate these conflicts. Their arguments cited a moral order pervading the universe, or an objective moral essence discoverable by rationality. They were Kantian in spirit. Mill pointed out that all knowing is grounded in a limited knower, and dismissed these arguments as no better than "God said so." Such claims appeared to have moral authority, but in fact had none.

Folks like Whewell and Green claimed that moral intuitions reveal ends that are superior to those of our worldly nature, superior to mere pleasure and self-interest, and this is why we have conflicted desires. Mill agreed that our moral feelings often conflict with our inclinations of self-interest. Any drug addict on the street, with any personal awareness at least, would agree. But these feelings are not feelings that are contrary to our pleasure, Mill responded. Intentions based on such feelings, like all ends, are sought to the extent to which they are enjoyable. It is just that different, and conflicting, things are enjoyable.

Mill accounts for these divergent feelings and inclinations by means of his psychological account of human being. This account agrees with Jeremy Bentham that pleasure and pain are the prime motivators. Other things are sought, at least initially, as means to pleasure or the avoidance of pain. Mill posited associative mechanisms in the human mind that connect things that are sought, initially as means to other, pleasurable ends, with those other, pleasurable ends. Things originally sought as means come to be sought as ends in themselves, as parts of pleasure, through constant association with the pleasure of the original end. A consequence of this associative mechanism is that the group of things that come to be sought as ends in themselves conflict with other such ends, all of which are sought because they are associated with pleasure. Therefore, the various ends people consider necessary due to their moral intuitions are just things they have come to associate with pleasure. These conflict with one another. Some are genuine, pleasure-giving ends, while others seem to be genuine, but have simply become associated with pleasure. Even genuine, pleasure-giving ends are not necessarily consistent with one another. Therefore, appealing to moral intuitions does not solve the issues of moral philosophy. Methods for resolving value conflicts lie elsewhere. Mill considered consequentialist utilitarianism to be the appropriate "elsewhere."

Mill believed that *all* ends pursued by human beings are either pleasure or parts of pleasure. This means that pleasure is the end of moral intuitions, indeed of morality itself. Be clear about this. Mill says, "[t]o desire anything, except in proportion as the idea of it is pleasure, is a physical and metaphysical impossibility."[1] This claim is very often misunderstood, as it was by G. E. Moore, a famous 19–20th century British ethicist. Moore thought that when Mill consistently said that the only evidence that anything is desirable is that it is, in fact, desired, this amounted to deriving from "is desired" that something "is worthy of desire." Mill indeed made such an inference, but in a legitimate manner. He did not say that if Bill wants to kill George, then wanting to kill George is a worthy desire. Rather, Mill said we *must* seek pleasure in the same way we *must* make inductions to make sense of language and the world, and *must* accept certain basic perceptual judgments in order to live practically in the same world others do. If the "musts" are justified in the latter two cases, then it is justified in the former case. Mill thought all of these "musts" justified. He also considered that a person who would not admit that could not be convinced that it was so. It was just blindingly obvious to him. Asking anything other than desiring pleasure and wishing to avoid pain of a person was morally unreasonable.

The maximization of pleasure, or happiness, which Mill considered the end of morality was not, however, the maximization of anything crude or simple. Sensual pleasure, for instance, was certainly not the aim of Mill's hedonism. His thinking is to be compared to that of Epicurus, in his letter to Menoeceus:

> By pleasure we mean the absence of pain in the body and of trouble in the soul. It is not an unbroken succession of drinking-bouts and of merrymaking, not sexual love, not the enjoyment of the fish and other delicacies of a luxurious table, which produce a pleasant life; it is sober reasoning, searching out the grounds of every choice and avoidance, and banishing those beliefs through which the greatest disturbances take possession of the soul. Of all this the beginning and the greatest good is prudence.

Mill goes on to say that from prudence comes all the other virtues. Prudence is tied to honor and justice and cannot be separated from them. From those virtues comes a pleasant life. A pleasant life is bound to those virtues. For Mill, happiness is the satisfaction of desire, and the relevant pleasure is the pleasure that comes from satisfied desire. He also strongly insisted that the quality of a particular pleasure counts. In this he disagreed with Bentham, who thought it only necessary to consider the quantity of pleasure. Mill thought reading Coleridge was simply better, as an experience of pleasure, to, say, that of playing tic-tac-toe. As he said, better Socrates dissatisfied than a pig satisfied. Higher pleasures must be planned for, as they are not just a sum of lower pleasures, but are qualitatively different at a chemical level in psychological processes. Among the qualitatively highest ends are moral ends, part of why people think their "moral intuitions" are better than mere self-interest. But they are mistaken. A happy person with a good enough life has both a reasonable balance of relaxed repose and moments of intensely pleasurable events. But how should these people treat others?

Persons are by nature social, Mill believed, and they naturally develop communities. In these communities, rules developed to maximize their collective happiness. Each person in the community wanted enough material goods to satisfy their material needs, but these were scarce, producing conflict, so norms for distributing material goods developed. Conflict did not mean people wished to maximize material goods, but rather that everyone wanted a satisfactory level of goods with some sort of assurance that access to those goods would continue. Mill never met the Koch brothers, or anyone else who thought their goods should be multiplied infinitely. So, norms or rules for distributing scarce goods came to be naturally. And with those norms or rules came ways to enforce them. This is where law enforcement fits in Mill's analysis, as a naturally developing social phenomenon. Police punish those who violate the norms or rules.

These norms or rules, together with their sanctions, became the norms of justice in a community. These norms of justice, in turn, became the means to procuring a satisfactory level of goods and some assurance that they would continue to be available. This level of goods with assurance is pleasure, or the satisfaction of desire. Through associative mechanisms, these norms of justice become sought as ends or parts of pleasure. Their connection to human well-being resulted in their being felt by people as stronger than simple utility in terms of moral demands, but this was an illusion. The principle of utility judges norms of justice.

Some claim that, since Mill insisted that utility judged norms with sanctions attached, Mill was neither an "act utilitarian" nor a "rule utilitarian." He was not an act utilitarian because utility did not judge the rightness and/or wrongness of each individual act. And he was not a rule utilitarian because utility did not function as a second-order principle to determine which norms of justice produced the greatest happiness for the greatest number. In spite of this, Mill did consider that there were two occasions in which utility must judge individual acts directly.

First, utility must judge directly concerning exceptions to norms or rules, or conflicts between them that require subsidiary rules. For instance, Jean-Paul Sartre gave a famous example of a student who came to him during WWII with a question. Should he stay where he is and care for his sick and frightened mother, or should he join the resistance and fight for his country, then occupied by Nazi Germany? Sartre refused to answer the question, perhaps because he considered it a self-defining moment for the young man. The question involved incommensurable norms or rules for living justly. On the one hand, filial loyalty and care for aging parents was expected. On the other hand, bravery and fighting for one's country was also expected. Some subsidiary norm or rule is required, for instance filial requirements trump nationalistic requirements or some such. This situation, Mill observed, would require direct application of utility. As we shall see in the interpretation section below, these situations do not always make utilitarianism attractive.

Second, utility must judge directly actions meant to challenge or change the social structure or norms of justice themselves. Mill betrayed a bit of elitism by not considering such actions as coming from below, perhaps in the form of revolution, but rather considered such actions as coming from above. The "ruling portion of the community," he said, must consider and plan for such changes. Mill thought those in positions of economic or political or moral power (are these different?) could determine, influence at the very least, public feeling concerning social/political/economic change.

Clearly Mill's focus was on using utility as a policy tool for making decisions affecting large numbers of people. He was not so much focused on personal ethical decisions. But there is no denying he did consider, as did Bentham, personal decisions to be subject to the same utilitarian desiderata as public policy decisions. Any number of and very different institutional structures, or norms of justice, might serve well, Mill thought, such large changes serving legitimate ends of justice. Such changes took place over time and through periods of "crisis and consolidation." Mill believed such processes were making progress toward greater justice, or greater utility, as time went on. But what should we say about personal behavior and responsibility? There is not as much to go on in Mill's description of utilitarianism.

Mill seemed to consider, in spite of the fact that individuals almost never acted in the public interest, as it contradicts the principle of utility, that maximizing personal happiness or utility automatically led to maximizing general happiness. If my task, as given to me by utilitarianism, is to maximize my own happiness, then there is no reason for me to consider the general happiness at all. Norms for the social whole are not simply the sum of norms for individuals, so it is difficult to see how this works. It is difficult to see that the principle of utility itself has secure grounds. This does not mean necessarily that humans are incapable of developing norms for resolving conflicts between individuals. Norms of justice, which lead to the satisfaction of both our own and others' needs, can indeed become part of the pleasure of both others and us. In complex modern societies, rules for making change are often built into the norms for justice.

Further, and Mill mentioned this, in contrast to the previous generation of atomistic utilitarians, there is a natural sympathy, a sort of social/political counterpart to Adam Smith's "invisible hand," between people, at least between those who are close. If we are inclined to feel as others feel, which neuroscience calls "mirroring" these days, then each is inclined to feel as others feel, making common rather than conflicting ends more likely. Perhaps, if each of us could move in unity with our fellows, then the good of each and all becomes possible. At the same time, sympathy and particular norms of justice sometimes conflict. You might think women are terribly mistreated in another culture, but not be moved to do or say anything about it because the norms of justice and expected behavior, including religion, are different between that culture and yours.

Mill tended to interpret history as including effective and affective personalities who, in times of crisis and transition, could embody the general sympathy present in a society to bring about better social structures. Had Mill lived in a different time, it is reasonable to consider he would have included not only Socrates and Jesus as fulfilling this role, but Mohammed as well, given that he improved the lot of women in his time, giving them the right to own property, sue for divorce, etc., rights they had not hitherto enjoyed.

INTERPRETING MILL'S CONSEQUENTIALIST UTILITARIANISM

Rather than pursue Mill's utilitarian vision for politics writ large, we shall take advantage of utilitarianism as a source of endlessly discussible, and cussible, moral puzzles. These examples seem to fit straightforward utilitarian reasoning and yet ignore rights we tend to think of as, well, inalienable. Yet straightforward utilitarian reasoning also makes intuitive sense, and there are real-life examples in which most would defend it.

Medical Triage

A situation in which most people would defend utilitarian analysis is medical triage. In my classes, I suggest that a fragmentation grenade has gone off in a certain location in the room. In freshman classes, I usually choose the section containing the least ready for college and least engaged students. Sorry if that is too much information. Medical professionals are usually trained to behave so that, if they are the first persons on the scene of such a disaster, they are to "tag" people. There are usually three categories: (1) people who are dead or soon will be dead, so no medical resources, including time of course, should be spent on them; (2) people who may live if given reasonable first-aid, a quick tourniquet, etc.; (3) people who need aid but can wait till others are treated. The tags are sometimes red, orange, and green. When more medical professionals, say an EMT team, arrives, then this initial classification helps save valuable time. This is clearly a strategy that serves saving the greatest number of people possible, given obviously scarce medical resources, including trained personnel and time. Most people would approve of it, even knowing that mistakes could be and have been made, that a victim classified as beyond hope might be found, after all others are treated, still breathing. And she might be treated and transferred to medical facilities with greater resources, and respond to treatment and survive.

Of course, the reason a strategy is necessary in such a situation is that more could be saved if an EMT team showed up quickly for each individual. But that does not happen, and would be a practically unreasonable expectation. Absent that ideal treatment scenario, decisions regarding who gets the limited medical resources actually available must be made. And no one, generally speaking, has any issues with that.

Transplant

But let us stay with medical resources and propose a different problem. A common illustration is called Transplant. For this, imagine each of five patients in a hospital will die without an organ transplant. The patient in Room 1 needs a heart, the patient in Room 2 needs a liver, the patient in Room 3 needs a kidney, and so on. The person in Room 6 is in the hospital for a routine physical, which she has just passed with flying colors. Her tissue is compatible with the other five patients, and a specialist is available to transplant her organs into the other five. This operation would save their lives, while killing the "donor." There is no other way to save any of the other five patients.

Add that the organ recipients will emerge healthy, the source of the organs will remain secret, the doctor will not be caught or punished for cutting up the "donor," and the doctor knows all of this to a high degree of probability. It looks as if cutting up the "donor" will maximize utility, since five lives have more utility than one life. If this is so, then classical utilitarianism implies that it would NOT be morally wrong for the doctor to perform the transplant and even that it would be MORALLY WRONG for the doctor NOT to perform the transplant. Most people find this result disgusting because it ignores the healthy patient's right to life.

Lifeboat

This is a variation on the Lifeboat illustration, an actual case in which a cabin boy, named Richard Parker, was eaten in a lifeboat in 1883, after the foundering of the ship *Mignonette*, resulting in the famous 1884 British legal case, *R v Dudley and Stephens*. In that case, the problem is set by the issue that all of the occupants of the lifeboat would have starved had the murder and cannibalism not occurred. The case is weakened in real life by the fact that a third passenger in the lifeboat, named Brooks, dissented from the plan and survived, apparently without participation. Brooks was the owner of the ship. Dudley and Stephens were convicted of murder, establishing a precedent that hunger was not a defense against a charge of murder. But of course the question is whether one would condemn the cannibals on utilitarian grounds. If it were established that the threat of starvation were reasonable, then it seems the cannibalism would be morally justified. And indeed not to engage that solution would be immoral. Again, this seems to ignore Richard Parker's right to life.

Transplant Again

An interesting sidelight to the discussion so far would be to modify the Transplant illustration. Suppose the five patients need a kidney, a lung, a heart, etc., because they were all victims of attempted murder. That means five killings will occur if they die, worse than the one killing if the transplants occur. Most people still think it would be morally wrong for the doctor to kill the one to prevent the five killings. This seems to be because the doctor does not kill the five, but does kill the donor. A doctor's duty is to reduce the amount of overall killing, and not doing the transplant operation means the doctor kills no one, which is ideal. But, the utilitarian argues, this means the doctor has no obligation to either promote life or decrease the number of deaths overall, whether by herself or other people. Perhaps your class can decide whether the utilitarian counterargument holds water. Remember, there are at least two different points: (1) does the counterargument properly express the utilitarian point of view, and (2) is that point of view morally correct.

Trolley Car

The question of personal proximity to the cause of death or misfortune is a surprisingly predictive element in cases of moral praise and blame allocation, especially regarding moral praise or blame for one's self. Another common illustration can be given and then modified to make this same point: the Trolley Car. In this illustration, you observe an out-of-control trolley hurtling toward five people who will surely die if hit by the trolley. You can throw a switch and divert the trolley down a side track saving the five but with certainty killing a different innocent bystander. There is no opportunity to warn or otherwise avoid the disaster. Do you throw the switch? You may wish to discuss this in class.

Fat Man

A variation on Trolley Car is Fat Man. In this one, you stand on a bridge with a fat man. The only way to stop the trolley car from killing five is to push the fat man in front of it. He will die, but his body will stop the trolley car before it reaches the five. Do you do so? In an extension of this problem, you are confronted with the same out-of-control trolley car hurtling toward five people who will certainly die. You can throw a switch and divert the trolley car onto a side track that this time joins back up with the main track before it gets to the five people. But, on the side track is the fat man who will certainly die, but the fat man's body will stop the car in time to save the five. What would you do in either of these situations? Are they different? Why?

Is Neuroscience Helpful?

Joshua Greene[2] has done some research concerning what the brain is doing while it is thinking about such ethical problems. Greene found that, when making the decision to divert the trolley, there is activation in brain regions associated with abstract reasoning and cognitive control. On the other hand, he found that, when making the decision not to push the fat man in front of the trolley, there is more activation in areas associated with emotion and cognition. He refers to this discovery of different areas of brain engagement as his "dual-process theory of moral judgment," and notes different answers are given to the problems depending upon which systems of the brain are activated. Perhaps obviously, the decision is more likely to be "do it" when abstract reasoning and cognitive control systems were engaged than when emotion and cognition systems are engaged. Greene suggests the former system is more utilitarian than the latter.

Crying Baby

In further studies, Greene went beyond two different types of responses to two different types of situations to study two different types of responses to the same situation. His illustration or problem is called the Crying Baby Dilemma. The word "dilemma" is just a fancy word for problem. In this thought experiment enemy soldiers have invaded your village, with orders to kill all civilians they find. You and a group of other villagers have found refuge in a cellar of a large house. You have a baby who begins to cry loudly, so you cover its mouth. If you remove your hand from your baby's mouth, the enemy soldiers will hear it, and will kill you, your baby, and all the villagers. But if you keep your hand covering your baby's mouth, the baby will suffocate and die. Is it appropriate for you to smother your baby in order to save yourself and your fellow villagers? You may wish to discuss what you would do in this situation.

Well, this is no longer very amusing in a way. And Greene's research is interesting concerning what happens in our brains when we consider the Crying Baby Dilemma. Greene explains out thought process when considering the dilemma, putting into action the dual process theory. In much the same way as the scenario about whether to push the Fat Man off the bridge to stop the Trolley Car, the Crying Baby Dilemma makes us first react strongly to save the baby, not kill it. At the same time, however, there is a competing response—if you save the baby, everyone gets killed. The brain responds to a difficult dilemma such as this by increasing activity in the anterior cingulate cortex. This area of the brain handles "response conflict." There is an increase in activity in anterior regions of the dorsolateral prefrontal cortex when decisions are made in response to such difficult dilemmas.

So What?

Of course, this indicates there may be no consensus concerning what to do in such situations. Remember Sartre's student, who came to him for advice? The student lived with his aged, depressed mother, whose only comfort was her son's care. But the young man was also moved to fight against the German and Italian fascists, that alliance of business and government interests that wished to enslave the common people. He wished to journey through Spain to England, and join the French resistance. Sartre told the student there was nothing that he, Sartre, could say. The young man was forced to choose between his options, to define himself existentially. There was nothing that Sartre or any other authority could tell him. Sartre has been mercilessly attacked for having no existentialist ethic, when in fact it seems he was acknowledging the validity of both brain systems, or competing moral systems, filial and national loyalty one might call them, corresponding to the two neural systems identified by Greene. Subsidiary rules seem necessary even for personal morality.

Greene found that increased activity in brain areas responsible for abstract reasoning and cognitive control corresponded to utilitarian judgments (i.e., it is appropriate to smother the crying baby). Correspondingly, he found the decision to let the baby cry correlated with increased activity in the emotional center. What you will do appears to depend upon which area is activated most as you consider what to do. Such brain research is new. It does not necessarily explain more than we already knew. Correlation is not causation. The decision is difficult. Either horn of the dilemma can be defended. Nonetheless, the research is interesting and promising.

Brain Damage

In studies focused on patients with damage to their emotional centers, utilitarian thinking appears to increase.[3] These patients have intact capacities for general intelligence, logical reasoning, and knowledge of social and moral norms, but where they suffer is in exhibiting standard emotional response and regulation, often exhibiting reduced levels of compassion, shame, and guilt. They made logical and rational decisions, but without their emotional center pulling them in a particular direction, they tended to make moral judgments that many people would find troubling.

Really, So What?

Is any of this neuroscience helpful? Perhaps it is not. Human consciousness might be more usefully explained by concentrating on the objects of direct experience, including feelings, moods, etc. There is no reason, prior to experience, for elevating science into any sort of authoritarian position regarding particularly moral decisions. Since consciousness itself is not physical or material, perhaps data that is limited to the empirical is not to the point.

Are You Tired Yet?

At the end of this chapter on ethics, you should be learning, at least, that knowing what the "right" thing to do is can be thought about in many ways. Some people, unfortunately, adopt a position more out of thinking fatigue than anything else. Arguments and evidence simply go by the wayside for these folks. But the ancient skeptical position would seem more in line with what these same people have experienced. Critically, Skeptics cataloged three kinds of thinkers who searched for truth. First were the dogmatists, who thought they had discovered truth. Second, there were those who confessed they had not found the truth and claimed the truth could not be found, which could also be classified dogmatist. Third were those who continue the search for truth having not yet found it, which are the Skeptics, who properly suspend belief but do not reject it. If you find that you are unsure what to think, I definitely recommend the Skeptic position. It completely changes the game to consider how few beliefs are necessary to live a very successful life. You might even decide such an approach would produce a successful law enforcement official.

REFERENCES AND FURTHER READING

Beauchamp, T. L. (2000). *Philosophical Ethics: An Introduction to Moral Philosophy*. McGraw-Hill College.

Benn, P. (1997). *Ethics (Fundamentals of Philosophy)*. Routledge.

Darwell, S. (2002). *Consequentialism*. Wiley-Blackwell.

Driver, J. (2011). *Consequentialism (New Problems of Philisophy)*. Routledge.

Kleinig, J. (2008). *Ethics and Criminal Justice: An Introductions (Cambridge Applied Ethics)*. Cambridge University Press.

Lippert-Rasmussen, K. (2005). *Deontology, Responsibility, and Equality*. Museum Tusculanum Press.

Mill, J. S. (2002). *The Utilitarianism* (2nd ed.). Hackett Publishing Company, Inc.

Mill, J. S., & Bentham, J. (1987). *Utilitarianism and Other Essays*. Penguin Classics.

Rachels, J., & Rachels, S. (2011). *The Elements of Moral Philosophy* (7th ed.). McGraw-Hill Humanties.

Scheffler, S. (1988). *Consequentialism and Its Critics*. Oxford University Press.

Shafer-Landau, R. (2014). *The Fundamentals of Ethics*. Oxford University Press.

Turvey, B. E., & Crowder, S. (2013). *Ethical Justice: Applied Issues for Criminal Justice Students and Professionals*. Academic Press.

ENDNOTES

1. J.S. Mill, *Utilitarianism*, Ch. 4.
2. See http://www.wjh.harvard.edu/~jgreene/.
3. See http://www.ncbi.nlm.nih.gov/pmc/articles/PMC2244801/.

Aristotle: A Virtuous Man

"These virtues are formed in man by his doing the actions . . . The good of man is a working of the soul in the way of excellence in a complete life."

—*Aristotle, The Nicomachean Ethics*

The last two chapters concerned deontology, ethics based on duty, and consequentialism, ethics based on consequences, in that order. Both of these ways of thinking are results of the Enlightenment, a period in the history of Western thought and culture stretching roughly from the mid-decades of the seventeenth century through the eighteenth century, characterized by dramatic revolutions in science, philosophy, society, and politics. One of those dramatic revolutions produced the United States. People who pretend to have a college education without understanding the Western Enlightenment are frauds, to put it bluntly. They may have degrees, but they do not have a useful education. Explaining that Enlightenment, however, is beyond the scope of these three chapters. I mention the Enlightenment because there was obviously a way of doing ethics that involved neither deontology nor consequentialism in any narrow or self-conscious way before the seventeenth century. This way, called virtue ethics, either crosses cultures or is a naturally evolving human point of view. China exhibited it even before the Greeks, the usual reference point for us, were born.

VIRTUE ETHICS

This dominant way of thinking morally, virtue ethics, briefly disappeared as a consequence of the Enlightenment, but re-emerged in the middle of the twentieth century, partially at least by means of an article by Elizabeth Anscombe in the journal *Philosophy*, titled "Modern Moral Philosophy." This essay expressed very effectively a frustration with deontology and consequentialism, namely that they gave precious little attention to topics in ethics that had been considered central for thousands of years: the motives and moral character of persons, the moral education of children, the discernment or moral wisdom of persons, the virtues themselves, friendships between persons, family relationships, a reasonably deep concept of happiness, the role of the emotions in the moral lives of persons, and the fundamentally important questions of what sort of person we should be and how we together should live.

The difference in point of view is enormous. Consider that we have happened upon a drowning child. A deontologist would consider some rule like "Do unto others as you would be done by them," and move to help the child out of a duty to obey that rule, whether they consider their rule rational, like Kant, or a matter of religious obedience. A utilitarian would consider that helping the child would increase the amount of well-being or pleasure in the world and reduce the amount of suffering or pain, and is therefore a rational requirement. A virtue ethicist would move to help the child because she had habituated herself over years of discipline to acting benevolently, or charitably, toward others. All three *do the same thing*, but the reasons they give for so doing are very different indeed.

ARISTOTLE

Note the virtue ethicist does not mention rationality, a primary theme of the Enlightenment. Aristotle, the primary source of virtue ethics in our culture, was not particularly distracted by rationality, in spite of his constant talk of rationality and the rational soul, as discussed below. Aristotle rejected the supposedly rational thought castles his friend and teacher, Plato, built in *Republic*, an extremely influential book. Aristotle observed that people were not naturally good or bad. People simply exhibited different characters, depending on what their habits of behavior were. In fact, a habit of behavior was all a virtue was for Aristotle. It might be rational, under some definition, or just natural, to adopt the habits of behavior of the people around whom one grows up. Aristotle in fact advises his son, Nichomachus, hence the *Nichomachean Ethics*, to adopt the habits of the people in his culture who make the decisions, whether he grew up around them or not. In this way one can be upwardly mobile. The point is that you want to be in the group that makes decisions for your culture. And Aristotle does not presuppose that these people, nor their habits of behavior, are good. We are left to guess whether he considers that you stand more of a chance of changing your culture in a good direction if you are a member of the deciding group, no matter whether their habits are good or bad. He did agree with Plato that an individual could not be good in a bad state or community.

But we get ahead of ourselves. If we do not begin where Aristotle began, given the distance between his culture and ours, and his language and ours, we may become misled about crucial issues if we do not go back.

How Did Aristotle "Do" Virtue Ethics?

Aristotle almost immediately gave us a deeper, more satisfying version of happiness than was available in deontology or consequentialism. Neither the dour, joyless duty of deontology nor the calculating, chess machine-like nature of consequentialism seem even central to a good life, as Anscombe so persuasively argued. Aristotle thought everything had an end or purpose, a *telos*, including persons. So, whatever he says about the good for man, or ethics, will be couched in teleological terms. This gives us a single word for virtue ethics. It is teleological. So we have deontology, consequentialism, and teleology. Note right away that teleological thinking obviously overlaps with consequentialism. But also be sensitive to the differences as we explain Aristotle's approach to virtue ethics.

A teleological system of thinking is one that assumes final causes in nature. It is important we understand what a "final cause" was for Aristotle. He thought there were four causes, or "becauses," that explained any and every physical object. First, there was the stuff of the object, that of which it was made. In the case of a person, this was flesh, blood, and bone. In the case of a marble statue, it was marble. Second, there was the way in which the object came to be. In the case of a person, this was sexual reproduction. In the case of a marble statue, it was the activities of the sculptor. Third, there was the shape and function of the object. In the case of a person, this was the human body's shape and both reproducing and becoming rational, presumably to include living and doing well. In the case of a statue, the shape might be the same, but the function is to honor, memorialize, decorate, or whatever the statue was supposed to do. Fourth, there was the end or purpose of the object's existence. *This is the final cause.* In the case of a person, this was to achieve adult shape and function.

That is all, and the final cause is different for every species. But every species has a *telos*, an end toward which its activity aims.

To get at what happiness for a human being is, something Aristotle called *eudaimonia*, he asked what the natural good for humans was. Well, they want to live well and do well. This is simple enough, although richer and fuller than Enlightenment deontology or utilitarianism. Aristotle goes to some pains to make sure his son understands what he means, and following the way he does this will be helpful.

Discovering what the good of man is can be done, for Aristotle, by considering the nature of man. He began teaching his son with an illustration designed to define the subject matter of the inquiry. What are we investigating, this "Good of Man"? He suggested we contrast *instrumental* ends with *intrinsic* ends, which is to say *acts accomplished as means for other ends* with *acts accomplished for their own sake* respectively.

A good way to think about this, Aristotle said, predictably given the warring nature of his society and ours, was to consider "every action associated with war." If we considered all of the many acts which are involved in the total activity of preparing for and executing a war, Aristotle contended, we would notice a series of acts which have their own intermediate ends but which, when finished, can be seen as having been accomplished as instrumental or means for still other ends. The carpenter constructs barracks. When he is finished, he might say he has fulfilled his function as a carpenter. He might be a good carpenter, but this is not the same as being a good man. He might be a good carpenter and a lousy man, after all. But of course the barracks are not an end in themselves, but rather a means for safely housing soldiers, protecting them from the elements, so that they can pursue the war. Likewise the bridle maker might make a set of bridles and say he has fulfilled his function as a bridle maker when he is finished. But the bridles are not ends in themselves, but means to the end of controlling horses. And controlling horses is not an end in itself, but a means for using the horses effectively in battle. The shipbuilder is finished when the ship launches, but it is a means for transporting troops to the battlefield. The doctor fulfills his function by keeping the soldiers healthy, but they are kept healthy in order for them to be effective fighters/soldiers. The military officer aims at winning the war, and fulfills his function as an officer if he does win, but this winning is a means to peace.

Peace is sometimes taken to be an end in itself, but it is not in Aristotle's view. Peace is a means for creating conditions under which men can fulfill their function as men, not their function as carpenters, bridle makers, ship builders, doctors, officers, or even soldiers. When we can say what men aim at as men, then we will have arrived at an action done for its own sake, an intrinsic good. All other activity will be explainable as means to this end, which will be the Good of Man. This is how Aristotle explains the subject matter of ethics. By the way, there is nothing that can really be done about Aristotle's male chauvinism. The word "man," he would say, includes all persons, but he really thought of females as defective males. There it is. Defending it would be ridiculous. Not much has really changed.

What Is the Function or Nature of Man?

Now that we know what it is we are investigating, we should be careful with the words we use to describe it. What does the word "good" mean in "the Good of Man"? Aristotle agreed with Plato that the adjective "good" refers to the particular function of a thing. A good knife did what knives were supposed to do, cut things, for which they needed to be sharp and hold an edge. A good doctor or carpenter fulfilled his function as a doctor or builder. It was the same for all professions and crafts. But being a good carpenter or doctor did not mean the same as being a good man. A good carpenter might not be a good man, as we mentioned earlier. To know what a good man was, we needed to know what the particular function of human nature was. A good man would fulfill his function as a man.

Speaking as a biologist, Aristotle said, if "the eye, hand, foot and in general each of the parts evidently has a function, may one lay it down that man similarly has a function apart from all of these?" What was the distinctive activity of a man? It was not living, because man shared that activity with vegetables. It was also not sensation, for animals share that. The something else that all men aimed for involved the rational part of the human soul.

Small Interlude on "Rationality" and the "Soul"

Oh no, rationality again, not to mention the human "soul." I will run through this quickly. The word "soul" was not something exclusively human for Plato or Aristotle. Anything that moved, generally, had a soul. Even plants move toward the sun, and had souls for Aristotle. What made the human soul different was that it had a rational component. Aristotle in particular thought the capacity for language was essential to human rationality, or the rationality in a human soul. He was not aware of the capacities of the chimpanzee, Lana, at the Yerkes Center. Lana amassed a vocabulary of more than a thousand words, and used language with some skill, in an experiment done during the 1970s. In any case, the word "soul" had nothing like the religious connotations it carries today.

Further, Aristotle more or less adopted Plato's tripartite description of the soul, or human essence. First, there was the appetitive part, the part that wanted food, drink, sex, money, etc. Second, there was the spirited part, NOT to be confused with a "spiritual" part. The spirited part of the soul was the part that valued honor, military honor. It was the "Death before Dishonor," real Marine part of the soul. Thirdly, there was the rational part of the soul. A "just" soul, for Plato, was a soul in which the appetitive and spirited parts were dominated by the rational part. The lower two parts of the soul, in a just soul, acquired and consumed food and drink, engaged in sexual activity, acquired money, and acted honorably and bravely, but accomplished all this activity within boundaries set by the rational part of the soul. That was Plato.

Aristotle spoke of the irrational parts of the soul and invoked Plato's desiring or appetitive notion in addition to Aristotle's own vegetative notion as the two irrational parts of the soul. Moral action was action. Function could not manifest unless there was action. The irrational parts of the soul led to bad actions, while the rational part led to good actions that accorded with the Good for Man, which we have not yet fully named. Aristotle thought of the moral playing field in terms of sport and said, "as at the Olympic games it is not the finest and the strongest men who are crowned, but they who enter the lists, for out of these the prize winning men are selected; so also in life, of the honorable and good, it is they who act rightly who win prizes." So, "an active life of the element [of the soul] that has a rational principle," so long as the actions are "in accordance with virtue," indicates a well functioning soul. This activity was the Good for Man. Why develop the habits that led to the Good for Man? We develop them in order to live well and do well. Finally, we have described happiness, *eudaimonea*, as living well and doing well, and as that toward which all persons intend their actions. This is the function or nature of man, to live well and do well.

What is this "Virtue" in the Phrase "In Accordance With Virtue"?

What did it mean to act in accordance with virtue, or what was virtue for Aristotle? The appetitive part of the soul, or human consciousness, was affected and influenced by objects and persons outside of the self or soul. The way in which the appetitive soul reacted to these outside influences was with passions (e.g., love and hate). Aristotle thought of concupiscence as a passion to possess or be close to objects and/or persons, whereas irascibility was a passion to avoid or destroy objects or persons. These passions for creation and destruction could clearly have gone wild were there no boundaries brought to bear on them. In themselves, they contained no rational principle of measure or selection. What should a person love/hate? How much? How should a person relate himself to wealth, pleasure, honor, or other persons? What difference do circumstances make? Aristotle thought persons did not automatically act rightly regarding these issues, but that a person could develop virtuous habits of thought and action that addressed these issues. He said, "none of the moral virtues arises in us by nature; for nothing that exists by nature can form a habit contrary to its nature."

Since the threat of the passions was that they could constitute extreme feelings and provoke extreme actions, Aristotle conceived of the virtues as means between extremes. He spoke of excess and defect in feelings and actions. This presupposed a balanced mid-point or mean. We might feel fear, confidence, lust, anger, compassion, pleasure, or pain either too much or too little. Virtue is to feel these things when we should, toward whom we should, and in the right strength between too much and too little. For instance, courage is a virtue. I can miss the mark of having this virtue in two ways. I can be so concerned that others perceive me as courageous that I act in foolhardy ways, challenging people for no real reason.

In my classes I sometimes suggest the thought experiment that Hulk Hogan, a giant person, is a friend of mine. He has asked permission to sit in on a class, just to get a feel for philosophy. He sits in the back of the classroom, for anyone sitting behind him would be unable to see the front. In the first case, he sits passively and respectfully through the class. But, about twenty minutes in, his huge bulk generates in me a feeling I am not being perceived as male enough by the class, and this in turn causes me to think my status as a virtuous and courageous male is being threatened. So, in spite of his passivity, I run back and punch him in the face. Aside from the fact that I likely have seconds to live, have I demonstrated the Aristotelian virtue of courage? No. This is not courage, but rather foolhardiness. It is too much dependence on my interpretation of other's impressions, if you like, or not enough personal fear.

In the second case, Hogan sits passively through twenty minutes of the class and *he*, for whatever reason, becomes threatened and reacts by grabbing the nearest young person and flinging her up against a side wall, saying "Bah, humbug." The class, including me, is stunned for a moment, so he grabs another young person and flings him against the other side wall. We all just sit there, thinking, "Wow, he is huge," and he flings several more people around and leaves, barely squeezing through the door but slamming it in disgust. We finally recover our wits enough to call 911 for ambulances for the victims. Have any of us demonstrated the Aristotelian virtue of courage? No. We have all failed to act because we were afraid. That is called cowardice.

For Aristotle, courage is a virtue that indicates knowing what to fear and when to be afraid. Cowardice, too much fear, and foolhardiness, too little fear, are both vices. In similar ways, Aristotle categorized all virtues as a mean or middle between two vices or raw passions. Through the rational capacity of the soul, passions like fear are controlled and actions are guided. Through practice, we can form habits of rationally controlling of our feelings and creating our character, or normal state of being, "a state apt to exercise deliberate choice, being in the relative mean, determined by reason, and as the man of practical wisdom would determine." The cardinal moral virtues for Aristotle were courage, temperance, justice, and wisdom.

Practical Wisdom for Aristotle

The sort of reasoning that controls the passions and measures actions in the practical world is practical reason, *phronesis* for Aristotle. This is different from theoretical reason, which gives us fixed principles and scientific knowledge. Practical reason gives us rules of thumb to guide our actions in various circumstances. Theoretical reasoning gives us philosophical wisdom and practical reasoning gives us practical wisdom. Without practical reason, man would have no capacity for moral action.

Though Aristotle thought man had a natural capacity for right action, he did not think man acted rightly by nature. Goodness or right action was in man potentially, but its actualization resulted from a process of knowing what he must do, deliberating about how to do it under infinitely varying circumstances, and choosing. It is not as if man would act rightly in the same mechanical and inevitable way the acorn would become an oak tree. This meant that Aristotle disagreed with Socrates and Plato that knowing what was good was sufficient for doing what was good. It was possible for someone who knew what she should do to not do it through weakness of will, *akrasia*. This was a large part of his advice to his son. Be aware, he suggested, that you could, at any point in your life, and no matter how habituated you have become to acting rightly, suddenly act wrongly. And the price may be high. Your entire life could be denied the adjective "happy," if you die badly, as for instance Socrates did in Aristotle's opinion. See the section on luck below. Such advice seems well placed for a career in law enforcement, as many outstanding careers have been ruined by one case of poor judgment.

Assigning blame and praise assumed choice for Aristotle. It made no sense to him to blame a person for something he had no choice but to do or not do. A person should be held accountable only for a voluntary act. An act done out of ignorance of particular circumstances is not voluntary, for instance opening a steel door that sparks an explosion without knowing a volatile gas was present. An act done from external compulsion was also not voluntary, as was an act done to avoid a greater evil, such as burning a wheat crop to prevent the spread of wheat blight to other fields.

The Unabashed Inclusion of Luck in the Well-Lived Life

This well-lived life was to be taken in the long run. Aristotle said, "it is not one swallow or one fine day that makes a spring, so it is not one day or a short time that makes a man blessed and happy." The ultimate end was a well-lived life, a life characterized as *eudaimonia*. So long as a man's actions were rationally directed and in accord with virtue, he might, if he were lucky, live well. Aristotle did allow for the possibility that a good man might not live well. He said:

> For there is required, as we said, not only complete virtue but also a complete life, since many changes occur in life, and all manner of chances, and the most prosperous may fall into great misfortunes in old age, as is told of Priam in the Trojan Cycle; and one who has experienced such chances and has ended wretchedly no one calls happy.

Politics as An Extension of Ethics

Aristotle agreed with Plato that politics was an extension of ethics. As man had a purpose, so had the state. In fact, the nature of man entailed the state. He said, "it is evident that the state is a creature of nature and that man is by nature a political animal." Man and the state were so closely related for Aristotle that he classified anyone who could not live in a state a beast, and one who did not need a state a god. The purpose of the state was analogous to the family, which has the purpose of preserving life for its members. In the case of the state, members were families and villages. Families and villages are not self-sufficient, but need protection and an economy. Beyond this, the state existed for the purpose of ensuring the supreme good of man, his moral and intellectual life. Aristotle did ultimately choose the intellectual life as the highest form of life, above political life. But this intellectual life required peace and order in political life, and he would have agreed with Plato regarding the necessary function of law enforcement at a political level.

Not only did Aristotle not create any sort of plan for an ideal state, as did Plato in his *Republic*, but he thought most political writings were impractical. A politician needed to understand what could and could not be done in a particular situation and be willing to compromise to achieve what was more or less best and would preserve the state. Aristotle thought Plato's notions of abolishing the family for the guardian class, establishing a public nursery for their children, and having them hold their property communally were just ludicrously impractical. In his opinion, this did away with natural loyalties of familial affection that the state should naturally strengthen as serving its own purpose of cooperation toward common ends of successful economies. The trick of being a good statesman or politician was to line up personal and private interests in such a way that the majority of the energy was headed in the same direction and toward the fulfilling of the function of the state, which was to provide economically and socially for the people and protect them from other states.

Aristotle did consider there were three basic sorts of governments: rule by one, a few, or many. These were monarchy, aristocracy, and polity respectively. Any of these, when functioning rightly, governed for the common good of all the people. Rulers who govern for their own private gain or interest are perverted and unnatural. Perverted and unnatural forms of these types of government were tyranny, oligarchy, and democracy. Aristotle's own preference was aristocracy, though he recognized the superiority of a single ruler with exceptional excellence, he thought such persons in short supply. In aristocracy, a group of men whose excellence, achievement, and ownership of property made them responsible, able, and capable of command could pool their skills to rule for the common good of all the people.

Natural Slaves?

Aristotle's elitist tendencies led him to make mistakes in the estimation of many people. He thought there were natural slaves, for instance, and he owned slaves. In fact, Herpyllis, the mother of Nicomachus, may have been a slave. Some he freed in his will. He distinguished between natural slaves and those enslaved as conquered peoples. He thought the latter to be unjust. He also thought citizenship should not be extended to laborers, because citizens should take their share in ruling and being ruled in turn. This required presence in the assembly and law court, not to mention appropriate temperament, character, and preparation. Laborers did not have time for any of this, and so should not have been citizens in his view.

Political Revolution?

Aristotle thought of political revolution as a fact, something that happened due to "the desire of equality, when men think they are equal to others who have more than themselves." Revolution might also occur due to insolence and avarice or fear and contempt. He thought a state would be well advised to take precautions against revolution, primarily by ruling in the common interests of all the people. Kings should avoid despotic acts. Aristocracies should avoid rule by a few rich men in their own business interests. A polity should provide ample time for its abler members to share in governing. He also thought the beginnings of change should be discouraged and respect for and obedience to the law should be jealously guarded. People will criticize a state that does not provide conditions of living in which they can achieve happiness and what they consider to be a good life.

Aristotle and Plato Disagreed on the Moral Usefulness of Art

Plato's negativity and suspicion concerning art was almost completely lacking in Aristotle. While they agreed that art was an imitation of nature, Plato thought art was several steps removed from the truth and therefore to be avoided as distorting knowledge. In *Republic*, Book X, Plato attacks poets as dangerous and destabilizing to the state. They use the language of the Forms, but they have not gone through the education necessary to understand the Forms, which education he has described in the earlier nine books of *Republic*. Since they use the language of the Forms in an uninformed manner, they represent a danger of leading other ignorant people to disobey their leaders, who have received proper knowledge of the Forms. Aristotle rejects Plato's Forms as proper objects of knowledge in the first place and thus develops his own view of poets and other artists.

Aristotle straightforwardly accepted that art communicates information about nature even as it imitates nature. Since universal forms existed only in particular things for Aristotle, artists were reporting information when they studied natural objects and produced artistic versions of them. For Aristotle, art was deeply psychologically significant. The instinct for imitation obvious from very early in a child's life was a way of learning about the world and how to behave in it. On top of this instinct is the pleasure people experience when contemplating art. So, "the reason men enjoy seeing a likeness is that in contemplating it they find themselves learning or inferring and saying perhaps, 'ah, that is he.'"

In his *Poetics*, Aristotle compared history to poetry and found poetry "more philosophical and a higher thing than history; for poetry tends to express the universal, history the particular." The sort of universality he meant was "how a person of a certain type will on occasion speak or act, according to the law of probability or necessity." The poet comes closer to dealing with the basic human, the natural thing, as opposed to a series of events in which they participated.

Aristotle also offered detailed, careful analyses of epic poetry, tragedy, and comedy. His remarks about what tragedy consists of and what its function is have most influenced contemporary aesthetic theory. He says, "A tragedy is the imitation of an action that is serious and also, as having magnitude, complete in itself; in language with pleasurable accessories, each kind brought in separately in the parts of the work; in a dramatic, not a narrative form; with incidents arousing pity and fear, wherewith to accomplish its catharsis of such emotions." Much ink has been spilled over whether catharsis means we somehow purge ourselves of and do away with the emotions of pity and fear or we have the opportunity to feel and express these emotions in a deep and satisfying, albeit vicarious, manner. Whatever it means, Aristotle clearly thought tragedy was an artistic experience that ennobled and purified the audience morally, perhaps by educating the passions concerning extremes to be avoided, encouraging virtue.

Do you think art, say plays and/or movies, do or could serve any moral purpose? Do you think a law enforcement officer who thought about the natural ends of humans in the way Aristotle did would be a good officer?

CONCLUDING QUESTIONS

There we have it: deontology, consequentialism, and teleology, or duty ethics, utilitarianism, and virtue ethics. Have this reading and the discussions you have had in your class been useful to you? Do you think they will serve you well as a law enforcement officer? Do you have a favorite way of thinking about ethical behavior? Can you defend it? As you worked your way through his material, did you recognize and categorize the dominant way in which you were taught to think about moral issues as a child? Do you see both strengths and weaknesses in making decisions according to the way you were raised? Do you know people who were raised differently and think about issues differently? Did you recognize their methods of thinking in the three offered here? Can you think of some other way to think about ethics? Is awareness of different approaches to issues useful to a law enforcement officer? What is the proper end or *telos* of a law enforcement officer? Is it appropriate to end these three chapters with a series of questions rather than a summary of how a law enforcement officer should act?

REFERENCES AND FURTHER READING

Ansombe, G. E. (2006). *Human Life, Action and Ethics: Essays by G.E.M Anscombe.* (M. Geach, & L. Gormally, Eds.) Imprint Academic.

Aristolte. (2009). *The Nichomachean Ethics.* (L. Brown, Ed., & D. Ross, Trans.) Oxford University Press.

Crisp, R., & Slote, M. A. (1997). *Virtue Ethics.* Oxford University Press.

Gardiner, S. M. (2005). *Virtue Ethics Old and New.* Cornell University Press.

MacIntyre, A. (2007). *After Virtue: A Study in Moral Theory* (3rd ed.). University of Notre Dame Press.

Plato. (1992). *Republic.* (C. D. Reeve, Ed., & G. M. Grube, Trans.) Hackett Publishing Company, Inc.

Richter, D. (2010). *Anscombe's Moral Philosophy.* Lexington Books.

Statman, D. (1997). *Virtue Ethics: A Critital Reader.* Edinburgh University Press.

Ethics and the Police

CHAPTER 6

"Relativity applies to physics, not ethics."
—*Albert Einstein*

By all accounts, Officer Larry DePrimo did not want to be a hero in the way we envision our police officers—let alone one of New York Police Department's finest—taking such strides. However, one cold, nighttime patrol beat in November 2012 offered him an opportunity, and when he bought a pair of boots for a shoeless citizen that evening, his act of simple generosity became a reflective moment for police-public relations in New York City and across the United States. As Officer DePrimo kneeled and assisted the citizen in putting on the boots he had purchased him, the act was captured at a distance by Arizona tourist Jennifer Foster, herself a sheriff's department dispatcher, and subsequently "went viral" after Foster posted the photo to the NYPD Facebook page. Within a week, Officer DePrimo had become a national celebrity as accolades poured in for his act of selflessness from places around the world. In a city where the relationship between the police and the public had been through trial and tumult, Officer DePrimo initiated a discussion about police behavior—and ethics—that continues to intrigue criminal justice professionals and students as well as citizens everywhere (Goodman, 2012).

In a sense, Officer DePrimo's act and the national dialogue that followed raised interesting questions about police ethics in the digital age. One simple act, whether generous or violent, captured by ever-present cameraphones and immediately posted to social media, can carry huge repercussions for individuals and organizations in criminal justice. The attention given the NYPD and Officer DePrimo could have been less positive and even critical had his act been an arrest, or even a casual encounter with a citizen that caused notice because of language, tone, or tactic. The DePrimo case indicates the degree to which individual officers' and their departments' ethical orientations are on a global stage at all times. It is this critical transformation, in technology as well as in the police role, that were captured in Jennifer Foster's now-iconic photograph that November evening.

The term "transformation" is used above with caution, but with confidence. The police profession has yet to come to terms with the manner by which ordinary citizens, even in the last decade or less, have used everyday devices to revolutionize the police ethical landscape, placing ethical responsibilities at the forefront of police-citizen interaction. Such technological changes are indicative of the current volatile and rapidly changing police ethical environment that has allowed for greater scrutiny and accountability. The ethical foundations of the police profession have never been more visible, and the risks are more accentuated. Consider the current police ethical climate:

- Albany (New York) Sheriff's Deputy Stan Lenic is publicly celebrated as a hero for refusing to remove two citizens from the Albany Airport who were passing out flyers informing travelers of their rights to opt out of Transportation Security Administration search policy. The citizens filmed the incident and posted it to the internet (Seiler, 2012).

- Tennessee State Trooper James Moss is fired and subsequently indicted for misconduct and evidence-tampering after he allegedly received oral sex from a motorist and filmed the encounter. After Trooper Moss sent the motorist the video, she posted it to her weblog, leading to his arrest (Schoetz, 2007).

- Changing generational preferences—and laws—with regard to marijuana use are highlighted as the Seattle, Washington police department determines, after Washington state citizens voted to legalize recreational marijuana use, to relax restrictions for police recruits whose personal histories reflected prior use of marijuana. A partial explanation given for the rule change is to make the department more reflective of the community it serves (Kaminsky, 2012).

- Dallas, Texas police chief David Brown maintains a Twitter feed where he publicly shames Dallas police officers whom he fires for wrongdoing, stating their offense and using their proper name, and earning a mixed reaction from employees, media, and citizens (Matyszczyk, 2014).

These are but a few of the more high-profile recent incidents underscoring the urgency and importance by which police ethics have been shaped by shifting public opinion, often fueled by technology and social media. Within each, a central moral question with regard to how police should and should not behave, interact with the public, enforce the law, and conduct themselves professionally is hidden. This chapter will focus on these moral underpinnings, and examine ways in which the current police ethical landscape can be interpreted and understood.

POLICE ETHICS: DEFINING THE FOCUS

There are many variations of working definitions of ethics, and as ethics pertains to policing it can incorporate many dimensions. But in a practitioner context, ethics may imply *activity* and *behavior*, as noted from some of the above examples. One interpretation of the "action" component of ethics is Hoban's emphasis on "moral values in action" (Hoban, 2012), in which critical thinking ability and evaluation of moral behavior intersects with moral duty and action. The popularity of Hoban's warrior-like ethical interpretation with police practitioners should be of interest: long-persisting discussions of the "battle" and "war"-inspired aspects of the police role, and police organizations that resemble paramilitary structures, continue to have varying degrees of effect on the public image of police themselves, especially contemporarily (Balko, 2013; Fry & Berkes, 1983). An American Civil Liberties Union report which recently portrayed United States police agencies as being increasingly militarized illustrates the degree to which police officers' ethical orientations are increasingly distant from public approbation (ACLU, 2014). What this chapter intends to illustrate is that ethical orientations in postmodern society, specifically in an era when disparate "realities" are interpreted through the lens of democratized media and social media, have an explicit effect on the police profession at large as it struggles continually to provide justification for the behavior of its participants. Police want and need to convince the public that their actions, beliefs, and behaviors are morally just and in the best interest of those whom they serve, but these "morals in action" are structurally difficult to justify in the face of an increasingly fragmented and disbelieving population. Adding increasing calls for accountability and fluctuating budgetary and fiscal concerns only illustrates how hard it is to examine police ethical behavior objectively. But it appears historically that, to varying degrees, this has always been the case in our nation's history.

THE HISTORICAL ROOTS OF POLICE ETHICAL CHALLENGES

At what point in the past history of the United States, namely with regard to police training and education, did the study of ethics become important for the police profession? This is an important question, because police ethical scholarship is a relatively recent phenomenon, especially to the degree that it is highlighted in the public conscience as it is today. It is difficult to pinpoint, but with the ascent of criminal justice scholarship and its effect on police policymaking, police scholars began to turn their attention from impressionistic portrayals of authoritarianism (Niederhoffer, 1969) to more academic examinations of police moral content. The classic study by Muir (1977) of police moral codes, specifically Muir's focus on how police morals are created and reinforced by police organizations themselves, generated a branch of criminal justice scholarship which still impacts both academic and practitioner audiences (Muir, 1977). Police officers in training environments, and students of policing, have probably been studying what constitutes "police ethics" for only a generation.

That does not mean that the issue itself has been of no concern until now, especially since police history is fraught with lapses in ethical orientation. The long past of police-citizen interaction, specifically with surging immigrant populations in the pre-professional era and the African-American civil rights movement, offers opportunities to examine the foundation upon which police ethics have evolved. Students of police history understand the impact of high-profile events such as the Haymarket Riot and the Birmingham civil rights campaign as signposts of gradual improvement in police-public relations; but what of the ethical orientations of the profession at those moments? If we use Hoban's definition of "moral values in action" as an indication of what was occurring along the historical trajectory of police behaviors, is it simplistic to say that police ethics have always been a reflection of society's ethics at those times?

BOX 6.1

POLICE ETHICS AND THE POLICE-PUBLIC PARTNERSHIP: *FIVE CRITICAL HISTORICAL EVENTS*

Haymarket Riot (1886), Chicago, Illinois. From a different era in American society, a labor strike results in outright combat as protestors volley explosives at police, who strike back with gunfire, killing 11 and injuring hundreds.

Wickersham Commission (1931), "Report on Lawlessness in Law Enforcement." An ironic title hides cold truths about the relationship between the police and the public in this 1931 report introducing the word "brutality" into the police lexicon. It acted as the foundation for police reform movements throughout the 20th century.

Birmingham, Alabama Civil Rights struggle (1963). Portraying the relationship between the police and the public as one of mutual distrust and anger, and with a newly attentive global media at hand, this flashpoint represents a critical moment for American police ethics and the initial struggle to craft a mutual partnership from chaos.

Chicago Democratic Convention (1968). With the whole world indeed watching, police misconduct is placed on full view as an acceptable political impulse for probably the final time in American history. Police unprofessionalism's Waterloo.

(Continued)

BOX 6.1 (Continued)

Herman Goldstein's Problem Oriented Policing (19790). Returning the focus of the police role to the community and service was a gradual byproduct of the 1970's urban malaise and violent crime crisis, but the publication of Goldstein's work framed the discussion in terms of specific tasks police could perform. Its impact on discussions of police ethics is incalculable, and it serves as the watershed moment for future research and policy development in this category.

For further reading on these events, see:

J. Green (2006), *Death In the Haymarket: A Story of Chicago, the First Labor Movement, and The Bombing That Divided Gilded Age America*. Toronto, ON: Pantheon Books.

J. Q. Wilson (1968), *Varieties of Police Behavior*. Cambridge, MA.: Harvard University Press.

T. Branch (1989), *Parting the Waters: America in the King Years, 1954–1963*. New York, NY.: Simon & Schuster.

N. Mailer (1968), *Miami and the Siege of Chicago*. New York, NY.: Donald Fine Publishers.

H. Goldstein (1990). *Problem-Oriented Policing. New York, NY.: McGraw Hill Publishers.*

Consider two illustrations that may put the historical roots of police ethics into perspective. During the Gilded Age in the United States (roughly 1870's to 1900), an era that police historians call the "preprofessional era," police training as we know it was nonexistent. The apparatus of police supervision and accountability known to us was absent, and patrol technique consisted mostly of urban areas covered on foot. A two-way relationship of distrust between the police officers themselves (who were largely uneducated) and the public persisted. Political corruption saturated police behavior, from the urban political machines to the violence of the Prohibition Era (Alpert et al., 2006). Quite simply, policing in the United States reflected the brutal nature of life in urban America and its whims, populations, and growing pains one generation removed from the Civil War. What passed for "ethics" on the part of police officers themselves, their moral values reflected in behavior, would be difficult to quantify without referring to these constructs, let alone compare to our current age. But it can be said that examining the growth in interpretations of police roles and responsibilities since then has been fundamental to reinforcing what we seek to call "police ethical responsibilities" today. A second illustration helps us understand further: in 1967, in the metropolis of Detroit, a city fractured by urban dislocation (caused, ironically, by the tremendous economic growth of the automobile industry), racial animosities were inflamed to the point of violence during the "long, hot summer" of that year. Detroit police officers responding to an illegal nightclub provoked protest as they dispersed the crowd, many of whom responded with violence. What followed was the worst race riot in American history until that point, and long-standing anger toward the city's police department and its tactics was unleashed (Herman, 2005). But the moral values of urban police officers in 1967 stood opposed to the expectations and needs of the population of Detroit, specifically African Americans, at this time: police behavior in Detroit in 1967 was notoriously without consequence, brutal, and violent (Westley, 1970). Using these two examples, police ethics resembles an arc extending from different time periods in American history that, when examined historically, embodied values and morals that appear unjust by today's moral standard.

The irony of the foreword to Westley's classic work *Violence and the Police* should resonate with anyone examining police ethics in the 21st century. Writing at the cusp of the 1970's, which represented an era of turmoil, violence, and political upheaval, Westley described police officers as living in a

"world . . . spawned of degradation, corruption, and insecurity. He sees man as ill-willed, exploitative, mean, and dirty; himself a victim of injustice, misunderstood and defiled. Hungry for approval, uneasy as to his own worth, wrathful and without dignity, he walks alone—a pedestrian in Hell." (Westley, 1970, foreword).

This shocking assessment indicates the difficulty in examining police ethics as a linear historical progression, yet also the importance of recognizing it and studying it as a progression at all. On the one hand, it can be read as a historical artifact, a relic from a time when police knowledge was stunted and officers themselves distant from the public they served. On the other hand, it could in many ways be applicable to certain officers, locales, and departments today as they struggle to define what moral actions are proper—and permissible—for their communities.

ETHICAL REFORM IN POLICING: LITIGAPHOBIA AND PROFESSIONALIZATION

Recalling the long past of police ethical changes, it is difficult not to envision a slow pendulum swing, influenced by community mandates, political winds, crime increases or decreases, and leadership shifts. Ethical questions may be raised by these ripples in the police pattern: a recent *New York Times* article called into question the ethical foundation of following the city's tried-and-tested "broken windows" crime policy during times of less violent crime (Goldstein, 2014). Police ethics, tactics, and policies appear to be part of a dynamic pattern that adapts to change as well as it influences changes that occur. This impression is critical to examining police ethics over time, because although they appear linear, litigation and professionalization appear cyclical in the wake of technological changes, a system of continual ethical checks and balances.

The Impact of "Litigaphobia" on Police Ethics

Court cases supporting ethical reconsiderations in policing are numerous, but the principle behind such efforts and the effect of litigation on the psyche of American law enforcement deserves attention. "Litigaphobia," or the fear of being sued (in police contexts civilly, but also potentially criminally), has been seen as supportive of better training and subsequently of a "watchdog" mentality that has transformed the American police landscape. Speaking long before the advent of pervasive cellphone cameras and YouTube videos which provide tools for citizens to "watch" police more closely, Alpert and Dunham (1996) saw a link between civil lawsuits and police training, with litigation potentially leading to better ethical standards and practice. Also, Kappeler (2006) recognized that judgments resulting from civil lawsuits had resulted in increased training standards, educational levels, and stronger ethical foundations for the police profession. Unexpectedly, the culture of litigation has contributed to maintenance and improvement of police ethical standards.

The Push for Professionalism and Standards

One of the pervasive criticisms of police ethics brought by the reform movement of the late 1970's and early 1980's was that the very police bureaucracy and apparatus which hires, trains, and inculcates values to officers exerted a form of control that hindered the development of better police ethical standards (Brown, 1988). Often, departmental expectations of their officers (and therefore, of their behavior and actions) were seen as undefined, even ambiguous, leading to an interpretation of policy directives as inviting dispute or, at worst, invalid. Throughout the 1980's, emphasis on the police order-maintenance role (coupled with, possibly, the failure to adequately implement community policing through stronger training for the requirements of that role) stunted ethical standards improvement because of bureaucracy and organizational indifference (Chappell, 2009). Endangered because of poor implementation, community policing was supported more by external forces that assisted departments in navigating the new police ethical landscape. Organizations such as the Police Executive Research Forum (PERF), International Association of Chiefs of Police (IACP), the National Organization of Black Law Enforcement Executives (NOBLE), the Commission for Accreditation for Law Enforcement Agencies (CALEA), and the United States Department of Justice's Office of Community Oriented Policing Services (COPS) are but a few of the organizations seeking to support and promote ethical standards through increased law enforcement agency professionalism. In particular, by supporting research, publications, training opportunities, and accreditation practices, these and other organizations helped push police ethics into new territory through the post-community policing era.

DISCRETION: THE ETHICAL MOMENT

The impulse of professionalism exemplified by the above organizations draws focus to a central question with regard to Hoban's initial concern for action: *how adequately are we preparing officers to make ethical discretionary decisions on the job?* This is an intriguing issue which casts light on the practice of police discretion and how such events intersect with moral integrity and action. By examining discretion, we can see how the moral content of police behavior can be shaped by various factors, long studied in police scholarship.

To illustrate, consider the high-profile example of the Danziger Bridge Incident, an ethical breakdown in police discretion that took place in New Orleans, Louisiana in September of 2005. After Hurricane Katrina ravaged the Gulf Coast, the city of New Orleans in particular suffered infrastructure devastation and near-anarchy in the face of widespread flooding. The New Orleans Police Department, long struggling with community outreach and police legitimacy, responded to untold numbers of reports of crime, looting, and gunfire as the community struggled to regain its footing. Responding to a report of "shots fired" in the city's Gentilly neighborhood, a unit of officers (arriving in a rental truck in lieu of police vehicles that were unusable) shot unarmed civilians, killing two citizens and injuring four others (Robertson, 2012). The officers concocted a cover-up for the shootings, alleging that civilians were actively shooting at the responding officers. In an issue with multiple avenues of discussion for ethical decision making and discretion, two intriguing comments emerged from a PBS *Frontline* episode of "Law and Disorder" that addressed the Danziger Bridge story. First, Retired New Orleans Police Officer David Benelli raised the possibility that the post-Katrina moment represented a "holocaust," incompatible with standard operating environments by which one can judge other police discretionary decisions (PBS, 2012). Secondly and counterpoint, Attorney Mary Howell, who represented one of the surviving victims in a lawsuit against the NOPD following the incident, claimed that such volatile circumstances as the Katrina disaster steered police towards relying on training—and their ethical and moral foundations—as backup, or "default," during times of intense stress. "Why did some lose their bearings?" asked Howell in one critical segment, calling to mind past police scholars' attempts to grapple with the issue of how best to train ethical orientations that may be absent in some employees to begin with (PBS, 2012).

The function of these discussion points in the Danziger Bridge example is to focus our attention on how specifically officers' discretion can be affected by environments (such as the extreme stress of post-hurricane urban chaos), by pre-existing moral standards in persons (such as the "bearings" Howell probes above), or by some organizational effort such as training or departmental guidelines. Howell raises an important question in her assessment of the discretion used by New Orleans officers in a time of crisis: were the ethical and moral "bearings" lost during a moment of error, or did the officers have no "bearings" to begin with? More importantly, can police officers be trained to exercise ethical conduct during discretionary decision making? Or at the front end, can police agencies screen applicants for open positions during the recruitment process to ensure that moral and ethical standards exist in individuals to not only prevent Danziger-like behavior, but also enhance their department's overall quality and ethical orientation?

These are hot-stove questions that have fueled police scholarship from the earliest focus on discretion as a byproduct of political impulse (Brown, 1988). We know from contemporary example that organizational factors impact the police role through crime control, appointment, and policy-making (Chappell et al., 2006). We also have seen a slate of research focusing on use of force continue as emblematic of a specific organizational ethic (Terrill et al., 2011). There is current work examining the moral ambiguity of training programs (Delattre, 2011). We have also seen a growing concern with recruitment techniques which either address, or fail to address, specific ethical considerations inherent in the applicant pool, including motivation for police work and potential for excellence and performance (Orrick, 2008; White, 2008; Wilson et al., 2010). This breadth of knowledge portrays police discretion as an organic and evolving feature of police ethics, as susceptible to external forces (training, department policy) as it is internally driven (officers' innate ethical orientation) and impacting on others (i.e., as part of an organization or group, as in the Danziger Bridge case). Models from the field of psychology have examined the interaction of each of these forces in synergistic operation (Jones, 1991); we can see them evident in the police examples mentioned here. Police scholarship disentangling discretionary decision making is fascinating as it impacts all others: training, recruitment, accountability, and officer wellness are but a few of the areas that stand to gain from continued exploration of police discretion and its ethical foundation and impact.

THE "NEW NORMAL": CONTEMPORARY CHALLENGES

One summary argument of this exploratory chapter looking at police ethics is that all police decisions are somehow affected by ethics, from officer recruitment to retirement. Few specific issues, tools, strategies, or approaches pertaining to police behavior are not in some way ethically endowed. This section intends to bring the issue of ethics to a more current focus by raising specific current controversial issues that consist of "ethical decision making" in some fashion, to illustrate the extent to which organizations, officers, and citizens exist in an interdependent ethical relationship. The following are but a few of the vistas in which contemporary police technologies and issues carry heavy ethical weight, some of which incite controversy by trading concern over ethical implication for cost savings and the lure of new technological advance.

Evidence-Based Policing, Hot-Spots, and Prediction

In the post-community policing era, the ethical implications of hot-spot policing are often lost in the enthusiasm for data-driven solutions. Empiricism has driven police departments to enact policies that target specific crimes in specific areas, and policing "space" and "territory" exist as interchangeable positives in an evidence-based practice police world (Crank, 2004; Herbert, 1997). But when police state that they are targeting specific crimes in specific neighborhoods, armed with zeal for cost-efficient policing and a data-infused technological approach, what are they exactly saying about the neighborhoods they are targeting and the people who live there? Where are these crime hot-spots, and who are the persons who are spotted as "hot"? Casady (2011) raises the issue of police legitimacy with regard to the phenomenon of predictive policing, another form of hot-spot technology that weds data to policy by presupposing that police agencies can prevent future crime in existing neighborhoods where crime has or is occurring. In its infancy, PredPol ("Predictive Policing," a vendor-operated software and mapping technology that can attach future criminal behavior to existing data patterns) has aroused deep concerns over constitutional and legal ethics, as well as constituent concern over pervasive data gathering for presumed social good (Gordon, 2013).

The Effect of the Economic Downturn on Policing

Many police scholars have grappled with the effect of the 2008 economic recession and its aftermath on American policing, going so far as to say that its hold on police organizations is more permanent than economic fluctuations may suppose by teaching police to "do more with less." But what if the "less" implies leaving behind traditional training mechanisms, patrol styles, and citizen interaction that allowed for greater ethical advantage? What if the economic recession steered police departments to embrace vendor-driven training programs thrust upon them by the companies behind the technologies themselves? Two recent PERF reports about the effect of the economy on police organizations detected noticeable shifts toward technologies that allowed for less patrol contact with the public (crime cameras, website-based crime reporting, and license plate readers, to name a few) which leave the citizen outside the policing process (PERF, 2010; PERF, 2012). Cost-efficacy studies probing advantages and disadvantages of adopting these technologies for perceived fiscal savings, and assessments about what is lost, have yet to capture the attention of police scholars. However, this shift toward a more streamlined technological reality and the risk of reduced community involvement serves as the backdrop for essays that suggest technology is not an end unto itself in police work (Glensor & Peak, 2012; Treverton et al., 2011). It is evident from the robust discussion about *what* may be happening, as opposed to the much-needed discussion about *how*, that a knowledge gap exists about the relationship between the political economy of policing and police ethics.

The Ethics of Current Workforce Management

Prior to the 2008 recession, police recruitment was in a state of crisis (Wilson et al., 2010). This subsided temporarily as the recession eliminated many police hiring and recruitment budgets, but the crisis reignited as the economy slowly improved and retirements from the ranks exposed deep divisions between police agencies' and the new generation's career expectations. Many questions about recruitment remain: how may police departments hire for the future, and do so with an eye to training a new workforce ethically? Can they maintain a workforce that is reflective of the community it serves, which is an ethical cornerstone to representative democracy and police legitimacy? Also, what is police training's impact on inculcating a police organizational ethic?

The importance of proper workforce management and good police training in solidifying ethical orientations in police organizations cannot be understated. In 2007, police misbehavior in the North Charleston (South Carolina) Police Department led to firings and community embarrassment, with one officer proclaiming "this is how I learned to behave" when asked about her misdeeds (Findlay, 2007, pp. A1). A link between training and ethical behavior has always been assumed in police training literature, and its effect is seen as contributing to employee retention and the avoidance of organizational stagnation that comes with eliminating training for career advancement (Haarr, 2001; Marion, 1998). Addressing the needs of new generations of officers, and allowing their career intentions to come to fruition with proper leadership, training, and opportunities, can strengthen the ethical bonds between these persons and long-term psychological capital (Batts et al., 2013; Castaneda & Ridgeway, 2010; McCafferty, 2003).

The Attractions of Policing without Borders

Conflict has persisted with regard to emerging police technologies: "no-boundaries" policing, portrayed as mobile, fast-paced, remote, and flexible, is contrasted with "bricks and mortar" methods that represent traditional patrol mechanisms and patrol deployment patterns derived from formal office-based approaches (Etue, 2012, p. 51). These two appear incompatible: mobility and flexibility are the new standard by which police will expect the unexpected and train for uncertainty, and accept the volatility of everyday police challenges (Scheer, 2014). But is the excitement of revolutionizing policing to incorporate new strategies, and the subsequent abandoning of "bricks and mortar" policing, a proper ethical approach? The contemporary police technological landscape appears to be endlessly and rapidly reinventing itself. Thermal imaging attachments for cell phones alert police to weapons and contraband on persons using heat sensors. TASER and other conducted electronic devices have become commonplace in police agencies, often replacing entire use-of-force continuum strategies such as citizen interaction and "verbal judo" techniques. Lapel and uniform cameras record entire shifts from patrol officers' perspectives, and record citizen behaviors. Red light and speed cameras, initially developed to augment existing traffic strategies, may replace patrol efforts as they drive up revenues, displeasing the public. The use of social media for criminal investigations may suppose a degree of privacy violation which the public may see as unethical. And even some technologies such as mobile unmanned vehicles used for surveillance, years ago a seeming impossibility in American police departments, have become popularized quickly, raising ethical concerns.

The potential value of "bricks and mortar" and community outreach approaches are in danger of being discarded wholesale in favor of a "no boundaries" approach that holds much potential promise, but in the absence of more comprehensive discussion of the ethical risks involved in this revolution, no sense of what is either lost or gained can be assumed.

American policing is evolving rapidly, and without borders, as some have enthusiastically championed from multiple standpoints. What has not followed technological changes, and what has always been consistently present in the long past of policing progress, is a careful consideration of the ethical balance between police tactics and approaches and the needs and rights of the communities served by police officers. It is critical to remember that these officers are in fact people, with their own career goals, interpersonal skills, desires to protect and improve the human condition, and ways of negotiating public interaction. They may respond to differing varieties of training and supervision. They bring their own morals and values to the police culture, and transform these values into actions and behaviors in a manner that is unique to each one. The groundwork for continual examination of the ethics of police behavior has been established through significant events and flashpoints, all of which teach the police and the public about which actions are of benefit to all communities.

REFERENCES AND FURTHER READING

Alpert, G.P. & R.G. Dunham. (1996). *Policing Urban America.* Long Grove, IL: Waveland Press.

Alpert, G.P., R.G. Dunham, & M.S. Stroshine. (2006). *Policing: Continuity and Change.* Long Grove, IL: Waveland Press.

American Civil Liberties Union (ACLU). (2014). *War Comes Home: The Excessive Militarization of American Policing.* New York: American Civil Liberties Union. Retrieved June 22, 2014 from https://www.aclu.org/war-comes-home-excessive-militarization-american-policing

Balko, R. (2013). *Rise of the Warrior Cop: The Militarization of America's Police Forces.* New York: Public Affairs.

Batts, A. W., S.M. Smoot, & E. Scrivner. (2012). *New Perspectives in Policing: Police Leadership Challenges in a Changing World.* Cambridge, MA: Harvard Kennedy School in Criminal Justice Policy and Management.

Brown, M.K. (1988). *Working the Street: Police Discretion and the Dilemmas of Reform.* New York: Russell Sage Publishers.

Casady, T. (2011, March). Police legitimacy and predictive policing. *Geography and Public Safety, 2* (4), 1–3.

Castaneda, L.W. & G. Ridgeway. (2010). *Today's Police and Sheriff Recruits: Insights from the Newest Members of America's Law Enforcement Community.* Santa Monica, CA: RAND Corporation.

Chanen, D. (2014, July 27). Minneapolis police outreach to Somali community offers a national model. *Minneapolis Star-Tribune.* Retrieved July 27, 2014 from http://www.startribune.com/local/minneapolis/268749491.html

Chappell, A.T. (2009). The philosophical versus actual adoption of community policing: A case study. *Criminal Justice Review, 34* (1), 5–28.

Chappell, A.T., J.M. MacDonald & P.W. Manz. (2006). The organizational determinants of police arrest decisions. *Crime & Delinquency, 52* (2), 287–306.

Crank, J.P. (2004). *Understanding Police Culture (Second edition).* New York: Anderson.

Delattre, E.J. (2011). *Character and Cops: Ethics in Policing (Sixth Edition).* Washington, DC: American Enterprise Institute for Public Policy Research.

Etue, K.K. (2012, September). No boundaries policing. In *American Policing in 2022: Essays on the Future of a Profession* (Eds. D.R.C. McCullough & D.L. Spence). Washington, DC: Office of Community Oriented Policing Services.

Findlay, P. (2007, February 13). Chief tells of police misconduct. *Charleston Post & Courier*, pp. A1.

Fry, L.W. and L.J. Berkes. (1983). The paramilitary police model: An organizational misfit. *Human Organization, 42* (3), 225–234.

Glensor, R.W. & K.J. Peak. (2012, September). New police management practices and predictive software: A new era they do not make. In *American Policing in 2022: Essays on the Future of a Profession* (Eds. D.R.C. McCullough & D.L. Spence). Washington, DC: Office of Community Oriented Policing Services.

Goldstein, J. (2014, July 24). Safer era tests wisdom of 'broken windows' focus on minor crime. *New York Times*. Retrieved July 26, 2014, from http://www.nytimes.com/2014/07/25/nyregion/safer-era-tests-wisdom-of-broken-windows-focus-on-minor-crime-in-new-york-city.html

Goodman, J.D. (2012, November 28). Photo of officer giving boots to barefoot man warms hearts online. *New York Times*. Retrieved June 22, 2014 from http://www.nytimes.com/2012/11/29/nyregion/photo-of-officer-giving-boots-to-barefoot-man-warms-hearts-online.html?_r=0

Gordon, L.A. (2013, September 1). Predictive policing may help bag burglars, but it may also be a constitutional problem. *American Bar Association Journal*. Retrieved May 22, 2014, from http://www.abajournal.com/magazine/article/predictive_policing_may_help_bag_burglars--but_it_may_also_be_a_constitutio/

Haarr, R.N. (2001). The making of a community policing officer: The impact of basic training and occupational socialization on police recruits. *Police Quarterly, 4* (4), 402–433.

Herbert, S. (1997). *Policing space: Territoriality and the Los Angeles Police Department*. Minneapolis: University of Minnesota Press.

Herman, M. A. (2005). *Fighting in the Streets: Ethnic Succession and Urban Unrest in Twentieth-Century America*. New York: Peter Lang Publishers.

Jones, T.M. (1991). Ethical decision making by individuals in organizations: An issue-contingent model. *Academy of Management Review, 16* (2), 366–395.

Kaminsky, J. (2012, December 29). Seattle police recruits get a break on past pot use. *Reuters*. Retrieved April 2, 2014 from http://www.reuters.com/article/2012/12/20/us-usa-marijuana-seattle-idUSBRE8BJ00J20121220?irpc=932

Kappeler, V.E. (2006). *Critical Issues in Police Civil Liability (Fourth Edition)*. Long Grove, IL: Waveland Press.

Marion, N. (1998). Police academy training: are we teaching recruits what they need to know? *Policing, 21* (1), 54-79.

Matyszczyk, C. (2014, January 7). Dallas police chief proudly announces firings on Twitter. *C-Net*. Retrieved May 17, 2014, from http://www.cnet.com/news/dallas-police-chief-proudly-announces-firings-on-twitter/

McCafferty, F.L. (2003). The challenge of selecting tomorrow's police officers from generations X and Y. *Journal of the American Academy of Psychiatry and the Law, 31*, 78–88.

Muir, W.K. (1977). *Police: Streetcorner Politicians*. Chicago: University of Chicago Press.

Niederhoffer, A. (1969). *Behind the Shield: The Police in Urban Society*. Garden City, NY: Doubleday Anchor Books.

Orrick, W.D. (2008). *Recruitment, Retention, and Turnover of Police Personnel: Reliable, Practical, and Effective Solutions*. Springfield, IL: Charles C. Thomas Publishers.

Police Executive Research Forum (PERF). (2010). *Critical Issues in Policing Series: Is the Economic Downturn Fundamentally Changing How We Police?* Washington, DC: Police Executive Research Forum.

Police Executive Research Forum (PERF). (2012). *How are Innovations in Technology Transforming Policing?* Washington, DC: Police Executive Research Forum.

Public Broadcasting Service (PBS). (2012, January). *Frontline: Law and Disorder. Case Six: Danziger Bridge Incident (video)*. Retrieved April 3, 2014, from http://www.pbs.org/wgbh/pages/frontline/law-disorder/case-six-danziger-bridge/

Robertson, C. (2012, April 4). 5 ex-officers sentenced in post-Katrina shootings. *New York Times*. Retrieved June 18, 2014 from http://www.nytimes.com/2012/04/05/us/5-ex-officers-sentenced-in-post-katrina-shootings.html

Scheer, C. (2014). *Adaptive Expertise in Police Work: The Role of In-Service Training*. East Lansing, MI: Michigan State University, Ph.D. dissertation.

Schoetz, D. (2007, May 21). Porn star's blog has Tennessee Trooper in hot water. *ABC News*. Retrieved May 20, 2014, from http://abcnews.go.com/US/story?id=3196477

Seiler, C. (2012, November 29). Deputy won't take action against TSA pat-down opponents at Albany airport. *Albany Times-Union*. Retrieved June 20, 2014 from http://www.timesunion.com/local/article/Deputy-won-t-take-action-against-TSA-pat-down-4074103.php

Terrill, W.M., E. Paoline, & Ingram, J. (2011). *Final Technical Report Draft: Assessing Police Use of Force Policy and Outcomes*. Washington, DC: National Institute of Justice.

Treverton, G.F., M. Wollman, E. Wilke, & D. Lai (2011). *Moving Toward the Future of Policing*. Santa Monica, CA: RAND Corporation.

White, M.D. (2008). Identifying good cops early: Predicting recruit performance in the academy. *Police Quarterly, 11* (1), 27–49.

Wilson, J.M., Dalton, E., Scheer, C., & Grammich, C.A. (2010a). *Police Recruitment and Retention for the New Millennium: The State of Knowledge*. Santa Monica, CA: Rand Corporation.

Police Deviance

CHAPTER 7

"The police must obey the law while enforcing the law."
—*Justice Earl Warren, United States*
Supreme Court

"The police are the public and the public are the police; the police being only members
of the public who are paid to give full time attention to duties which are incumbent
on every citizen in the interests of community welfare and existence."
—*Sir Robert Peel (1788–1850)*

In the postmodern, internet-media era, it is not difficult to locate stories of police officers who, for
many reasons, behave in a manner inconsistent with their sworn oath to protect the public. Across
the United States, untold numbers of police-public interactions a day are potentially recorded either
by citizens or by the police departments themselves. The technology they use for this culture of
monitoring has led to more stringent observation and important capture of this critical feature of
police career behavior. Along with this increasing scrutiny brought by the mobile media age, an
accentuated distrust of police themselves, of their motives and manners, has captured the attention of citizens who can monitor police behavior and misbehavior in ways never before accessed.
Internet websites are devoted to reporting police misconduct, YouTube channels have been specifically created to report and discuss cases of police deviance, and entire strains of police research are
devoted not only to studying police deviance but also to capturing the social importance of public
attention to police deviance. It can be said that watching the police and monitoring what they do,
and critiquing it—an exercise often called "Monday morning quarterbacking" by seasoned patrol
officers—has become a cottage industry in the era of democratized media extremes.

But along with the increased emphasis on critiquing police behavior and rooting out "deviant"
activities by the police, the new modes of observation have altered the landscape of organizational
and social controls of police misconduct. In an environment where everyone is now watching each
other, it would seem easy to project simplistic statements about "what happens" when police engage
in deviant behavior. Courts, police supervisors and leaders, police trainers and officers themselves,
watchdog organizations and the public, and future officers enrolled in education programs all have
sudden and immediate access to video footage shot from different angles and often in high-resolution
quality of every aspect of police behavior. The legacy of this important opportunity in creating a new
ethic about what constitutes "proper" police behavior is important, because one can visualize that

this increased ability to critique the police and learn from everyday acts of police misconduct, and improve, has actually helped the police-public relationship.

But this has so far proven untrue. As a field of study, police scholarship has only just begun to come to terms with the new realities of increased public scrutiny of police behavior. This massive technological and ethical shift has produced fear in some corners, among police managers who believe that increased scrutiny will drive away potential applicants for the job, among chiefs who fear erosion of service quality, and among police officers who feel burdened by ever-increasing demands of a distant and misunderstanding public (Wilson et al., 2010). It is not enough to fuel concern that an active search for "police deviant behavior" is being conducted by certain social circles, but the digital and mobile media era has indeed provided those who have long suspected police as being inherently deviant or abusive of power with a new avenue of interpretation (Allen & Kearney, 2014). However, aside from providing some citizens with ammunition by which critique of police behavior may become easier, the new standard of observation has already had an important impact on fostering better police conduct by increasing police organizational accountability. This is reflected in a much improved standard of training that has yet to be evaluated empirically, but can use existing technology to tell a clearer story of events that occur and how they may be learned from. Before discussing the underpinnings and locations of these events in police settings, a working understanding of the various terms commonly used to portray police deviance is needed.

WHAT'S IN A NAME: DEVIANCE, MISCONDUCT, CORRUPTION

Do citizens, or police themselves for that matter, know when police are behaving in a manner inconsistent with their sworn duty to protect the public? Is specific behavior or action classified as "deviant" defined along a continuum? Is deviance a means, or an end, to a specific goal? There are several theoretical descriptions and bases for the classification of police deviance and misconduct that have been used by police scholars, and each serves a distinct purpose. One reason why it is important to identify and classify such behavior properly is that statements about the context and source of such behavior are made depending upon the designation used. Deviant events are often classified according to specific features, such as the size or severity of the presumed act (Newburn, 1999), or the system or mechanism which defines and gives support to it (Klockars et al., 2000, Kutnjak-Ivkovic, 2003).

Classifying deviance by event strength or size has historically been a feature of police scholarship on deviance. Since Barker and Carter's (1994) typology of police deviance, police *corruption* has been viewed as distinct from police *deviance* or *misconduct*.

Barker and Carter suggest that the designation *police corruption* carries an assumption of occupational or organizational support, and that corrupt activities, from small incidents of dishonesty and transgressions to large events, carry support mechanisms in the form of organizational reinforcement or occupational benefit. These acts make strong implications about the individual's membership in and participation among peer groups and system-wide reinforcement mechanisms. These are rare and profoundly serious indications of pervasive wrongdoing, and usually involve multiple members and levels of the police organization. And although smaller events such as accepting free meals may be classified as "corruption," what makes them distinct is that such events take place in isolation from larger organizational support mechanisms (Newburn, 1999).

Therefore, police *deviance* or *misconduct* would be defined as events along a continuum of severity that persist outside the classification of *corruption*, which implies pervasive organizational resistance to protection of the constitutional rights of the public. This definition is helpful in distinguishing between what is commonly referred to as a "corrupt police department" or a "corrupt cop," because those labels tend to evoke more serious and pervasive patterns of disruption of the public good. Among events that can be classified as police *deviance*, then, are specific opportunistic points of exit from non-deviant or conforming behavior, or simply put, ways police can suddenly find themselves with an opportunity to behave improperly. Roebuck and Barker (1974) offered a conceptual typology of police deviance in an earlier era of police scholarship; this chapter uses their suggestions in contrast to what are more common, modern police events familiar to many.

What is critical about the activity of placing acts of police deviance into tractable categories is that organizational policies to deal with each of these transgressions can be crafted specifically to target their root cause. By placing them along a continuum of severity, causes and organizational and community controls can be exercised to respect the pattern of behavior in proper context. This assists police leaders in pinpointing problems and devising opportunities to solve them.

BOX 7.1

FORMS OF POLICE DEVIANCE

Corruption of authority. Using one's badge or authority as an officer to glean a variety of gifts or perks from businesses or individuals constitutes an ethical compromise of police authority. For instance, how soon after accepting a discounted meal from a restaurant would a police officer be expected to give preferential services to that venue, as opposed to elsewhere? This is seen as an initial entry point into various forms of deviance which may follow.

Kickbacks. Short of outright bribery, kickbacks in many jurisdictions may imply courtesy, such as an officer receiving partial compensation for referral of services to businesses. This category includes behaviors such as extra security checks of businesses that may result in discounts or even monetary compensation, as a corollary to the first category above.

Opportunistic theft. Stealing is one potential point of entry into deviance for many officers who realize that their authority and access produce opportunities for theft. This avenue to deviance may also depend upon the officer's stature in the department, or specific detail or unit such as a narcotics or investigations unit.

Shakedowns. Far from a relic of an era of Popeye Doyle and other classic Hollywood portrayals of police corruption, there are many contemporary examples of police asking for outright favors in exchange for refusal to enforce the law. These quid-pro-quo arrangements may be context-specific, such as traffic stops or even investigations that carry more serious penalty.

Protection of illegal activities. In large urban environments as well as small towns, illegal activities associated with a number of specific crimes may engender police complicity through conspiracy.

The Fix. Roebuck and Barker's use of this form of corruption may seem antiquated to our modern police context, but specific behaviors that undermine prosecution of criminal cases can take many forms.

Direct criminal activities. There are rare but documented cases where police officers, either on the job or within their capacity of knowing the law, have been involved in direct criminal activities such as theft, drug operations, or sex crimes.

Internal payoffs. In what ways have police acted within their departments to negotiate for enhanced status, services, or even promotional opportunities among other employees or within the organization? While many of these cases may not appear in the public eye, internal forms of deviance can be just as disruptive to police legitimacy in the eyes of the public when exposed.

(Continued)

BOX 7.1 (Continued)

Other forms. Roebuck and Barker's typology was seen as an initial foray by police scholars into defining varieties of deviance and misconduct. In the forty years that have passed since their typology, many new opportunities for police to enter into deviance have occurred. Are there any that you can identify that have developed out of an era of different ethical responsibilities and technologies?

Adapted from Roebuck, J. & T. Barker (1974. A typology of police corruption. *Social Problems,* 21, 423–437.

THE LOCUS OF DEVIANCE: INDIVIDUAL VS. ORGANIZATIONAL

Does it make a difference in the eyes of the public if police deviance is exhibited by one individual or is endemic to the entire organization? There are many ways in which police chiefs and managers can jettison the casual, or even severe, case of the "deviant officer." They can be labeled as passive "grass eater" types who engage in deviant behavior if it is opportunistically presented to them, or more serious "meat eater" types who seek out opportunities to deviate from ethical codes over a period of time (Knapp Commission, 1973). But although the severity of the deviance is reflected in the metaphor of what is "eaten," interestingly, the Knapp Commission identifying deviance and corruption in the New York Police Department in the mid-1970's states that the "grass eaters" were more prevalent within the overall population of New York officers because the variety of deviant behavior itself was smaller and more ingrained in the work culture at the NYPD (Armstrong, 2012). This interesting addendum to the "grass eater"/"meat eater" framework presents a critical challenge for police agencies grappling with any form of deviance within their ranks: it is an opportunity not only to frame discussions of deviance with the public differently, but also in crafting policy. If small, passive events are much more prevalent than high-profile deviant acts which persist over time, it may necessitate different strategies for dealing with each from a managerial standpoint.

FACES OF POLICE CORRUPTION: WHEN A "BAD APPLE" IS REALLY BAD

Corruption, as we have acknowledged earlier, implies a more severe form of deviance that involves levels of police organizations beyond one person. This follows Punch's (2009) typology as well as classical interpretations of police corruption mechanisms derived from the earliest eras of police work. Sherman's (1974) typology of police corruption, which has been manipulated over its 40-year existence by many scholars of police deviance, focused on three distinct types of corruption. In the first, lone-wolf-style "rotten apple" officers act alone in their behavior without any organizational support or assistance in their misdeeds. This is the classic case of an officer who, Sherman would say, is wholly alone both before and after the disclosure of his or her act, since the police leadership will discard the officer and cut all formal ties to his or her behavior in an effort to terminate public concern that the person was part of a larger culture of corruption. The second level of corruption is when the behavior is *pervasive* but is *unorganized,* as in the case of a specific pattern of behavior that happens without any ringleader or structural organization. However, the third form of corruption, *pervasive* and *organized,* is most severe and normally involves support from different levels of leadership, often engulfing the entire department's culture and constituting an alternative organizational mission (Sherman, 1974).

One of the salient features of Sherman's typology is how over time police scholars have used it to explain strategies for dealing with deviance and more severe corruption within a police department, especially in the case of the "bad apple" who is easily labeled. But an interesting question remains: what if the activities of the deviant "bad apple" are more abhorrent than the standard fixed tickets, stolen items, and low-level behavior one normally ascribes to a single deviant officer? Consider the example provided by former Santa Fe (NM) Police Sergeant Michael Eiskant. For years, Eiskant had allegedly assaulted women, even sexually, and bribed them in order to produce pornographic videos. He harassed female citizens, stalked others, and kidnapped one woman (Rodgers, 2013). His behavior was far outside the conduct one would expect a police department could explain away with a "bad apple" designation. As the department found out in the social media era, Eiskant would quickly become the public face of the Santa Fe Police Department. In today's Twitter and Facebook-wired social landscape, events that years ago were seen as "bad apple" or "grass-eating" low-level events that were easily dismissible are now taken more seriously because of social media exposure. In the case of Eiskant, although the behavior was exemplary of type-I corruption on Sherman's typology, the activity was so severe and unacceptable to the public eye that the department was suspected of being summarily complicit. The city of Santa Fe, in attempting to reduce public outcry regarding Eiskant's behavior, simply stated in response to multiple lawsuits that it had lacked sufficient cause to pursue the various complaints it had received about Eiskant's behavior. Departmental attempts to label Eiskant a "bad apple," strategies that may have worked in another era, failed to placate the demands of a more social-network and accountability-conscious public in the present day. This illustration is used to indicate how typologies of corruption and definitions of deviance may seem semantic in nature, but carry weight in defining how organizations can strategize and negotiate public outcry when police deviance occurs.

SYSTEMS, EARLY WARNING AND OTHERWISE

It is critical to consider how police departments have dealt with deviant officer behavior in the past and how the manner by which they will deal with it in the future will be distinctly different. Much has been said in literature about police accountability mechanisms, early warning systems to "catch" officer misbehavior before it becomes a chronic problem, mechanisms departments use to predict officer misbehavior through comprehensive psychological screening and profiling at an early (even recruitment) stage, and the way that these early warning systems have held officers accountable to department standards prohibiting deviance (Alpert & Walker, 2000; Walker & Alpert, 2002). But external standards have likewise been developed with regard to how police agencies are supposed to inculcate "ethical behavior" and hold their officers to a set standard. One such mechanism for control is the threat of civil liability, as expressed through large monetary judgments given to individuals who have sued police departments and officers for wrongdoing (Kappeler, 2006; Kappeler & Alpert, 1994). The ease by which one can sue the police in civil court has streamlined informal control mechanisms, such as the public embarrassment of having been sued regardless of the foundation of the case. The accelerated manner by which these cases are publicized in social media add to feelings of scrutiny for police agencies and officers.

In an intriguing explanation of the new accountability landscape, Walker and Archbold (2014) state that social media has reinvented mechanisms of police accountability for deviant behavior by acting as a public shaming tool which keeps police and police organizations above an ethical standard. In an age when even reporting mechanisms have become intertwined with social media, some jurisdictions have implemented phone applications for reporting police behavior—both negative and positive. As accountability systems return to the hands of citizens, and venues for public display of such behavior increase in the form of YouTube and other video websites, it has become increasingly hard for police departments to respond to criticism and to keep track of what the public sees as "deviant" and what is permissible. Consistency of policy has become irrelevant if a police chief spends time responding to perpetual outcry over behavior that the agency used to consider minor, manageable, or even acceptable.

This implies an urgent and difficult task for the police leader. It used to be that the department could control what was defined as a "type-I" or "type-II" variety of corruption, or who was a "grass eater" or a "bad apple." But these designations are now out of the control of police departments and firmly under the control of the individuals armed with blogs, cameraphones, and video-recording devices. Years ago, a police officer's deviant act would be "disclosed" by the department in a carefully worded statement or press release, often accompanied by planned explanation and a united public front of outrage and understanding. This allowed the police department to control the discourse of what constituted deviance and a proper response to it. But that era is behind us; a police officer doing something as seemingly non-deviant, albeit potentially unprofessional, as smoking on the job can become the target of irate citizens who see opportunities to right perceived ethical wrongs, even if these wrongs exist only in their minds. Years ago the apparatus of complaint consisted of a phone call to the officer's supervisor; now, within minutes public embarrassment can be levied on police departments for untold numbers of perceived "deviant behaviors," whether they are of a serious nature or not.

This critical moment leaves the police agency with choices, some of which have not yet been fully explored, such as police department social media pages and other attempts to meet these concerns head-on. But in the age of increasingly democratized media where police officer behavior is more commonly tried in the court of public opinion, are department attempts to play the same game going to produce intended results? The era of constant change and adaptation to changes in progress may ensure that no one answer exists for how best to keep officers accountable while responding to public perception of their behavior, even if it is seen as deviant by a few.

CASE STUDY: THE LOS ANGELES POLICE DEPARTMENT RAMPART SCANDAL

"Across the board" failure is a cliché often reserved for the most pronounced events, catastrophic occurrences where not only simple behaviors, but also organizational oversight, early-warning systems, routine supervision, and sanctions become inert. For some event to meet such "across the board" negligence is to assign the event a sort of cultural iconography, when events become a literal ball and chain which can bring down the systems attached to it, and to necessitate similar "across the board" measures to root out causes and right wrongs while ensuring permanent and preventive cultural change. Such was the acknowledgement of the Los Angeles Police Department in their multiple internal assessments of their most tragic case of corruption and deviance, one that exposed deep inadequacies of the police paradigm at work in Los Angeles in the 1990's (LAPD, 2004).

In the decades since its resolution, the Los Angeles Police Department's scandal involving the Rampart Division's special CRASH anti-gang unit has grown to become a cultural phenomenon in its own right. From dramatic Hollywood movies, to hip-hop songs, to countless television programs and even a video game, the "Rampart Scandal" has grown from being one of the most notorious examples of police corruption in Los Angeles Police history to a phrase exemplifying the overall thrust of police ethical misconduct, corruption, and intrigue in the United States (Boyer, 2001; Golab, 2000). It has become the default event for those who wish to label all police as somehow corrupt, and an event which has yet to undergo a much needed historiographical scrutiny. The Los Angeles Rampart Scandal has entered the cultural realm of a near-present-day pulp fiction episode, commanding as much subcultural attention in L.A. as the murders of rap moguls Tupac Shakur and Notorious B.I.G. (events to which the scandal itself has even been linked by some authors) (Golab, 2000).

The pop-cultural spotlight inhabited by the Rampart Scandal distracts from the critical importance of examining the case from the perspective of organizational upheaval and community demands for change. Entrenched corruption of the sort demonstrated by Rampart Division officers in the 1990's, the relationship between corrupt behavior and the nature of the CRASH unit, and benign LAPD leadership are test cases for how quickly cultural influences can impact the spread and trajectory of deviance. Beginning with opportunistic behavior and expanding eventually to consume anti-gang efforts in the disadvantaged, predominantly immigrant Rampart section of Los Angeles, the scandal provided a window into the socio-legal culture of the LAPD as it struggled to maintain order amidst chaos, eventually supplanting one chaos for another (Skolnick, 2005).

The scandal was disclosed in 1999 when former officer Rafael Perez, himself implicated in theft of narcotics from evidence, secured immunity from prosecution and spilled the beans on wrongdoing surrounding the CRASH anti-gang unit (an acronym that stood for Community Resources Against Street Hoodlums, a designation steeped in irony). The unit operated in the city's deep end of gang violence, its elite officers embracing a war-metaphor approach (derisively labeled "thin blue line policing" by the subsequent LAPD summary report) while committing crimes ranging from evidence and weapons planting to perjury and physical violence (Boyer, 2001; Skolnick, 2005). But more urgently, Perez also pointed out the deeper institutional failures and culture which allowed the wrongdoing to continue. In many police scandals, the scandal ends with the behavior itself, and spin control (in conjunction with sound organizational theory) can limit public outrage along with demotions, firings, and resignations of "bad apples" (Klockars et al., 2000). But in Los Angeles' unique socio-political environment, the corruption exhibited by CRASH was more than just racketeering by fiat. The "breaking news" of the CRASH unit's misdeeds, as egregious as they were, was not perceived as a surprise by many Los Angeles communities, notably the city's African-American community, still simmering from the outbreak of violence in response to the Rodney King verdict mere years earlier (Boyer, 2001). Kaplan (2009) poses an intriguing question about the interplay between the unit's behavior and the resulting public perception of the LAPD itself: could the tough, combative stance taken by the LAPD, as well as other departments throughout the nation during the 1990's heralded "war on crime," create the very environment in which Rampart-style scandals are allowed to fester and grow?

The belief that get-tough police organizational responses to crime waves brought by crack epidemics of the late 1980's constituted a separation between the police and the public is a continuation of the critique of other similarly styled pendulum swings in criminal justice, such as mass incarceration and mandatory-minimum sentencing (Kaplan, 2009). But, as with those concerns, the Rampart Scandal can be seen in this regard as much more than rogue police misbehavior. At the least, it is suddenly viewed as a major malfunction in the public faith in the police crime-fighting model, and at worst an exposure of the failures of community policing as a cover for the violent extremes of a police culture gone awry. The CRASH unit was certainly a brutal fringe element of the LAPD, but the perspective offered by distance has led many to have misgivings about the police mission inherent in the model followed by CRASH itself, and by default the LAPD and its leadership. The denial of due process, beatings, and framings associated with CRASH were not widespread at the LAPD. But is it possible that the attitude embraced by police in the environment of the mid-1990's, including disregard for the welfare and rights of perceived "hoodlums" (which finds its way into the acronym CRASH itself), fueled a tolerant and ignorant mindset that allowed such behavior to "metastasize" (LAPD, 2004)? The department itself has struggled to affirm that the culture that gave rise to the scandal is eradicated, even years after the lifting of a consent decree.

The Rampart Scandal's true legacy, at least in the long term for LAPD leadership, is to illustrate that "thin blue line" police rhetoric is counterproductive to positive interactivity between police and the public, and may even allow future scandals to evolve and take root. Conversely, the needed changes that may prevent scandals and deviance, and prevent them from spiraling out of control into chaos, require proactive leadership and consensus among police and public officials wired for change (LAPD, 2004). This unexpected critique of the modern police paradigm (which one can see evident in contemporary anti-terrorism concerns and public outcry against the "militarization" of police) has startling implications for police work 25 years on from the Rampart Scandal itself. Returning to the pop-culture familiarity of the scandal, and considering the culture of complaint, citizen expectation of police brutality in Los Angeles throughout the 1990's, and the department's humility in addressing the failure of the supposed "lessons learned," the Rampart Scandal appears to be a true watershed moment in the political career of "get tough" police tactics. It is still up for debate that those lessons have been learned.

THE CLEVELAND-AREA NARCOTICS SCANDAL AND THE ILLUSION OF POWER

As the Rampart Scandal was at its height in Los Angeles, a sting operation was under way that would expose a multi-jurisdictional drug-protection racket in northeast Ohio. In 1998, federal authorities exposed a wide-ranging network of police officers from five Cleveland-area jurisdictions who envisioned themselves to be a form of "Mafia" or organized-crime-style protective arm of a cocaine-distribution network. But the drug distributors they were sworn to protect were in fact federal agents (Belluck, 1998). Beginning with Cuyahoga County jail officer Michael Joye's sale of cocaine to undercover federal agents, the sting operation moved from corrections to street officers, and even narcotics enforcement officers themselves (one was actually late to a simulated transaction because he was giving an "anti-drug presentation") (Affleck, 1998). The brazenness of the officers' attachment to this simulated "drug culture" and the breadth of the sting operation shocked local communities. The scandal also portrayed law enforcement as inherently tempted by money and wealth resulting from the drug trade, where jurisdictions appeared embroiled in greed (Belluck, 1998).

Along with the Rampart affair, this entire era of police ethical misbehavior demonstrated widespread abuse of power across a spectrum of national police agencies struggling to reconcile the relatively new dictates of community policing with political and community demands to "take back" communities from spiraling crime. These philosophies appeared irreconcilable; so many police agencies dabbled in one and specialized in the other with different degrees of "success." In the Cleveland scandal, FBI agents even conducted simulated "Mafia-style" initiation exercises to provide the illusion that the "network" was creating "drug lords" from street cops (Belluck, 1998). Lines between illusion and reality were blurred in every direction.

What is startling about this era in American policing history is that the Cleveland case (and similar corruption incidents in Philadelphia, New Orleans, Detroit, and elsewhere around the same time) demonstrated police officers' almost theatrical fascinations with power. This desire for power took root in multiple police roles, from narcotics trafficking enforcement, to the use of force, to routine patrol. Drug-related police corruption created "bushels" of bad-apple deviants entrenched at the shift or unit level (such as in the Rampart affair), or embedded in different levels throughout multiple organizations (such as in the Cleveland area scandal), but sublimely focused on monetary wealth at all cost. Civil rights abuses by New York police officers in the same era reinforced the illusion of power provided by the badge. When NYPD officers beat and sodomized Abner Louima in 1997, they were effectively asserting their sexual and racial authority over an immigrant; the shooting of Amadou Diallo two years later reinforced the display of power through use of force (Kappeler & Gaines, 2011). What was learned from these high-profile incidents, as reinforced by the comprehensive lessons of the Rampart affair, was that police roles and the culture that enveloped them offered myriad opportunities for the unethical and dramatic seizure of power from individuals (Kaplan, 2009; LAPD, 2004).

It is helpful to use Crank's (2004) discussion of the seductive qualities of criminal behavior (by police themselves) to make sense of the mid-to-late-1990's police scandals. Crank states that criminals foster an emotional attachment to misbehavior; in the case of police protection, many feel an opportunity to "settle a score" or lash out in a personal vendetta at those perceived as bad or insulting to society at large, or the badge, or to a man (Crank, 2004, p. 191). Criminals act as a scapegoat for societal ills, and "thin blue line" police attitudes inherently place police in opposition to those responsible. The police officer is

> beckoned by [crime's] sensuous allure, the seduction by dark, secret places and violent revenges, to be princes of the city. To walk down Colfax Avenue in Denver and watch the pimps crawl back into the shadows, not just because you are a cop, but because you are one tough mother in a uniform (Crank, 2004, p. 191).

We can easily envision the 1990's corrupt cop as a living manifestation of Crank's immoral hero. And despite the personal desire for power, it is also important to consider the organizational attachment to the "crime fighting" ethic as well as public demands for "zero tolerance" that potentially allowed deviant behavior to evolve and continue (LAPD, 2004).

THE PHILADELPHIA NARCOTICS BUREAU SCANDAL: WHAT HAVE WE LEARNED?

"Right on schedule," says a current headline from the *Philadelphia Inquirer*, "another Philadelphia police scandal" in a city all too familiar with police scandals stretching back to the 1960's (Heller, 2014). But in 2014, all would indicate that this big city police department would be scandal-free, because certainly Philadelphia would have learned something from its past. The department has been under the supervision and culture of Commissioner Chuck Ramsey for nearly a decade, an iconic figure popular with many city residents. He has been the president of the Police Executive Research Forum (PERF), a think-tank of innovative police leaders from the nation's largest police departments and an agency that supports new approaches and research to improve police leadership and effectiveness. It can be also noted that the mayor of Philadelphia, Michael Nutter, has been supportive of the police department's efforts at community outreach and engagement in volatile times (Boyer, 2011). Surely this is not the monolithic police department of old that would allow a scandal to go undetected, or occur in the first place.

But in a city where 88 officers have themselves been arrested for a variety of crimes since 2008, the Philadelphia Police Department still struggles with corruption and innovative ways to prevent it (Gambacorta, 2014). In 2014, a federal probe into the department's narcotics unit resulted in the arrests of six officers who were accused of stealing over a half million dollars in cash, drugs, and other items, in addition to robbery, extortion, and kidnapping (Lattanzio & Stamm, 2014). The scandal was embarrassing: twice the officers were alleged to have dangled drug suspects over balconies in robberies, and the officers were accused of filing falsified police reports supporting discrepancies in money and drug amounts they were supposed to have seized (Heller, 2014; Lattanzio & Stamm, 2014). The commissioner echoed institutional embarrassment and a desire to eradicate the wrongdoing in a press conference in which the iconic leader sounded almost resigned, calling the officers' behavior a "malignancy" (Lattanzio & Stamm, 2014).

What is different this time, however, is that the public and media discourse following the scandal pushed a different viewpoint than in the past, one that placed significant attention on issues of prevention, renewal, restorative justice, and police legitimacy. These perspectives suggest that the department and the community absorbed the shock of the scandal, as though the headline lamenting "another scandal" may have been a statement uttered by nearly everyone, including leaders and officers in the department itself. But the abrasiveness gave way quickly in Philadelphia media to a more aggressive down-to-business approach. Gambacorta (2014) tells of a leadership summit where outside-the-box solutions, many of them technological, were being considered as new approaches to preventing further scandal. For instance, body-worn cameras that track officer behavior throughout the day, although expensive for a department of Philadelphia's size, have proven to be helpful tools in creating a culture of accountability. Traditional approaches also held sway in the suggestions, such as community review panels with subpoena power and extra oversight of the narcotics squad itself.

Even more intriguing across the spectrum of Philadelphia responses to this latest scandal is a focus on different recruiting strategies that can supplant unethical behavior over the long term (Heller, 2014; Lombardi, 2010). This strategy, while potentially not impacting immediate public opinion, requires institutional and public patience and faith to engender feelings of legitimacy and trust. Strengthening hiring requirements and ethical screening of applicants, rethinking ethics training, and hiring for potential are but a few of the strategies that can transform a workforce.

Lombardi (2010), writing prior to the latest Philadelphia scandal, based his reconsideration of police recruitment and screening techniques on a general feeling that the Philadelphia Police Department suffers from a sort of scandal "fatigue." He lists practical strategies that are used in private industry that can potentially invigorate police organizations by shifting personnel screening processes from a "weeding out" approach to a more proactive identification of potential "good cops." Specifically, Lombardi laments civil service examinations which do not constitute forecasting or predictive staffing, and urges that scenario-based training may be used to identify future "good cops" (Lombardi, 2010). This approach is not new to police workforce management research, but Lombardi's recognition of its merit is timely, and in the case of the most recent narcotics scandal in the department, adds to a growing chorus of tractable solutions, not just tired complaints about how perpetually corrupt the department seems to be.

Concerns over media portrayals of police deviance and increased civic scrutiny through electronic and mobile media served as the theme at the start of this chapter. But the discourse on the 2014 Philadelphia narcotics scandal yields anything but unfiltered complaints normally associated with the new democratic media. In fact, the discourse appears focused on solutions: technological "early warning systems" such as body-worn cameras, new recruitment and screening techniques, and frank discussions among stakeholders about how to transform the police ethical landscape are a welcome relief from the historical blame-game. Even in cities such as Philadelphia and Los Angeles, where scandal and policing appear historically synonymous, there is great hope for innovative solutions to steer policing toward a new ethical paradigm.

REFERENCES AND FURTHER READING

Affleck, J. (1998, January 22). FBI arrests 44 Cleveland cops. *Associated Press*. Retrieved August 1, 2014 from http://www.apnewsarchive.com/1998/FBI-Arrests-44-Cleveland-Cops/id-44f9a45643e0cf47e88c626d79a1ea36

Allen, J. & Kearney, L. (2014, July 24). New videos add to scrutiny of N.Y. police use of choke holds. *Chicago Tribune*. Retrieved July 24, 2014 from http://www.chicagotribune.com/news/sns-rt-us-usa-new-york-chokehold-videos-20140724,0,7084908.story

Alpert, G.A. & S. Walker. (2000). Police accountability and early warning systems: Developing policies and programs. *Justice Research and Policy*, 2 (2), 59–72.

Armstrong, M. (2012). *They Wished They were Honest: The Knapp Commission and New York City Police Corruption*. New York: Columbia University Press.

Barker, T. (1978). Empirical study of police deviance other than corruption. *Journal of Police Science and Administration*, 6 (3), 264–272.

Barker, T. & D.L. Carter. (1994). *Police Deviance (Third edition)*. Cincinnati, OH: Anderson Publishers.

Belluck, P. (1998, January 22). 44 officers are charged after Ohio sting operation. *New York Times*. Retrieved August 2, 2014, from http://www.nytimes.com/1998/01/22/us/44-officers-are-charged-after-ohio-sting-operation.html

Boyer, D. (2011, August 8). Philadelphia mayor talks tough to black teenagers after 'flash mobs'. *Washington Times*. Retrieved August 2, 2014 from http://www.washingtontimes.com/news/2011/aug/8/mayor-talks-tough-to-black-teens-after-flash-mobs/?page=all

Boyer, P.J. (2001, May 21). Bad cops. *The New Yorker*. Retrieved August 1, 2014, from http://www.newyorker.com/magazine/2001/05/21/bad-cops

Gambacorta, D. (2014, August 1). Wanted: Ideas to prevent police corruption. *Philadelphia Inquirer*. Retrieved August 24, 2014 from http://articles.philly.com/2014-08-01/news/52332162_1_narcotics-units-cops-body-camera

Golab, J. (2000, September 27). L.A. Confidential. *Salon*. Retrieved April 22, 2014, from http://www.salon.com/2000/09/27/rampart_2/

Heller, K. (2014, August 7). Another Philadelphia police scandal, right on schedule. *Philadelphia Inquirer*. Retrieved August 10, 2014 from http://articles.philly.com/2014-08-07/news/52519336_1_six-narcotics-officers-philadelphia-police-department-narcotics-bureau

Kaplan, P.J. (2009). A critical approach to the LAPD's Rampart Scandal. *Social Justice, 36* (1), 61–81.

Kappeler, V.E. (2006). *Critical Issues in Police Civil Liability (Fourth Edition)*. Long Grove, IL: Waveland Press.

Kappeler, V.E. & L.K. Gaines. (2011). *Community Policing: A Contemporary Perspective*. Waltham, MA: Elsevier.

Kappeler, V. E., R.D. Sluder, & G.P. Alpert. (1994). *Forces of Deviance: Understanding the Dark Side of Policing*. Long Grove, IL: Waveland Press.

Klockars, C.B., S. Kutjnak-Ivkovic, W.E. Harver, & M.R. Haberfeld. (2000). *The Measurement of Police Integrity*. Washington DC: National Institute of Justice.

Knapp Commission (1973). *Report on Police Corruption*. New York: City of New York. Retrieved April 3, 2014, from http://www.nyc.gov/html/ccpc/pages/home/index.shtml

Kutjnak-Ivkovic, S. (2003). To serve and collect: Measuring police corruption. *The Journal of Criminal Law & Criminology, 93* (2), 593–650.

Lattanzio, V. & D. Stamm. (2014, July 31). 6 Philadelphia Narcotics officers stole half a million dollars from suspects: Feds. *Philadelphia Inquirer*. Retrieved August 22, 2014 from http://www.nbcphiladelphia.com/news/local/6-Philadelphia-Narcotics-Officers-Arrested-269193381.html

Lombardi, L. (2010, August 9). How to recruit cleaner cops. *Philadelphia Inquirer*. Retrieved August 10, 2014 from http://articles.philly.com/2010-08-09/news/24971453_1_police-corruption-police-officers-philadelphia-police-department

Los Angeles Police Department (LAPD). (2004). *Rampart Reconsidered: The Search for Real Reform Seven Years Later*. Retrieved April 22, 2014, from http://www.lapdonline.org/home/pdf_view/32827

Moon, M. & C.L. Johnson. (2012). The influence of occupational strain on organizational commitment among police: A general strain theory approach. *Journal of Criminal Justice, 40* (3), 249–258.

Newburn, T. (1999). *Understanding and Preventing Police Corruption: Lessons from the Literature*. London: Policing and Reducing Crime Unit (Home Office).

Punch, M. (2009). *Police corruption: Deviance, Accountability, and Reform in Policing*. Portland, OR: Willan Publishing.

Rodgers, B. (2013, July 7). Santa Fe sued over ex-cop's actions. *Albuquerque Journal*. Retrieved April 3, 2014 from http://www.abqjournal.com/218434/news/santa-fe-sued-over-excops-actions.html

Roebuck, J. & T. Barker. (1974). A typology of police corruption. *Social Problems, 21*, 423–437.

Sherman, L. (1974). *Police Corruption: A Sociological Perspective*. Garden City, NY: Anchor Publishers.

Skolnick, J.H. (2005). Corruption and the blue code of silence. In Sarre, R., D.K. Das, and H. Albrecht (Eds.), *Policing Corruption: International Perspectives*. Lanham, MD: Lexington Books.

Stamm, D. (2014, August 6). 4th Philly narcotics officer accused of corruption put on house arrest. *NBC Philadelphia*. Retrieved August 11, 2014 from http://www.nbcphiladelphia.com/news/local/Narcotics-Officers-Bail-Speiser-270134571.html

Walker, S. & G.A. Alpert. (2002). Early warning systems as risk management for police. In Lersch, K.M. (Ed.), *Policing and Misconduct*. Upper Saddle River, NJ: Prentice Hall, 219–230.

Wilson, J.M., Dalton, E., Scheer, C., & Grammich, C.A. (2010a). *Police Recruitment and Retention for the New Millennium: The State of Knowledge*. Santa Monica, CA: RAND Corporation.

Ethics Within the American Judicial System

CHAPTER 8

"It is a pleasant world we live in, sir, a very pleasant world. There are bad people in it, Mr. Richard, but if there were no bad people, there would be no good lawyers."

—*Charles Dickens*

"No client ever had money enough to bribe my conscience or to stop its utterance against wrong, and oppression. My conscience is my own—my creators—not man's. I shall never sink the rights of mankind to the malice, wrong, or avarice of another's wishes, though those wishes come to me in the relation of client and attorney."

—*Abraham Lincoln*

As stated before, the word "ethics" is historically rooted in the Greek term *ethnos*. Its meaning can be defined as the habits, conduct, or disposition that characterize a demographic region, community, group, or ideology. Determining the best, right, or wrong way to live or act, as well as what obligations you have to societal events, is all within this concept. Morality, on the other hand, is a far narrower concept relating to our behavior. It is the distinction of good or bad as defined by our culture, religion, or philosophy. Morality may, therefore, be bifurcated into correct and incorrect conduct, as we see it. The process of departmentalizing the concepts into socially accepted or rejected behavior is marked by the benefits gained by society. It is therefore possible that ethically correct behavior conflicts with morality. This can occur when our moral rationalization is not congruent with an ethically accepted concept. In a diverse population, it is far more likely that this conflict occurs than in non-diverse groups. Because the United States consists of a diverse population, moral diversity, the method of evaluating the desire of individuals to employ different evaluative methods, as well as how they evaluate virtues, goals, and regulations, must be considered when analyzing the historical and present American judicial system.

HISTORY OF LEGAL ETHICS IN THE UNITED STATES

The inception of legal ethics for attorneys, in American jurisprudence, was initially established through fiduciary legal concepts. In other words, the attorney was held to the duty of a representative and the client was the beneficiary of this relationship. Consequently, a lawyer in essence was required to, at all times, do what was in the best interest of the client. That, however, was not the public's consensus. At a Harvard commencement speech, in 1905, President Theodore Roosevelt stated that lawyers hindered the public interest by their lucrative representation of corporations and wealthy business investors.[1] In 1906, the American Bar Committee on the "Code of Professional Ethics" found, as well, that commercialism was adversely affecting the reputation of the profession in the administration of justice. In response to this national concern, the American Bar Association (ABA) published its Canons of Ethics in 1908.[2] The intention was to bolster the dwindling reputation of the profession, as well as the dwindling reputation of attorneys, in the administration of justice. It was hoped that implementing ethical standards would enhance the confidence of the public in the profession's social and political contributions to our nation. It is important to note that prior to this time, no formalized national regulation pertaining to the conduct of American lawyers existed. By 1924, the vast majority of states had adopted these regulations, or similar versions, into their state laws. At the state level, the Alabama State Bar Association, Code of Ethics established in 1887, became the most influential document in the drafting the ABA's Canons of Ethics.[3] The Alabama code relied heavily upon an 1854 essay entitled *Modern Legal Ethics*, written by George Sharswood. In fact, several other states later used this essay to form their ethic codes. Yet, according to Louis Parley's article, "A Brief History of Legal Ethics," these rules were predominantly viewed by attorneys as a "professionalism" code. The American Bar Association, however, went far beyond the Alabama Code by obligating attorneys to a higher standard of accountability. Personal solicitation of clients and the passive solicitation of clients through advertising were unprecedented additions to 20th century American jurisprudence. It further presented professional self-regulation and exclusive admission rights to bar membership. This moved lawyering from a trade to a profession. Lawyers were now required to withdraw attention from capitalism, in all its unvirtuous representations. In order to accomplish this against the capitalistic pressures of the Industrial Age, the American Bar Association restricted entrance into the profession in order to establish a controlled monopoly, hence reducing competition and limiting violations of ethics caused by induced financial survival. From this beginning, the Ethics of the American Judicial System was formally established. In 1964, under the authority of Lewis F. Powell, Jr., the president of the American Bar Association, reformed the rules of conduct. In 1969, the ABA created the *Model Code of Professional Responsibility*.[4] It consisted of nine rules or "Canons." Each rule presented a fundamental principle supported by explanation. The disciplinary rules identified obligations of the practice of law and the grounds for discipline. From the inception, there was criticism because many of the rules lack clarity. The generalized language left many attorneys uncertain as to the meaning. Others believed that the *Code* created performance obligations, despite language to the contrary. The term "appearance of impropriety" was such a topic of confusion. Consequently, in 1977 the ABA revised the *Model Code of Professional Responsibility*, which was formally adopted as the *Model Rules of Professional Conduct* in 1983.[5] Thirty-five states adopted the rules while others adopted a similar concept. Thereafter in the later years of the 1980's, the American Law Institute also produced a document entitled *Restatement of the Law Governing Lawyers*, in an effort to have a uniform code for all states.[6] There have been numerous additions and modifications to the codes of conduct. However, the essential regulations that established the original models remain the foundation of the judicial system today. In addition to specific competency, a lawyer is obligated to maintain general legal competency and skill by knowing the changes in the law and practice. Understanding technology and its uses in the field as well as the risks and benefits are critical points of competency in a technologically savvy nation. The American Bar Association initially summarized the standard in 1988 and disseminated it as the "Lawyers' Pledge of Professionalism." The following paragraphs represent the present pledge of the organization.

BOX 8.1

AMERICAN BAR ASSOCIATION LAWYERS' PLEDGE
OF PROFESSIONALISM

I WILL encourage respect for the law and our legal system through my words and actions.

I WILL remember my responsibilities to serve as an officer of the court and protector of individual rights.

I WILL contribute time and resources to public service, public education, charitable, and pro bono activities in my community.

I WILL work with the other participants in the legal system, including judges, opposing counsel and those whose practices are different from mine, to make our legal system more accessible and responsive.

I WILL resolve matters expeditiously and without unnecessary expense.

I WILL resolve disputes through negotiation whenever possible.

I WILL keep my clients well-informed and involved in making the decisions that affect them.

I WILL continue to expand my knowledge of the law.

I WILL achieve and maintain proficiency in my practice.

I WILL be courteous to those with whom I come into contact during the course of my work.

I WILL honor the spirit and intent, as well as the requirements, of the applicable rules or code of professional conduct for my jurisdiction and I will encourage others to do the same.

Source: www.americanbar.org. Copyright 2010 The American Bar Association.

ETHICAL ASPECTS CHARGED TO ATTORNEYS UNDER THE ABA'S 1983 MODEL RULES

The Attorney-Client Relationship

Adopted by the ABA in 1983, the *Model Rules of Professional Conduct* are the model rules for most states in America. These rules carved out duties to prospective clients, whether retained or not. Rule 1.18 generally mandates that consultations in forming an attorney-client relationship impart confidentiality on the conversation and or information revealed. Therefore, an attorney, generally, may not represent an individual adverse to the prospective client who did not retain counsel. Additionally, the rule extends to additional members of that particular firm. They also may not generally represent an opposing party against a prospective client. However, in clarification, the Ninth Circuit held, as pertaining to Rule 1.18, that the attorney-client privilege "does not apply where the lawyer has specifically stated that he would not represent the individual and in no way wanted to be involved in the dispute."[7] In order to successfully claim harm, "A party claiming the privilege must identify specific communications and the grounds supporting the privilege as to each piece of evidence over which privilege is asserted."[8] Nonetheless, "An attorney is prohibited from accepting representation materially adverse to a former client in the same or substantially related matter."[9]

In highlight, the first rule relating to the attorney-client relationship is for an attorney to be competent in the area of representation. Rule 1.1 of the *Rules* relates to competency. This competency must be measured by the complexity of the topic, the specialization necessary, the experience required, the training obtained, as well as the time the attorney has to give to the client. Unless expertise is necessary, it is not mandatory for an attorney to have a specific knowledge at the moment of retention; what matters is whether he or she can obtain that skill or knowledge through reasonable preparation. In fact, many areas only require the standard of a general practitioner. It is also permissible for an attorney to obtain assistance from other counsel, so long as the client has been informed and has consented to such representation. Related to the issue of competency, Rule 3.1 mandates that an attorney shall not bring frivolous or non-meritorious claims in good faith. A frivolous appeal [24] is one which "involves legal points not arguable on their merits."[10] So long as a basis of law exists to raise an extension, modification, or reversal of current law, such topics are not a violation.

With regards to the attorney-client relationship, Rule 1.2 states, in essence, that both should know the boundaries of the obligation raised by the relationship. It is possible to restrict the representation to a specific task, and not the entire scope of issues, if the limitation will not jeopardize the clients, and there is consent. Foremost, an attorney must respect the client's decision to settle or proceed to trial, assuming the decision was a well-informed one. Steering a client to other choices is not representation but dictatorial counseling. Further, an attorney, as an officer of the court, should never counsel or assist a client in pursuing an action the attorney knows is criminal or false. Regardless of the type of legal representation, the rules mandate that it should be conducted in a diligent manner. To that end, attorneys are required to inform the client promptly of any decision or situation affecting the representation or issue. In order to do so, quick compliance to a client's request for information is necessary. Failing to adhere to this model is a dereliction of Rule 1.4, Communications. With regards to legal fees, several points determine reasonableness. Certainly the time necessary, the labor involved, lost opportunities to the lawyer, the customary fee rate charged, experience of the attorney, reputation, and whether it is a fixed or contingent amount are all factors.

The *Model Rules of Professional Conduct* Rule 1.6(a) protects against the disclosure of client "confidences," which is defined as information protected by the attorney-client privilege, and the disclosure of client "secrets," which is defined as "other information gained in the professional relationship that the client has requested to be held inviolate or the disclosure of which would be embarrassing or would be likely to be detrimental to the client."[11] The issue of confidentiality is a fundamental duty in the judicial system. Consequently, a lawyer should never, unless permitted by client, disclose information relating to the representation. This is a difficult issue for parents of clients to understand. Many times they are paying for the child's representation and feel that they have the right to know the details of the case. However, without the client's consent, and subject to the aforementioned exceptions, this is a violation of Rule 1.6. Other general exemptions are also applicable. For example, an attorney may reveal information if it is reasonably necessary or to prevent death or substantial bodily harm. Should a client allege acts against an attorney, counsel may disclose information to raise a defense to a civil or criminal charge or grievance. It is also permissible to release confidential material in order to comply with a judicial order or to resolve conflicts relating to an attorney's change of employment or composition or ownership of a firm unless it compromises the attorney-client relationship. Consent by the client is certainly a viable exception. Rule 2.3 of the *Code* provides additional scenarios. In certain circumstances, beneficial to the client, third parties may be given relevant information. Rule 2.3 expressly authorizes the rendering of third-party opinions when the client consents and when the attorney believes that the making of the evaluation is compatible with the other aspects of the lawyer's relationship with the client.[12] Providing title opinions, for example, in support of a client's claim, or, in criminal matters, providing a pre-sentence investigatory report regarding pertinent information in support of an appropriate punishment are both clearly acceptable ethical conduct.

Conflicts of Interest

Conflicts of interest are another major aspect of the ethical practice of law. Lawyers are prohibited from representing a client if that representation involves a "concurrent" conflict of interest. The word "concurrent" is defined in Rule 1.7 as the representation of a client that will adversely affect another client of counsel. It can also occur where a significant risk exists that one or more client's representation will be affected and or limited by the responsibilities he or she has to another client. That said, the lawyer may competently represent multiple clients if there is no collateral limitation of representation to each. Additionally, the client must consent to the representation, should it not be illegal and one client is not exerting a claim against the other. An example is representing the plaintiff and the defendant. Another is representing the state and the defendant. Finally, and in a more likely scenario, representing co-plaintiffs or co-defendants may raise unexpected issues. It is likely, for example, that there will be liability and/or accusatory points that may create conflicts between the representations. Similarly Rule 1.9 prohibits counsel who previously represented an individual from representing another in the same or substantially the same matter whose interest are materially adverse to the former client.

In summation, changing sides, in a legal matter, in essence, is generally prohibited under limited exceptions. Similar regulations are applicable to government officers and employees under Rule 1.11. Judges, arbitrators, mediators, or third-party neutrals are held to Rule 1.12 of the *Rules*. Corporate attorneys are required to follow Rule 1.13 when faced with corporate personnel acting in a matter that affects the legal obligations to the entity. The attorney is ethically required to report this act, as necessary, if it is a legal obligation to the organization or is a violation of law. If counsel reasonably believes that it is not necessary, in the best interest of the organization, to act, then he or she will remit this information to a higher authority in the organization. For example, in a situation in which legal counsel for a law enforcement agency finds that an officer is behaving in a manner that may cause injury to the entity, counsel would be mandated to report such behavior individually, or, if counsel reasonably believes it is in the best interest of the agency, to report such infraction to a higher authority in the organization. Failure to report at all, however, would constitute an ethical violation under the rule. It is permissible, however, under the rule, to jointly represent an individual officer and the entity if authorized by the clients, contingent upon Rule 1.7 compliance. There are times in which an attorney is required to maintain a safekeeping of property. Rule 1.15 defines the requirements to comply with this ethical obligation. Specifically, an attorney has an ethical responsibility to hold property of a client or third party, should such be connected to the representation. Prompt notification of the funds to clients or third persons is necessary. Accordingly, these funds must be deposited in a client trust account. Earned legal fees shall be withdrawn from the client trust account as they accrue.

Terminating or Declining Representation

The 1983 *Rules* brought clarity to a convoluted area of responsibility and conflict, applicable to the attorney-client relationship. Specifically, this area was codified by Rule 1.16., to provide a guideline to terminating or declining representation. When an attorney is faced with violating a conduct rule or representation, an attorney is obligated not to accept the client, or, if the attorney is already representing the client, to cease representation of the client. Such circumstances may arise where the client has used the attorney to perpetrate a crime. Another is where the client persists in committing continual offenses using the lawyer's services. This can be related to civil harm to counsel. If a client fails to fulfill an obligation to the lawyer regarding the lawyer's services and has been given warning that the lawyer will withdraw unless the obligation is fulfilled, the lawyer may ethically withdraw. Similarly and in conjunction, a lawyer may withdraw from representation where the representation will result in an unreasonable financial burden on the attorney. This right to withdraw is subject to court approval. Consequently, an attorney may be required to remain on a case unless good cause for terminating the representation exists. The obligation to the past client does not end with the withdrawal. Counsel remains responsible to protect a client's interest, such as giving reasonable notice to the client, sufficient to retain new counsel.

Third-Party Neutrals

Turning to lawyers serving as third-party neutrals, Rule 2.4 defines such an individual as a person who assists two or more non-clients in reaching a settlement or closure in a disputed matter. This includes arbitrators, mediators, and others who assist in conflict resolution. The unrepresented parties must be informed of the neutrality of the lawyer. Failure to be neutral is a violation of the *Code*.

Candor Toward the Tribunal

Perhaps the most comprehensive rule of ethics is that of Rule 3.3: Candor Toward the Tribunal. The term is defined by Rule 1.0(m):Terminology. "Tribunal" denotes a court, an arbitrator in a binding arbitration proceeding, or a legislative body, administrative agency, or other body acting in an adjudicative capacity. A legislative body, administrative agency, or other body acts in an adjudicative capacity when a neutral official, after the presentation of evidence or legal argument by a party or parties, will render a binding legal judgment directly affecting a party's interests in a particular matter.

In reviewing highlights of ethical conduct mandated by the *Model Rules of Professional Conduct*, it is evident that candor is not an issue when the rules of ethics have been followed. Consequently, truthfulness is the least difficult when proper conduct exists and the most difficult when it does not. Yet a failure to follow the rules may establish additional disciplinary consequences, far beyond the initial violation. It is incumbent upon counsel to be truthful to non-clients, in whatever represented or non-represented capacity, on his client's behalf. This includes non-party third-party individuals. Rule 4.1 cites misrepresentation, statement of facts, and crimes of fraud by clients as the three major subcategories where statutory truthfulness is mandated. Rules 5.1–5.7 of the *Model Rules of Professional Conduct* concentrate attention on the ethical obligation of supervising and subordinate attorneys to comply with the rules of practicing law in certain jurisdictions. It is prohibited for counsel to violate practice requisites or to assist someone in doing so. For example, an attorney should not practice in a jurisdiction in which he or she is not licensed to practice. Additionally, an attorney should not assist someone to practice in such a situation. Consequently, if an attorney is aware that an individual is not authorized to practice law in a jurisdiction and assists him or her in doing so, without approval, that attorney has not only violated an ethical rule but may have criminally conspired to assist someone to commit the criminal act of "practicing law without a license."

Advertising

Lawyer advertising has become a lightning rod of controversy, as it pertains to ethical behavior. Rules 7.1 generally covers communications, advertising, solicitation of clients, firm letterhead and name, and political contributions to obtain legal engagements or appointment of judges. Lawyers have a constitutional right to be involved in the political process, including the making and soliciting of political contributions for candidates for judicial and or other public office. However, this action may raise legitimate public concern as to the fairness of the judicial system and whether the act contributed to that lawyer's selection or appointment by a judge. Consequently, the integrity of the profession is undermined in the eyes of the public. Therefore, attorneys must show caution in their conduct.

ETHICAL ASPECTS CHARGED TO JUDGES

"The bedrock of our democracy is the rule of law and that means we have
Ito have an independent judiciary, judges who can make decisions independent
of the political winds that are blowing."

—*Caroline Kennedy*

Just as the *Model Rules of Professional Conduct* sets a bright line for U.S. attorneys to follow, it is similarly indispensable for the United States to have an honorable and independent judiciary. In order to maintain this standard, a judge must monitor and expect the highest standard of conduct in order to preserve the integrity of the judiciary. Without this standard, the public would lose trust in the independence of judges. The judiciary must follow the law and the code of ethics. To accomplish this they must act without fear or favoritism. At no time should a judge be swayed by political, social, or critical opinions held by the public. Consequently, it is necessary for a judge to hear all cases assigned to him or her, unless restricted by ethics conflicts. Further, judges must afford dignity, respect, and courtesy to all parties, their lawyers, and to the jurors. All parties should be given a right to be heard. The obligation to show respect includes commentary or actions that could reasonably be interpreted as harassment, prejudice, or bias.

With regards to information obtained improperly though ex parte communications, a judge has an absolute obligation to notify the parties of the content of the communication and allow them the right to reply individually. This restriction applies to any communication from non-participating lawyers, law teachers, and others to a proceeding. The exception to the restriction are other judges and law clerks in adjudicative duties.

Litigation is generally protracted and, as such, a judge should direct parties to settle matters. However, that should not be seen as coercive. The prompt administration of justice must coexist with the constitutional right of the parties to be heard in court. This is inclusive of prompt disposition of docket caseloads, punctuality in court attendance, and court cooperation of all personnel involved. The failure, generally, of a judge to comply with the ethical rules and duties reduces the trust or confidence that the public has in our system of government. The rules of conduct applied to judges and the laws of the land must coexist in such a way that they do not infringe on the neutrality of judicial decisions. Further, the mere impression of improper conduct should be avoided. This occurs when reasonable minds with knowledge of all the relevant facts would conclude that a judge's honesty, integrity, impartiality, temperament, or fitness to serve as a judge is impaired. This applies to professional and personal conduct. Impropriety that is certain includes violations of the law, court rules, or other specific provision of the code of conduct. Similarly, with regards to impropriety or hints thereof, a judge's responsibility also extends to his family. On a personal level, the judiciary should not allow family social, financial, or other relationships to influence or appear to influence a judge. Similarly, voluntary testimony as a character witness, by a judge, is unacceptable behavior because it lends the office for personal and private advantage. Likewise, a judge should not be a member of an organization that discriminates on the basis of race, sex, or national origin. This, however, relates to the ongoing practice of an organization. The method used to select members or the purpose may be restrictive to religious, ethnic, or cultural values of legitimate common interest to its members, or it may be in fact and effect an intimate, purely private organization whose membership limitations could not be constitutionally prohibited.[13] Other concerns may include the size and nature of the organization. Non-diversity of the membership is not automatically a violation unless it is shown that a reasonable person with knowledge of all the relevant circumstances would expect that membership to be diverse but for discrimination. An organization is generally said to be discriminatory if it, without reason, excludes membership on the basis of race, religion, sex, or national origin persons. Additionally, it would be an ethical violation for a judge to set up meetings at a location where the judge knows discrimination of membership is practiced. In essence, this creates an impression on the part of the public that the judge approves of the conduct of this organization.

Performance of Duties by the Judiciary

"Apparently a great many people have forgotten that the framers of our Constitution
went to such great effort to create an independent judicial branch that
would not be subject to retaliation by either the executive branch or the legislative
branch because of some decision made by those judges."

—*Justice Sandra Day O'Connor*

Above all, the judiciary must uphold the highest standard of conduct in order to preserve the integrity and impartiality of the position of trust. This is accomplished by acting without fear or favor and the application of the ethical regulations created for that purpose. Judicial compliance with the law and canons of ethics helps to promote confidence in the system of justice. The Judicial

Council Reform and Judicial Conduct and Disability Act of 1980 (28 U.S.C. §§ 332(d)(1), 351–364) was established to assist judges and nominees for judicial office. Determining if disciplinary action is required, and to what extent, should be decided through a reasonable application of the language. It should depend on the gravity of the alleged act, intent of the judge, frequency of improper action, and the ultimate effect it may have on others or on the judicial system.

While the Act is not the basis for civil or criminal liability, it nonetheless establishes a standard in proceedings against judges. It is important to note that not all violations *per se* rise to the level of disciplinary hearings. Reasonableness is required in comparing the action to the language of the relevant canons. These rules of judiciary conduct provide a template to guide the public and judge. In order to accomplish this, the duties of a judge take priority over all other events. Therefore, a judge should be loyal to the profession by maintaining competence in the law. He or she should not be moved by public interest, public complaints, or the possibility of being criticized. In order to represent the sanctity of the office, judges should be patient, dignified, and respectful to lawyers, witnesses, and jurors and expect the same from all court staff and lawyers. All individuals who have a right to be heard should be allowed to do so, individually or through counsel. However, judges should not allow ex parte (without the opposing side being present) communications. If a judge were to unwantedly receive ex parte communication, the judge has the obligation to notify the parties of the communication promptly and allow the parties an opportunity to respond. A judge or persons within his or her authority should not make public comments about the strength or merit of a case pending in his or her or any other court. To maintain the integrity of the court, a judge should dispose promptly with all business before it. Administratively, a judge should, in the most diligent manner, complete his or her responsibilities, maintain professional competence in judicial administration, and assist in that activity with other judges and court personnel. Nepotism and favoritism should be avoided in appointments of the court that may be perceived as such. The power to appoint individuals to conduct court business should be done fairly and on merit alone. Appointees may include assigned counsel, officials such as referees, commissioners, special masters, receivers, guardians, and personnel such as law clerks, secretaries, and judicial assistants. Consent of the parties, unlike financial managerial interest of a judge, in the appointment or granting of compensation, does not relieve the judge of the obligation prescribed by the canons of ethics. To that end, compensation for such appointments should be fair and impartial and not excessive.

Judges who are in a supervisory position over other judges should reasonably monitor the performance of those subordinates. By so doing, should it become reliably apparent to a judge that another judge's conduct is contrary to the canons or that an attorney is violating the *Rules of Professional Conduct*, a judge must take proper action by addressing and reporting the alleged conduct. If a judge believes his or her impartiality may be legitimately questioned, he or she must disqualify him or herself from that proceeding. This may occur in instances where the judge has a personal bias or prejudice on a party, or has personal knowledge of disputed issues in the proceeding. Another is where the judge served as a lawyer in the case. Where a judge previously practiced law with an attorney who is before the court, or where the judge or lawyer have been material witnesses to the case, a judge must recuse him or herself. Similarly this is applicable in cases where the judge's family has a financial interest or the judge's spouse or relative within the third degree of relationship, or the spouse of that individual. This applies to a party to the proceeding, officer, trustee, or director of a party. It also applies to a lawyer in the proceeding or to individuals the judge knows may be called as material witnesses in the case. When a judge has served as a governmental employee and as such was a previous judge, counsel, advisor, or material witness concerning the facts of the case, he or she must also recuse him or herself. In order to be informed about possible conflicts arising from family relationships, a judge is charged with the duty to keep informed about personal, financial, and related financial interests such as that of a "fiduciary." The latter term is defined as an executor, administrator, trustee, and guardian. Within this context, the word "family" is defined by civil law. It includes individuals within the third degree of consanguinity. Specifically it includes parents, children, grandparents, grandchildren, great-grandparents, great-grandchildren, sisters, brothers, aunts, uncles, nieces, and nephews either as whole or half-blood relatives and step-relatives. The term "financial interest" relates to any ownership, regardless of significance, as a director, advisor, or active participant in the affairs of a party. Excluded generally from this category are non-managing mutual funds. However, it is possible within this exclusion for a judicial full disclosure of a managing mutual fund position and stipulations on the record of the parties to allow a willing judge to preside over the case. Generally excluded, as well, are office positions in an educational, religious, charitable, fraternal, or civil organization. Mutual insurance interest and mutual savings associations may be disqualifying factors only if the outcome of the proceeding would substantially affect the value of the interest of the judge or that of others previously mentioned as judicial disqualifications. Similarly, ownership of governmental securities is a financial interest in the issuer only when a resulting outcome may substantially affect the value of the securities. In this context, "proceeding" is inclusive of all stages of litigation including but not limited to pretrial, trial, and appeals. However, if the judge would be disqualified by a financial interest in a party, divestment by the judge and or his family does not require disqualification unless the financial interest could substantially be affected by the outcome of the ruling. In a proactive expectation, the judiciary should refrain from involvement in businesses and or financial actions that may interfere with impartiality. Therefore, the mere possibility of future conflict sometime in the judge's career are violating actions.

That said, it may appear that there is nothing a judge can do without violating ethical conduct. It is not intended for judges to be quarantined from society and all extrajudicial activities. Further, it is not expected that a judge become a recluse or hermit. Rather, because a judge is in a unique position in society to contribute to the law and the judicial system, it is encouraged. Teaching and serving on not-for-profit law school boards in furtherance of the profession is clearly an acceptable contribution. The experience and knowledge obtained by the judiciary is an imperative aspect toward positive legal evolution. Logically, if a judge accepts excessive extrajudicial assignments that place excessive strain on a judge and his or her duties, it is a violation. That said, it is encouraged for judges to contribute to bar associations and the administration of justice. Procedural and substantive changes to the law that improve the civil and criminal process are necessary in the furtherance of the judicial system. Participating in a family business is acceptable unless, logically, it interferes with the efficient administration of judicial duties.

There are no requirements under The Ethics Reform Act of 1989 for judges to disclose their income, investments, or debts, except as a disclosure under the rules. However, a judge must be cautious and should seek consultation before receiving compensation from outside sources. These restrictions include (1) a prohibition against receiving "honoraria," (2) a prohibition against receiving compensation for service as a director, trustee, or officer of a profit or nonprofit organization, (3) a requirement that compensated teaching activities receive prior approval, and (4) a limitation on the receipt of "outside earned income."

With regard to political activities, a judge may not hold any office in any political organization. Judges should not make any speeches for or against any political candidate or official. Additionally, at no time may a judge solicit funds, pay for access to, or attend or purchase a ticket for a dinner or other event that is sponsored by a political group. Such action can be construed as prejudicial to non-supporters of these entities or individuals. If judges become candidates for political office, they must resign their judgeships. Because of the hint of impropriety, a judge should not be involved in any political activity with very limited exceptions.

"Justice delayed is justice denied."

—*William E. Gladstone*

The *Model Rules of Professional Conduct* and the Judicial Council Reform and Judicial Conduct and Disability Act of 1980 stand as a testament of the judiciary branch of government raising the dignity and impartiality of the judicial system. Clearly, capitalism, as our preferred economic national model, contains forces that previously and presently strain the impartial and fair administration of justice. Nonetheless, such acts and power have generally been identified and a model of conduct is predominately uniform in America. As technology and society change, these rules and canon will inevitably evolve again in order to serve society's need for a fair and trustworthy system of justice.

BOX 8.2

BEING A PROSECUTOR IS A CALLING: ADVICE FROM A CRIMINAL JUSTICE PRACTITIONER

Phil Grant, JD

First Assistant District Attorney

Montgomery County, Texas

Prosecution is a calling. It sounds somewhat dramatic to describe it that way, but choosing this field as a career means committing to a life of short budgets, large caseloads, and long hours. Your salary will always lag well behind your peers and you will quickly realize that your civil lawyer contemporaries have no understanding of how hard you work and how emotionally taxing prosecution can be. You will be subject to election strife and political criticism. You will be part social worker, part police officer, and part judge. You will go weeks without a good night's sleep or proper nutrition. And yet, even though the alarm clock rattles your brain and summoning the strength to get up before dawn takes everything you have left in your mental and emotional tank, you will smile through it all. You have the best job in the world; you are a prosecutor. It is a calling, and it is a worthwhile one.

My name is Phil Grant and I am the First Assistant District Attorney in Montgomery County, Texas. I have been a prosecutor my whole career since I graduated from law school in 1996. My job functions include the management of a 7.2 million dollar budget, supervising the 40 other attorneys in our office, and investigating and prosecuting crimes involving official misconduct. I occasionally try cases that need some expertise such as cold cases and violent felonies. I became a prosecutor thanks to a creative eighth grade home economics teacher who turned a parenting project into a significant life lesson. We were assigned the responsibility of hard boiling an egg and carrying it around with us for a week to simulate parenting. A rambunctious boy in our class knocked one of the young girl's eggs out of her hand, "killing it." Our teacher brought a local lawyer into the classroom and held a mock trial. I had a crush on the egg victim's mother so I volunteered to be the prosecutor. I won the case after a few hours of testimony and was rewarded with a date to the spring dance with the egg's "mother." Good times. I enjoyed the experience so much that when I started college I applied for an internship with the Dallas District Attorney's Office. I spent the summer working with the Major Offenders group cataloging the local members of an outlaw motorcycle gang. Every day was interesting and challenging and I knew I had found my career. My college did not offer a Criminal Justice degree, but I continued to pursue internships that related to criminal law. I continued to work in the field during breaks from school and during my time in law school as well. My early commitment to the field was rewarded by admission to law school and by a job offer with the Harris County (Houston) District Attorney's Office when I graduated. Prosecution requires a college degree (as mentioned above, it does not require a criminal justice degree, mine was in economics) and three years of law school. Most states require some sort of exam at the conclusion of law school that tests you on your overall competency in all of the practice areas you might face. There is no specific bar exam for criminal law in most states, so you are required to demonstrate a broad knowledge of legal matters in order to be admitted to the legal bar. Once you have passed this exam you can be sworn in as a lawyer and begin to practice law. The local prosecuting attorney, usually an elected official, then appoints you to the position of assistant district attorney to act as his or her representative in the prosecution of criminal cases. Federal prosecutors are appointed by the local United States Attorney and if admitted to any state bar may practice in any federal district court across the nation.

Depending on the size of your jurisdiction, you may handle all facets of prosecution or you may be able to specialize. Prosecution includes two broad phases: the trial phase and the appellate phase. In large jurisdictions, each phase is handled by separate groups of attorneys working as a team. In smaller jurisdictions one attorney may handle a particular case throughout both phases. The life cycle of a particular case may vary based on the speed of your local jurisdiction and the complexities of the litigation, but the typical life cycle of a case is over a year. A criminal case starts with a complaint. This complaint is either from a citizen who feels he or she has been criminally wronged or is from a police officer who witnessed an offense occur. The local law enforcement agency investigates the crime and refers it to the local prosecutor's office for prosecution. The office then handles the case through plea bargaining or trial. The vast majority of cases are resolved by plea bargaining. The prosecutor and a defense attorney in most cases discuss the facts of the incident, the defendant's criminal history, and any other relevant information. Based on the punishment ranges set by the local legislature, they often can agree, with the defendant's confession, to an agreement that satisfies all parties and the interests of justice. In the cases that cannot be resolved through negotiation, a judge or jury will hear the facts and decide guilt and the appropriate punishment. Prosecutors must have a stomach for difficult situations. It is not uncommon for prosecutors to be called out to major crime scenes involving violence and death. Attending autopsies and reviewing crime scene photos may be a regular part of your job. You will need to have good interpersonal skills as you deal with law enforcement and victims who may or may not be cooperative. You must be able to make sound decisions quickly and think on your feet. Public speaking is the number one fear of most Americans, but it is a regular part of your job and a critical skill for effective courtroom litigation. You must have a quick wit and a curious mind as you will become minor experts in various scientific fields such as DNA analysis, psychology, and medicine. You must be able to negotiate difficult issues without taking them personally. It is a job that forces you to be a jack of all trades. Larger jurisdictions often allow prosecutors the luxury of specializing in a particular practice area. Some attorneys find that they are suited for certain criminal behaviors and can develop an affinity for that specialty. Some examples of specialized prosecution fields include: white collar crime, child physical and sexual abuse, family violence, and major crimes. As mentioned previously, most jurisdictions have a specialized appellate division that handles post-conviction appeals. Appellate prosecutors must have strong research and writing skills.

Prosecutors take an oath to seek justice, not convictions. Despite how we are sometimes portrayed in the media, I have never met a prosecutor who intentionally pursued a case against a person whom he or she knew in his or her heart was not guilty. Sometimes the most important job a prosecutor can have is to exonerate an accused individual or dismiss a case when it is in the interest of justice to do so. Crime is not committed in a vacuum, prosecutors often have to evaluate the real-life circumstances of individuals and temper their considerable discretion with mercy. There are times, however, when mercy is not called for. Some criminals who demonstrate a continued disregard for the law and act out in violent and unconscionable ways should be separated from society for the longest possible period of time. In those cases, it is incumbent upon the prosecutor to demonstrate effectively to the judge or jury the serious of the offense or the significant criminal history so the individual will be sentenced to the longest possible prison sentence.

Prosecutors serve a system that is not perfect. Guilty individuals are sometimes acquitted and innocent individuals have been convicted. Prosecutors have a duty to move on from difficult

(Continued)

BOX 8.2 (Continued)

circumstances such as a not guilty or exoneration and continue to seek justice on the next case in front of them. There is always a next case or victim waiting for you to do your best to bring them closure. The most important thing a prosecutor takes from case to case is his or her integrity.

Prosecution is a career that allows an individual to impact dramatically not only individual lives but also the community at large. Effectively targeting high crime areas or violent repeat offenders can make dramatic differences in the day-to-day lives of your constituents. Combining aggressive prosecution techniques with effective public relations campaigns can have a significant deterrent effect within a jurisdiction. Partnering with law enforcement, parent teacher organizations, and local service organizations can foster educational programs for youth that discourage delinquent behavior that may lead to adult criminality.

Students who desire a career in law or prosecution should begin their research and participation in the criminal justice community early. Seek out internships and service programs with local law enforcement agencies or prosecutor offices. Some police agencies have citizen academies that train local citizens how to be ambassadors of law enforcement into the general population and how to respond as a citizen in the case of an emergency. The importance of a good educational record cannot be stressed enough. Prosecutorial jobs are becoming harder and harder to come by. Local district attorneys in Texas are getting their pick of the best and the brightest of local law school graduates. A demonstrated interest in criminal law from an early age can be a tremendous asset when pursuing a prosecutorial job.

The calling of prosecution often leads to other careers. Many prosecutors move on to elected offices such as elected district or county attorneys, judges, legislative positions, or local government officials. Many go on to hold advisory or managerial positions in state and federal government. Many take the extensive trial experience they receive and go on to lucrative private practice careers. Often, prosecutors like me commit to a lifetime of public service in the prosecutorial field. Prosecutors are in demand in both the private and public sectors.

You'll have the best stories at family get togethers and social functions. You'll have a sense of purpose and satisfaction that will carry you through the long hours. You will go to bed every night with the knowledge that someone out there is going to bed in the safety of his or her own home because you cared enough to do your best at work. You will save lives and help the victims of crime gain closure and move on. There will be dark days, sad times, and difficult moments to be sure, but they will be worth it in the end. Prosecution is a calling, and it is a worthwhile one.

REFERENCES AND FURTHER READING

Alfini, J. J., & Shaman, J. M. (2007). Judicial Conduct and Ethics. LexisNexis.

Altman, J. M. (2003). Considering the A.B.A's 1908 Canons of Ethics. 71 Fordham L. Rev. , 2395–2508.

Braswell, M. C., McCarthy, B. R., & McCarthy, B. J. (2015). Justice. Crime, and Ethics (8th ed.). Anderson Publishing.

Chemerinsky, E. (1989). Ideology, judicial selection and judicial ethics. The Georgetown Journal of Legal Ethics, 643.

Kayffman, K. (2013). Legal Ethics (3rd ed.). Cengage Learning.

Kleinig, J. (2008). Ethics and Criminal Justice An Introduction. Cambridge University Press.

Pollock, J. M. (2010). Ethical Dilemmas & Decisions In Criminal Justice. Wadsworth Cengage Learning.

Prenzler, T. (2009). Ethics and Accountability in Criminal Justice: Towards a Universal Standard. Australian Academic Press.

Shaman, J. M. (1988). Judicial Ethics. The Georgetown Journal of Legal Ethics, 1.

Souryal, S. S. (2014). Ethics in Criminal Justice in Search of the Truth (6th ed.). Routledge.

Spurgeon Hall, R. A., & Dennis, C. B. (1999). The Ethical Foundations of Criminal Justice. CRC Press.

ENDNOTES

1. See Altman, 2003.

2. http://www.americanbar.org/content/dam/aba/migrated/cpr/mrpc/Canons_Ethics.authcheckdam.pdf

3. http://law.hofstra.edu/pdf/academics/journals/lawreview/lrv_issues_v34n03_cc17_b.pdf

4. http://www.americanbar.org/content/dam/aba/migrated/cpr/mrpc/mcpr.authcheckdam.pdf

5. http://www.americanbar.org/content/dam/aba/migrated/cpr/mrpc/mcpr.authcheckdam.pdf page 5

6. Memorandum from Charles W. Wolfram, Reporter of the Restatement of The Law Governing Lawyers, ALI, to Geoffrey C. Hazard, Jr, Director, *ALI* (Jan. 20, 1986) (on file with the author). 1998

7. Barton v. U.S. Dist. Court, 410 F. 3d 1104, 1111 (9th Cir. 2005).

8. United States v. Martin, 278 F. 3d 988, 999 (9th Cir. 2002).

9. In re American Airlines, Inc., 972 F. 2d 605, 610 (5th Cir. 1992), cert. denied, 507 U.S. 912, 113 S. Ct. 1262, 122 L. Ed. 2d 659 (1993).

10. "*Olympia Co. v. Celotex Corp.*," 771 F. 2d 888, 893 (5th Cir. 1985) (quoting *Hagerty v. Succession of Clement*, 749 F. 2d 217, 221–22 (5th Cir. 1984), *cert. denied*, 474 U.S. 968 (1985)), *cert. denied*, 493 U.S. 818 (1989).

11. New York State Bar Ass'n v. FTC, 276 F. Supp. 2d 110, 2003 U.S. Dist. LEXIS 13939, 2003–2 Trade Cas. (CCH) P74116 (D.D.C., 2003). Model Rule 1.6 contains limited exceptions to this general rule:

    (1) to prevent the client from committing a criminal act that the lawyer believes is likely to result in imminent death or substantial bodily harm; or

    (2) to establish a claim or defense on behalf of the lawyer in a controversy between the lawyer and the client, to establish a defense to a criminal charge or civil claim against the lawyer based upon conduct in which the client was involved, or to respond to allegations in any proceeding concerning the lawyer's representation of a client.

12. In re Ethics Advisory Panel Opinion, 554 A. 2d 1033, 1989 R.I. LEXIS 26 (R.I., 1989).

13. New York State Club Ass'n. Inc. v. City of New York, 487 U.S. 1, 108 S. Ct. 2225, 101 L. Ed. 2d 1 (1988); Board of Directors of Rotary International v. Rotary Club of Duarte, 481 U.S. 537, 107 S. Ct. 1940, 95 L. Ed. 2d 474 (1987); Roberts v. United States Jaycees, 468 U.S. 609, 104 S. Ct. 3244, 82 L. Ed. 2d 462 (1984).

The Rationale of Punishment: Moral Dilemmas, Human Rights, and Capital Punishment

CHAPTER 9

"Wisdom, compassion, and courage are the three universally recognized
moral qualities of men."

—*Confucius*

MORAL DILEMMAS

This chapter is concerned with the moral dimensions of punishment. How does someone shape a moral decision? What is the functionality and moral essence of punishment? Upon what moral values are punishment and capital punishment administered? These are just some of the questions that will be discussed. Before proceeding into the analysis of the topic, there is a distinction that has to be clarified: that between ethics and morals. Even though these two terms are commonly used interchangeably, several philosophical and sociological sources tend to distinguish them to enhance the differences in their meanings (Zygmount 1994, Gert 2012).

According to the *Stanford Encyclopedia of Philosophy*, morality has two dimensions, each of which indicates a different specified role in the theoretical discussion of ethics: the descriptive one and the normative one. When referring to morality in a descriptive way, one is discussing the common societal codes that have been defined by a group of people holding a common system of values—for example, people who share the same religious denomination or beliefs. On the other hand, when referring to morality normatively, one is describing a code of conduct that, by taking into account the specified conditions, all involved individuals would agree upon, based on the idea that they are rational and are capable of judgment (Gert 2012, Pollock 2007). The difference between the descriptive and the normative approach of morality lies on whether or not this code of conduct is considered universal. When looking at the descriptive aspect of morality, since the codes of rules and values are representative of specified groups of people, then morality in its very essence cannot be universal. In these terms, there are different codes of conduct that represent the systems of values of different groups of people, some—or all—of which share common moral elements. On the contrary, since the normative form of morality refers to rules of conduct as agreed upon by all rational human beings, then morality is considered to be universal and, therefore, morally based decisions should never be overridden (Gert 2012, Pollock 2007).

Regardless of the philosophical approach of morality, moral judgments and actions initiate from the willingness of individuals to hold—and eventually[1] apply—the codes of conduct which they

97

have decided are moral. Nevertheless, taking into account that human beings are social beings, one could claim that the personal inner code of conduct is a result of society's ethical system of beliefs and values that have directly or indirectly influenced the individual at a young age. In different words, personal moral beliefs and values are commonly shaped by the society where the individual has grown up and been socialized. Nevertheless, there are times when a person's inner moral values differ from the general ethics posed by society.

The Ethical Pyramid

In order to demonstrate this idea schematically, imagine a pyramid where its base represents the societal ethical system according to which the moral rules are built (the middle level of the ethical pyramid). From then on the moral rules stand as the source of each individual's moral judgments (the top part of the pyramid) (Pollock 2007). Each societal ethical system, regardless of the philosophical stance or moral philosophy it follows, is the foundation of everyone's moral beliefs and therefore cannot be doubted by any member of the society. That is, as Pollock underlines, *"although ethical decisions may became the basis of debate, the decisions are based on fundamental truths or propositions that are taken as a given by the individual employing the ethical system"* (Pollock 2007: 35). Even from 1977, Baelz indicated that there are four specific characteristics found in every ethical system: (1) they are prescriptive and therefore inflexible, in the sense that, on both the individual and the collective levels, a certain behavior is expected; (2) they are authoritative since in the societal territory no one can doubt the established ethical system; (3) they represent the universal application of what is considered right or wrong so that individual relativism cannot really take place,[2] and finally (4) they are not individual-driven, meaning that what is conventionally right or wrong applies for every individual without exception (Baelz 1977: 19).

Ethical systems can take many different forms according to the societal settings in which they are posed and established. Several philosophers, sociologists, and other theorists tried to describe and frame the ethical systems in accordance with their historical placements and philosophical stances. As discussed in Chapter 3, Immanuel Kant, for instance, supported that there are universal principles of right and wrong, indicating from then on that since rationality is a quality of the human race, then each individual should be able, capable, and rightful to follow and apply these principles (Kant 1949). This system can be briefly described as "ethical formalism" and is considered a rather deontological ethical system.[3] Therefore, based on the qualities of the deontological system, the act of assassination is considered immoral in all cases, even if there might be positive consequences out of it (as is, for instance, killing with the intention to protect oneself).

On the other hand stands the teleological ethical system according to which the consequences of an action determine if the action was inherently wrong or right. Jeremy Bentham, a British philosopher and legal scholar discussed in Chapter 4, was a supporter of the teleological ethical system. Bentham believed that an action should be defined as moral or immoral based on the good or bad consequences combined with the effects of that action on the majority of the people (Borchert & Steward 1986). An example of a teleological ethical system is that of utilitarianism. Utilitarianism maintains that if a somewhat immoral action results in a rather utilitarian or good consequence to the majority of the people, then this action should be defined as a moral/good one.[4] Taking the example mentioned above, the act of protecting oneself by killing someone who is dangerous to the community cannot be considered immoral under the teleological perspective of utilitarianism.

Ethical formalism and utilitarianism are only examples of the deontological and the teleological ethical systems. Nevertheless, as also identified by Pollock, there are numerous ethical systems that shape the individuals' moral rules (which represent the second stage of the ethical pyramid). Other ethical systems are detectible in the many different religions around the world, almost all of which have two common denominators: God's will and respect for others. Religions create moral values through the direct or indirect divine will. From then on, the powerful divinity stands as the moral supervisor of humans' actions according to each religion's prospects (Banks 2012). Additionally, one can identify ethical systems stemming from the natural law,[5] the person's virtues,[6] the ethics of care,[7] or even from the psychological perspective of egoism.[8]

The second level of the pyramid represents the individual's moral values as influenced by the ethical system within which he or she was born and raised. There are many different theories that attempt to explain how a person develops moral values. Some of the most essential ones are the biological theories, which support that moral behavior originates from biological predetermining factors (Ellis and Pontius 1989). Another theoretical perspective maintains that moral values are built according to the individual's observations of what is considered to be right and wrong while growing up. This perspective is recognized as *learning theory* and asserts that moral values are shaped either through the process of "modeling,"[9] or through "reinforcement"[10] (Pollock 2007). Finally, the developmental theories propose that the biological, psychological, and emotional growth of the individual are all responsible for the development of moral reasoning. Probably the most significant contribution to the discussion of moral development is that of American psychologist Lawrence Kohlberg (see Chapter 1). Kohlberg analyzed the process of moral judgment in relation to the individual's cognitive development, indicating that the conception of what is right transforms according to one's age (Kohlberg 1981).

The upper level of the pyramid represents the individual's moral judgment in specific situations and certain occurrences. All individuals who hold an adequate cognitive level are capable of moral judgments and have been asked to take a moral position on an ethical issue. Moral judgments are part of our everyday lives. We make decisions about committing immoral or unethical actions constantly: from the most common judgment of whether to lie or not, up to most critical decisions that are responsible for an individual's life—such as a jury's decision of whether or not to sentence a convicted person to death (Pollock 2007).

Moral Dilemmas

Most—if not all—moral judgments are dilemmas. The decision that has to be made lies between what is right or wrong, moral or immoral, good or bad. Moral dilemmas are raised by individuals during the process of decision making between two or more choices of behavior. Nevertheless, as Banks highlights, the personal approach toward a moral dilemma cannot be considered as "correct" or "wrong" since "different approaches are equally valid in ethical terms" (Banks 2004: 12). In different words, since the personal stance of morality is fluid and changeable according to the system of values that the individual shapes always in relation to his/her age and societal surroundings, the fact that the final decision on a moral dilemma has come through an equally rational and emotional procedure, does not permit any external criticism (from another person). The exceptions to this assertion are considered mainly with the actual actions, especially when these actions are thought to be harmful toward others. Nevertheless, even in these circumstances, the human psychological defense mechanisms may lead an individual to justify an immoral—based on both his or her and the societal moral rules—act by transferring the responsibility of an ethical decision. An example of this instance is commonly found in periods of war where soldiers try to justify their violent acts of torturing and killing by claiming that they were *simply following orders in committing those crimes* (Banks 2004:13). Arguing on a more philosophical level, however, even the decision of obeying an order to perform an action that is commonly regarded as immoral and inhumane could be considered as an unethical decision after all.

In order to resolve an ethical dilemma, the individual needs to proceed on a number of steps that will clarify his/her positioning. Following Banks' and Pollock's suggestions, there are five main phases to be followed: (1) One should examine all the facts that are possible to be known so as to avoid misunderstandings and misconceptions; (2) From then on one needs to identify the potential values of the members involved in the dilemma, including their personality characteristics (Aristotelian *excellences*) and the concepts relevant to the situation; (3) The third step includes the identification of the moral rules and actions of all the involved parties so as to clarify the intentions; (4) Next comes the decision of the immediate moral attitude, which, even though in most cases might be constructed from the moral values of the individual (see pyramid of ethics), there are other cases where the immediate moral attitude might deviate or completely differ from these values; (5) Finally, the individual resolves his or her ethical dilemma by taking into account both one of the previously discussed ethical systems as well as his or her moral values at that specific moment (Banks 2004, Pollock 2007).

As we see later on in this chapter, moral dilemmas are apparent quite often in the criminal justice system, especially during the process of punishment. In order to provide an example of an ethical dilemma, consider that your spouse has inherited a property where he found a large amount of ancient golden coins of great national value hidden underground. The property is located in a country where it is illegal not to report and return any national treasures found. At the same time, your spouse's brother is in a critical health condition, lacking the amount of money needed to obtain a life-saving treatment. Your spouse decides to sell the coins illegally and use the money to get his brother better care. Your knowing this fact would make you an accomplice. What would you do? Would you agree with his decision? Would you report the findings to the police? Following the steps suggested you should (1) examine all the facts. Is there any other way to support your brother-in-law financially? Are the coins really of national value? If the coins are returned to the authorities, will there be any compensation? Second (2), you should consider the relevant values and concepts. So, in this example, you should examine your spouse's character: values such as honesty and integrity and the value of life in regards to your brother-in-law's condition. From then on (3), you should identify the ethical issues involved in the situation. The first issue is apparent: whether or not your spouse should keep the treasure. Moreover, there is the issue of participating in the black market to sell the coins. Finally, there is the ethical issue of what you should do now if you believe an injustice may have taken place. The next step (4) is to resolve the immediate dilemmas, which are whether or not to report the findings to the police, and as a result to turn your spouse in for his illegal actions. Based on the ethical systems previously described, if you are holding an ethical formalistic system of values, you would have reported both actions to the police since keeping a national treasure is considered to be stealing and participating in the illicit sale of antiquities is also dishonest and unlawful. On the other hand, if you are maintaining a rather utilitarian ethical perspective, you would have weighed all the costs and benefits for all persons and situations concerned, including the health condition of your brother-in-law. The final step (5) is to proceed in making the decision that is relevant to your ethical system's values.

Nevertheless, one should not mistake moral dilemmas with ethical issues. As we have observed, moral dilemmas are the processes under which the individual has to decide how to act when two (or more) different moral options are present. On the other hand, as Pollock states, "... *ethical issues are broad social questions, often concerning the government's social control mechanisms and impact on those governed*" (Pollock 2007). Most of these questions are difficult since they carry an importance that deeply influences and affects people's lives. Inevitably, several ethical issues have concerned the criminal justice system's decision-making processes, taking mostly the form of passing laws and issuing certain sentences according to the crimes committed. Examples of these criminal justice ethical issues could be identified in regards to the decriminalization of soft drugs, abortion laws, whether to issue the death penalty or not, and mandatory DNA registries. Therefore, the typical individual does not have control over these issues.

THE RATIONALE OF PUNISHMENT

The Moral Aspect of Punishment

Following the analysis of how moral dilemmas could be approached, we should underline that a similar variety of views applies also on the philosophical, sociological, and criminological perspectives regarding punishment. The act of punishment is closely related to moral values, especially after taking into account that it represents an unpleasant process that follows a wrong or immoral action against society. Throughout the years and based on the ethical framework of the theorists, there have been different developmental models on the rationale of punishment, focusing mainly on questions like: Why punish? What is the purpose of punishment? On what moral individual and social aspects should we focus when a specific punishment is applied?

However, before exploring these different models, we should examine the moral aspect of punishment and punishment *per se*. The Oxford dictionary defines punishment as *"the infliction or imposition of a penalty as retribution for an offense."*[11] Within this framework, Bean portrayed the following five main characteristics of punishment: (1) the offender has to experience the punishment as an unpleasant practice, (2) the punishment has to stand as a reactive action toward a supposed or completed offense, (3) there must be an actual or supposed offender who will experience the punishment, (4) the punishment should originate from personal agencies capable of cognitive decisions,[12] and (5) only an agent or an institution holding the adequate authority is able to impose a punishment. In any other case, an act that comes as a response to an offense is considered to be either revenge or a hostile act (Bean 1981, Banks 2004). A solid definition of punishment is provided by Garland, who states that punishment is *"the legal process whereby violators of criminal law are condemned and sanctioned in accordance with specified legal categories and procedures"* (Garland 1990).

The philosophical aspect of punishment can take many paths according to the ethical framework that one supports. As we have observed, the two main ethical systems are utilitarianism and ethical formalism. Based on these ethical systems, the corrections philosophy pursues specific goals. Under the utilitarian philosophical perspective, we use the following rationales of punishment: deterrence, incapacitation, and rehabilitation. Since the utilitarian ethical framework maintains that an action can be criticized only by the consequences it causes, under this idea, punishing and treating an offender benefits society. This benefit, according to Pollock, overshadows the offender's negative feelings of unpleasantness (Pollock 2007). In other words, the main philosophical view of utilitarianism supports that *the end*—which includes the individual and societal benefits derived from the punishment of the offender—*justifies the means*—which is the punishment itself. Jeremy Bentham, who was the main contributor of the utilitarian theory, charged that, since punishment serves specific utilities toward both the offender and the society in general, the rationale of punishment is morally justified only when the offender is capable of understanding the consequences of his actions (Bentham 1970). That is because the utilitarian view of the purpose of punishment would lose its main point of benefiting the offender if he or she is not able to comprehend the reasons for the punishment. Borchert and Stewart note that punishment under these circumstances could not be justified (Borchert and Stewart 1986).

On the other hand, from the viewpoint of ethical formalism, corrections are taking the form of retribution. Ethical formalism, as we have noted, is concerned with the fundamental immorality of the illegal action (the offense) *per se*, and thus punishment is what the offender deserves. According to Pollock, punishment is part of the social contract where all members of society are aware of the potential consequences of their actions (Pollock 2007). Therefore, when an unethical, inappropriate, or illegal act takes place, the person responsible should expect that he will experience a relevant punishment according to the social contract he lives within (Gough 1978).[13] Another view which is consistent with the philosophical elements of ethical formalism is that punishment functions as a prerequisite to restoring the balance that has been disrupted by the illegal act (Pollock 2007).

All the previously mentioned rationales of punishment (deterrence, incapacitation and rehabilitation, retribution, and justice model) will be further analyzed in depth in order to expand our understanding of the different purposes of punishment. Moreover, emphasis will be given to whether the two different moral aspects of punishment (the teleological and deontological point of views) could be reconciled under the common philosophical spectrum of *restorative justice*.

Deterrence, Incapacitation, and Rehabilitation

Since the utilitarian ethical framework focuses on the general long-term benefit to society, punishment should also prevent immoral and illegal acts from reoccurring. Under this school of thought, punishment can prevent future criminal activity through its abilities to deter, incapacitate, and rehabilitate. Individuals, according to Banks' claim, "[a]re deterred from actions when they refrain *from carrying them out because they have an aversion to the possible consequences of these actions"* (Banks 2004: 106). Until the end of the 17th century, although the role of punishment had mostly a punitive, retributive character, the works of classical philosophers such as Cesare Beccaria (1738–1794) and Jeremy Bentham (1748–1832) greatly helped shape the foundation of deterrence theory in criminology. The purpose of punishment, as Beccaria asserts, is not vengeance but the deterrence and reformation of the person who committed the offense—which also discourages others from committing a similar offense. Therefore, the deterrent purpose of punishment has two goals: *specific* (individual) *deterrence*, which aims to prevent the offender from committing another offense, and *general deterrence*, which intends to prevent others from committing a similar offense (Beccaria 1764). Therefore, whatever the motives of the offender, the punishment imposed should have a cleansing, cathartic nature in order to maintain its admonishing role while abandoning the element of revenge. Following a similar line of thought, Bentham asserted that deterrence should be the main—if not the only—purpose of punishment. As found in Bean's treatise, Bentham supports that since pain and pleasure are the main motivators in life, *"When a man perceives or supposes pain to be the consequence of an act he is acted on in such manner as tends with a certain force to withdraw him as it were from the commission of that act"* (Bean 1981:30). In other words, if the pain involved in the punishment feels worse than the pleasure expected after performing an illegal act, then the offender will be prevented from engaging in this act again (Banks 2004).

According to many scholars, the element of deterrence is more of a philosophical desire of the punishment's purpose rather than an actual result (Hudson 1996, Blumstein et al 1978, Ten 1987). As Beyleveld noted, there is no scientific evidence supporting that general deterrence is effective in controlling the crime rate without the interference of human rights (Beyleveld 1979). Moreover, Andenaes point out that since offences vary widely, not only in terms of the offender's motivation but also in terms of the consequences of each offense, one should take into account the specific conditions under which the offense took place as well as the offender's moral attitudes (Andenaes 1972). After all, even though Bentham may support that the deterrent aspect of punishment may prevent rational individuals from engaging in criminal acts, the alternative position supports that not all crimes have been committed under rational decision-making processes, and not all offenders maintain self-control when committing illegal actions (Banks 2004). Closing the part on deterrence, one more issue is commonly discussed: how severe should the punishment be in order to deter effectively? Since the aspect of deterrence has two branches, the individual one and the general one, the balance between these two might become problematic. As Pollock notes, in the case of a violent crime of passion, deterrence is probably of no use to the specific offender, considering the limited likelihood that he will repeat the offense. Nevertheless, the punishment should be harsh so as to convey to the general public that this kind of act will not be tolerated. After all, *"under deterrence theory, the offender is only a tool to teach a lesson to the rest of us"* (Pollock 2007: 396).

In utilitarian theory, another positive consequence of punishment is incapacitation. As the terms suggests, incapacitation represents the inability of the offender to re-offend while being punished. What distinguishes this role of punishment is that it is not related to the possible unpleasantness that the offender may experience through the process of punishment; incapacitation is only concerned with the fact that the offender will not be able to commit any further crimes. The aspect of incapacitation is observed in certain types of punishment. According to Morris, custody is the most common type that incapacitates since it ostensibly restrains the offender from engaging in any further criminal activity, thereby protecting the public (Morris 1994). Another form which follows this thinking is parole, since even though the offender is not incarcerated, the level of supervision to which he is subjected is a restraining factor in his willingness and chance to re-offend (Ten 1987).

However, the policy of incapacitation faces one major issue: it is based on the idea of prediction. This means that incapacitation benefits the society by eliminating the possibility that an offender might recommit a crime. However, as Banks points out, this kind of establishment has two major issues. On one hand, it involves a serious level of unfairness, since in the effort of incapacitating dangerous criminals, a number of offenders who probably would not re-offend are facing punishment just to satisfy the probability of committing a serious crime. On the other hand, it is related with the quite immoral principle of punishing offenders based on the future possibility of re-offending (Banks 2004). As Morris has also stated, sentences that focus on the incapacitation of an offender should be backed up with evidence of a high likelihood that the specific individual will engage in criminal activity in the future (Morris 1994). Therefore, following the choice of incapacitation, one may be exposed to two mistakes: (1) to incarcerate an offender who would not engage in any further criminal activity and (2) to release an offender who commits further crimes (Pollock 2007). However, there are now practices that reflect the role of incapacitation: they are most commonly found in habitual-offender laws.[14]

One of the main elements of utilitarian theory proclaims the essence of the rehabilitative character of punishment. Following this perspective, punishment functions as a reformative means since the offender reconsiders his moral values as well as the consequences of his actions. Nevertheless, by "consequences of one's actions" we do not mean that the unpleasant experience of punishment may encourage the offender to re-commit a crime: that is the role of deterrence. The evaluation of the consequences applies on how and why a committed offense is considered morally wrong (Banks 2004). Based on Bean's notion that crime represents a symptom of a social disease, the rehabilitation aspect of punishment approaches the offender in order to provide him treatment, aiming ultimately at the cure of the disease (Bean 1981). Furthermore, as Pollock underlines, *"Treatment implies acceptance rather than rejection, support rather than hatred"* (Pollock 2007). Therefore, the rehabilitation perspective puts emphasis on offender treatment, and it stands as the only way for an offender to be truly convinced of his mistakes. The rehabilitation point of view motivates the offender to reconsider the illegal action through a more versatile, morally accepted standpoint, at the same time abandoning any petty individualisms which have previously prevented him from conforming to the societal moral rules.

The concept of treatment implies the presence of social experts who can not only diagnose a condition of malpractice, but also can provide the treatment in accordance with the offender's needs. However, this personalized aspect of treatment and rehabilitation is seldomly available. The programs offered follow a standardized format that rarely addresses the special needs of each offender. In addition, since the treatment perspective implies that because the disease initiates from social circumstances, the offender does not have full responsibility for his actions and becomes able to manipulate the system according to his interests (Banks 2004). On the other hand, several scholars support that the treatment aspect of punishment may be considered brainwashing, which is imposed by coercive use of power (Hudson 1996). We will further examine the concept of rehabilitation (treatment), as it is the only idea that cannot be applied in terms of imprisonment and capital punishment. This fact comes as no surprise when taking into account that rehabilitation is effective only when the offender re-enters society (Rotman 1990).

Retributivism and Justice Models

As mentioned before, under the ethical formalistic view, it is the social contract that dominates the rationale for punishment. Therefore, the offender has to be punished since he has violated rules of the contract and therefore he deserves to "pay the price" for his actions. An offender under this *retributive* model has fully accounted for his or her actions, and when these actions do not follow the societal moral and legal rules, he or she should be punished accordingly. This practice can be historically identified even from the Biblical expression "an eye for an eye, a tooth for a tooth, and a life for a life," which is commonly defined as *lex talionis* (Hudson 1996). Nevertheless, as van de Haag explains, the philosophy of *lex talionis* was not practiced as a demand for retribution. On the contrary, it provided limitations on the magnitude of the punishment imposed, aiming instead to prevent revenge (van de Haag 1975). The strict application of the *lex talionis* approach, however, presents several issues, especially when it comes to very violent crimes, killing due to accident or negligent acts, or cases of rape, since the society would disapprove of the imposition of the exact same punishment (Ten 1987, Banks 2004). However, the practice of capital punishment represents a current form of *lex talionis*, and even though it is still applied in several countries, there are many scholars who support its abolishment (Tabak 2000, Zimring 2003).

The retributivist perspective, in comparison to the utilitarian one, is not occupied with the consequences of punishment; instead, it focuses on the fact that the offender owes his punishment to society so the balance can be restored (Walker 1991). As Walker identifies, each society holds a specific attitude toward deviations from the set moral rules and values. Therefore, when an offender breaks these rules, he or she has to face the societal censure in practice (Walker 1991). This notion becomes apparent in von Hirsch's approach, as Banks identifies: "*For von Hirsch [. . .], censure is simply holding someone accountable for his or her conduct and involves conveying the message to the perpetrator that he or she has willfully injured someone and faces the disapproval of society for that reason*" (Banks 2004: 110). However, other scholars who discuss the essence of retributivism argue that punishment is more than just an expression of the societal disapproval: punishment should function as a moral lesson to the offenders so they understand the consequences of their actions in depth, presenting the vindictive aspect of punishment (Feinberg 1994, Morris 1994). Nevertheless, one should not confuse the retributivist approach with revenge. As Nozick points out, retribution is given when an action is considered morally wrong and it involves a specified excess of punishment; on the other hand, revenge can be associated with less severe cases and there is no limit to the magnitude of revenge or to the people—innocent or not—who might experience the consequences (Nozick 1981). The limitations that are posed by retribution can be found in Mackie's theoretical approach, which argues: (1) the non-guilty person must not be punished (*negative retribution*), (2) the actual offender should be punished (*positive retribution*), and (3) an offender might be exempt of punishment in some cases (*permissive retribution*) (Mackie 1982).

Two models which represent the retributive rationale are the *justice model* and the *just deserts* model. The *justice model*, which evolved as a reaction toward the rehabilitative era, supports that there is need for a degree of predictability and equality when punishments are imposed so that individuality is avoided when following the rehabilitative perspective. The implementation of the justice model, therefore, "*restricted the state's right to use treatment as a criterion for release*" (Pollock 2007). Following a similar line of thought, the *just deserts model* focuses on the idea that punishment should be implemented proportionately to the offenses committed and to the offender's previous criminal history (Hudson 1996). In other words, the most serious offenses should be punished more severely than the less serious ones, and the first-time offender should be punished less severely than the serial criminal. Von Hirsch, who was the main supporter of the just deserts model, claimed that the deterrent perspective of punishment removes the element of moral judgment from the offender, since it emphasizes compliance and acceptance of the consequences. The just deserts theorists, however, support that the process of censuring encourages the offender not only to recognize the wrongfulness of the action, but also to engage in feelings of regret, so as to avoid committing criminal acts in the future (von Hirsch 1998).

Restorative Justice

More recently, one more theoretical rationale on punishment has been identified and analyzed. By the second half of 1990's, the restorative justice model begun to garner interest in criminological discussions, evolving to its widespread examination and application by 2006 (Johnstone et al 2007). Nevertheless, as Braithwaite argues, restorative justice was almost always present in human history, emerging from as early as the Ancient Greek, Arabic, and Roman civilizations (Braithwaite 1998). As the name suggests, restorative justice concentrates on restoring not only any lost property or personal injury, but also all individuals involved in an offense: the victim, the offender, and the community. In different words, restorative justice aims to bring back the sense of security by emphasizing the social relationships and providing social support and control for offenders (Bazemore and Schiff 2001). As Van Ness and Strong suggest, restorative justice (1) focuses on the healing of victims, offenders, and communities that were affected by the crime; (2) permits all individuals involved to participate actively and comprehend the justice process; and (3) places the government as the party responsible for preserving a just order while the community holds the responsibility to establish peace (Van Ness and Strong 1997).

However, as several scholars indicate, restorative justice assumes that the agreement among offenders, victims, and community is secured, even though there have been several cases where that agreement was not achieved. Garland, for instance, notes that the fact that restorative justice avoids implementing the more "traditional" ways of the criminal justice system leads to the deprivation of the victims' and communities' feelings of relief, which is more prominent when other rationales of punishment are followed (Garland 1990). Nevertheless, despite its theoretical deficiencies, restorative justice is considered to be a newcomer in the rationale of punishment that has attracted a large body of support, including support from "*police officers, judges, schoolteachers, politicians, juvenile justice agencies, victim support groups, aboriginal elders, and mums and dads*" (Johnstone et al 2007).

CAPITAL PUNISHMENT

Human Rights

Both the rationale and the application of different types of punishment have evolved throughout time. Most criminal justice systems around the world have abandoned several practices that were acceptable in earlier times such as hanging, branding, stoning, flogging, or cutting off limbs. As these practices were discontinued, society's need for punishment has led us to impose penalties that focus primarily on depriving the offender of freedom. In different words, one of the most commonly used punishments is that of imprisonment. Even within prison, however, the preservation of most substantive human rights is considered a country's or state's legal obligation.

Human rights are moral values or principles that refer to specific standards of human behavior and help the protection of all people globally from any political, legal, and social abuse. They are regularly regarded as legal rights in both national and international law (Nickel 2013). Moreover, in accordance with the United Nations, "*human rights are inherent to all human beings, whatever the nationality, place of residence, sex, national or ethnic origin, color, religion, language, or any other status*" (The United Nations 2014). All humans are equally entitled to human rights without any kind of discrimination. These rights are all interrelated, interdependent, and indivisible.

Human rights cover a widespread spectrum in all aspects of social life. Nevertheless, some of the most fundamental human rights are the right to life, freedom from torture, freedom from slavery, right to a fair trial, freedom of speech, freedom of thought, freedom of conscience and religion, and freedom of movement (Nickel 2013). As one can imagine, in order to maintain all one's human rights, one has to sustain the right to life. According to the Article 6.1 of the International Covenant on Civil and Political Rights, "*Every human being has the inherent right to life. This right shall be protected by law. No one shall be arbitrarily deprived of his life*" (The United Nations 2014). Nevertheless, despite the fact that most rationales of punishment take into account all the substantive human rights, there is one type of punishment which, in accordance with many academics and human rights activists, violates the most essential human right: that of the right to life. This type of punishment is capital punishment.

Capital Punishment

What distinguishes this type of punishment is that it leaves no room to correct a mistake. Capital punishment, or the death penalty, is the legal process where an individual is put to death by the state, as a punishment for a crime. When someone is sentenced to death, he or she spends life in prison until the time of execution. Capital punishment, therefore, is considered to be an irreversible punishment. In the countries or states where capital punishment is enforced, the crimes that can result in this type of punishment are referred to as capital crimes or capital offenses.

There are some scholars who claim that both the utilitarian and retributive ethical rationales support capital punishment (Pollock 2007). For instance, a logical inference is that capital punishment incapacitates the individual from repeating the offense, since the punishment does not leave any other option available to the offender. This view agrees with the utilitarian perspective that the *"evil of capital punishment is far outweighed by the future benefits that will accrue to society"* (Pollock 2007: 407). Nevertheless, several aspects promoted by the utilitarian perspective actually condemn capital punishment. In the case of deterrence, for example, one should show proof that, given the chance of re-committing the crime, the offender would have taken the opportunity to commit another crime. Even though this indication seems to be impossible to predict, abolitionists of this type of punishment have presented evidence that capital punishment does not deter (Pollock 2007). Moreover, taking into account the fact that the offender will not have the chance for social reintegration, the aspect of rehabilitation (treatment) is not under any consideration. Consequently, we are safe to conclude that the utilitarian rationale of punishment cannot provide a clear argument for or against this viewpoint in regards to capital punishment.

On the other hand, the retributive model clearly seems to support the retention of capital punishment. In murder cases, where capital punishment typically applies, it is only just to implement this type of punishment. After all, as Pollock claims, the upset societal sentiment that such a heinous crime leads to is a disorder that can be rectified only by punishment of equal intensity to the seriousness of the offense (Pollock 2007). Abolitionists' response to this claim suggests that executions may contribute even further to the societal resentment, since even though the offenders might receive what they deserve, society is negatively affected by the brutality of the act of execution (Bedau 1991).

According to the Amnesty International Report, even though the figures suggest a significant decrease in the number of countries which carried out executions (from 37 countries in 1994 to 25 countries in 2004), there are still 22 countries around the world that are known to have carried out executions in 2013. Data for executions in China, Egypt, and Syria is unavailable. Executions in China are handled as state secrets, so Amnesty International is unable to measure accurately the number of executions, and executions in Egypt and Syria are difficult to categorize as judicial, vigilante, or otherwise. Excluding these countries, the number of executions that took place has increased from 682 in 2012 to 778 in 2013. From these 778, 80 executions were carried out in the United States (Amnesty International Report 2013).[15]

REFERENCES AND FURTHER READING

Amnesty International (2013) Death Sentences and Executions 2013 report – Amnesty International Publications, International Secretarial, United Kingdom http://www.amnesty.org/en/library/asset/ACT50/001/2014/en/652ac5b3-3979-43e2-b1a1-6c4919e7a518/act500012014en.pdf

Andenaes, J. (1972). Does punishment deter crime? In Gertrude Ezorsky (ed.), *Philosophical Perspectives of Punishment*, (pp. 342–357). Albany: State University of New York Press.

Baels, P. (1977). *Ethics and Beliefs*. New York: Seabury.

Banks, C. C. L. (2004). *Criminal Justice Ethics: Theory and Practice*. Sage Publications.

Beyleveld, D. (1979). Deterrence research as a basis for deterrence policies. *The Howard Journal of Criminal Justice, 18*(3), 135–149.

Bazemore, G., & Schiff, M. (2001). What and why now: Understanding restorative justice. In Gordon Bazemore and Mara Schiff (eds.), *Restorative Community Justice: Repairing Harm and Transforming Communities*, (pp. 21–46). Cincinnati, OH: Anderson.

Bean P. (1981). *Punishment: A Philosophical and Criminological Inquiry*. Oxford, UK: Martin Robertson.

Beccaria, C. (2009). On crimes and punishments. In Aaron Thomas (ed.), *On Crimes and Punishments and Other Writings*. Toronto: University of Toronto Press (original work published 1764).

Bedau H. (1991). How to argue about the death penalty. *Israel Law Review, 25*, 466–480.

Bentham J. (1970). The rationale of punishment. In R. Beck and J Orr (eds.), *Ethical Choice: A Case Study Approach*. New York: Free Press (original work published 1843).

Blumstein, A., Cohen, J., & Nagin, D. (1978). *Deterrence and Incapacitation. Estimating the Effects of Criminal Sanctions on Crime Rates.* Washington DC: Panel on Research on Deterrent and Incapacitative Effects.

Borchert, D., & Steward D. (1986). *Exploring Ethics.* New York: Macmillan.

Braithwaite, J. (1999). Restorative justice: Assessing optimistic and pessimistic accounts. *Crime and justice*, 1–127.

Dershowitz, A. (2004). *Rights from Wrongs: A Secular Theory of the Origins of Rights.* New York: Basic Books.

Feinberg J. (1994). The expressive function of punishment. In Antony Duff and David Garland (eds.), *A Reader on Punishment*. Oxford, England: Oxford University Press.

Garland, D. (1990). *Punishment and Modern Society.* Oxford, England: Oxford University Press.

Gert, B. (Fall 2012). The definition of morality. In Edward N. Zalta (ed.), *The Stanford Encyclopedia of Philosophy* http://plato.stanford.edu/archives/fall2012/entries/morality-definition/>.

Gough, J. W. (1978). *The Social Contract: A Critical Study of its Development.* Greenwood Press.

Harris, C. E. (1986). *Applying Moral Theories* (Vol. 1, No. 7). Belmont, CA: Wadsworth Publishing Company.

Held, V. (2006). *The Ethics of Care: Personal, Political, and Global.* Oxford University Press.

Hudson, B. (1996). *Understanding Justice 2/E: An Introduction to Ideas, Perspectives and Controversies in Modern Penal Theory.* Buckingham, England: Open University Press.

Johnstone, G., & Van Ness, D.W. (2007). *Handbook of Restorative Justice.* Devon, UK: Willan Publishing.

Kant I. (1949). *Critique of a Practical Reason.* trans. Lewis White Beck. Chicago: University of Chicago Press.

Kohlberg, L. (1958). The Development of Modes of Thinking and Choices in Years 10 to 16. Ph.D. Dissertation, University of Chicago.

Kohlberg, L. (1971). Stages of moral development. *Moral education*, 23–92.

Kohlberg, L. (1981). *Essays on Moral Development, Vol. I: The Philosophy of Moral Development.* San Francisco, CA: Harper & Row.

Kohlberg, L., Levine, C., Hewer, A. (1983). *Moral Stages: A Current Formulation and a Response to Critics.* Basel, NY: Karger.

Mackie J. L. (1982). Morality and the retributive emotions. *Criminal Justice Ethics 1*(1), 3–10.

Morris, H. (1994). A paternalistic theory of punishment. In Anthony Duff and David Garland (eds.), *A Reader on Punishment* (pp. 92–111). Oxford, England: Oxford University Press.

Nickel, J. (2013). Human rights. In Edward N. Zalta (ed.), *The Stanford Encyclopedia of Philosophy* URL = <http://plato.stanford.edu/archives/spr2014/entries/rights-human/>.

Nozick, R. (1981). *Philosophical Explanations.* Cambridge, MA: Harvard University Press.

Pollock, J.M. (2007). *Ethics in Crime and Justice: Dilemmas and Decisions.* New York: West/Wadsworth.

Prior W. (1991). Aristotle's Nicomachean ethics. In W. Prior (ed.), *From Virtue and Knowledge: An Introduction to Ancient Greek Ethics*, (pp. 144–193). New York: Routledge, Kegan Paul.

Rotman, E. (1990). *Beyond Punishment: A New View on the Rehabilitation of Criminal Offenders.* Westport, CT: Greenwood Press.

Shue, H. (1996). *Basic Rights*, Second edition. Princeton: Princeton University Press.

Tabak, R. J. (2000). Finality without fairness: Why we are moving towards moratoria on executions, and the potential abolition of capital punishment. *Conn. L. Rev.*, 33, 733.

Talbott, W. (2005). *Which Rights Should be Universal?* Oxford: Oxford University Press.

Ten, C. L. (1987). *Crime, Guilt, and Punishment: A Philosophical Introduction*. Oxford, England: Clarendon Press.

van den Haag, E. (1975). *Punishing Criminals. Concerning a Very Old and Painful Question*. New York: Basic Books.

Van Ness D., Strong K. H. (1997). *Restoring Justice*. Cincinnati, OH: Anderson.

Von Hirsch, A. (1998). Penal theories. In Michael Tony (ed.), *The Handbook of Crime and Punishment*. (pp. 659–682). New York: Oxford University Press.

Walker N. (1991). *Why Punish?* Oxford: Oxford University Press.

Zimring F. E., Hawkins G., Kamin S. (2001). *Punishment and Democracy: Three Strikes and You're Out in California*. New York: Oxford University Press.

Zimring, F. E. (2003). *The Contradictions of American Capital Punishment*. New York: Oxford University Press.

Zygmunt B. (1994). Morality without ethics. *Theory, Culture & Society*, 11, 1–34.

WEBSITES

The United Nations (2014), Office of the High Commissioner of Human Rights, What are human rights? Retrieved Aug. 14, 2014 http://www.ohchr.org/en/issues/pages/whatarehumanrights.aspx

ENDNOTES

1. The term *eventually* here, implies that an individual's actual behavior might sometimes conflict with his internal moral value or belief. As Pollock also indicates, recent studies show that several people will keep wallets or money that they find, even though they consider the action as an immoral one (Pollock 2007: 22). Their inner assuage from a possible guilt which might follow due to their moral beliefs could be detected in their rationalized justification of the act.

2. Especially taking into account that all individuals are part of a societal group.

3. According to Pollock, a deontological system is "one that is concerned solely with the inherent nature of the act being judged" (Pollock 2007: 37). In different words, according to the deontological ethical system, if the intent of an action was of a good character, the action is considered to be a good one regardless of the consequences.

4. As also identified by Pollock, one of the later utilitarians, John Stuart Mill (1806–1873), asserted that the benefits of an action do not hold the same value in each instance. Following Bentham's proposition that human beings seek to maximize pleasure while minimizing the pain, Mill claimed that not all thoughts and actions hold the same weight or value in doing so. An example provided was that art benefits society in a completely different way than alcohol. Nevertheless as Pollock reminds us, other theorists as Borchert and Steward (1986) claimed that no one is in such a position to determine which action values more than the other (Pollock 2007: 41).

5. The natural law ethical system, as the name suggests, supports that the essence of morality conforms to the natural law and vice versa, what is natural is by default the moral/right (Pollock 2007).

6. As per the Aristotelian point of view, the person's virtues, or excellences, are what one should really examine when talking about morality. Holding a rather teleological position, the ethical system that focuses on the person's virtues is concerned about whether an action resulted in a good/moral end or not (Prior 1991).

7. The ethics of care emphasizes the human ability to empathize, focusing therefore more on the needs of the others rather than the rights. For instance, as we shall revisit later, the philosophical

stance of the "restorative justice" which supports that both offenders and victims need to be approached with care so that fairness and rightness would be restored (Held 2006, Bazemore and Schiff 2001).

8. The ethics of egoism promotes the individual's self-interests. In particular, as Harris would claim, egoism is a system of ethics in which the emphasis that is placed on the individual's self-interest is not only moral but more or less impossible to avoid (Harris 1986).

9. As Pollock underlines "In modelling, values and moral beliefs come from those one admires and aspires to identify with. If that role model happens to be a priest, one will probably develop a religious ethical system; if it happens to be a pimp or a sociopath, an egoistic ethical system may develop" (Pollock 2007).

10. The reinforcement of the moral values takes place through the process of rewarding when the individual acts according to what is socially considered to be moral or through punishing when a person's actions are thought to be wrong/immoral (Pollock 2007).

11. http://www.oxforddictionaries.com/us/definition/american_english/punishment

12. The natural consequences of an action therefore cannot be considered as punishment.

13. According to Gough, the social contract theory is traced back to Greek political philosophy. The social contract asserts that individuals have agreed to sacrifice some of their freedoms and conform to the rules imposed by the authority or government in exchange for protection and conservation of social balance (Gough 1978).

14. A habitual offender is an offender who has engaged in a new crime and has also been previously convicted for other crimes in the past. An example of habitual-offender laws is that of the three-strikes law, which stands as a type of selective incapacitation. These laws, as Zimring et al. observe, encourage the practice of imposing longer prison sentences on repeat offenders who commit the same crime than on first-time offenders (Zimring et al 2001).

15. THE DEATH PENALTY IN THE USA IN 2013: 39 executions: Alabama (1), Arizona (2), Florida (7), Georgia (1), Ohio (3), Oklahoma (6), Missouri (2), Texas (16), Virginia (1) / 80 death sentences: Alabama (5), Arizona (3), California (24), Florida (15), Georgia (1), Indiana (3), Missouri (3), Mississippi (2), North Carolina (1), Nevada (2), Ohio (4), Oklahoma (1) Pennsylvania (4), Texas (9), Washington (1), federal (1), military (1).

Ethical Issues in Probation and Parole

CHAPTER 10

"In law a man is guilty when he violates the rights of others. In ethics he is guilty if he only thinks of doing so."

—Immanuel Kant

"Ethics is knowing the difference between what you have a right to do and what is right to do."

—Justice Potter Stewart

"Acting responsibly is not a matter of strengthening our reason but of deepening our feelings for the welfare of others."

—Jostein Gaarder

Community corrections comprise the largest portion of the correctional population in the United States. In 2012, an estimated 1 in every 50 adult residents were under some form of community supervision, compared to 1 in every 108 adults incarcerated in prison or jail.[1] And by the end of 2011, approximately 6.98 million offenders were under some form of adult correctional supervision with 4.8 million of those supervised in the community on probation or parole.[2] In the face of prison overcrowding resulting from increased incarceration rates, a greater number of offenders are being placed on probation in lieu of incarceration or being released from prison and placed onto parole prior to the end of their sentences. The growing number of offenders under non-residential supervision demonstrates their importance in the functioning of the U.S. criminal justice system.

Probation and parole officers are tasked with the supervision of offenders prior to serving a sentence or upon release from prison. Offenders under this type of supervision have been convicted of offenses ranging from more serious violent crimes and/or sex offenses to misdemeanors. Supervising officers are responsible for enforcing court-ordered conditions which allow offenders to avoid incarceration assuming they successfully demonstrate their ability to follow the rules of the court while under supervision. This is accomplished through complying with both the general and specific conditions of their supervision for the term specified by the court. If at any time the offender violates these conditions of release, the supervising officer is obligated to report and track the violation to ensure an accurate record is kept of the offender's behavior while under supervision. In this capacity, the officer also has the ability to begin the revocation process in which case the offender would face additional penalty up to and including incarceration.

While the primary task of the supervisory officer is to ensure compliance with the court-ordered conditions of release, part of their duties also include competing goals of providing the offender with the services necessary for them to successfully complete their supervised release while simultaneously acting in the best interest of the community to ensure public safety. For an officer to accomplish these goals, the relationship they develop with offenders on their caseload must be centered on trust and honesty. The supervising officer expects offenders to be forthcoming with information regarding their adherence to court-ordered conditions, and in return, the offender expects their supervising officer to behave in an ethical manner. While this seems a straightforward and simple approach to successful case management and completion of conditions of supervision, these interactions do not occur in a vacuum and there are often other factors that influence the relationship between offenders and their supervising officers. The following discussion provides an overview of ethical considerations in probation and parole, with a specific focus on the probation and parole officer.

PROBATION

Probation can be defined as "a court-ordered period of correctional supervision in the community generally used as an alternative to incarceration."[3] Probation officers are responsible for supervising the probated sentence of offenders by ensuring they are compliant with the conditions of their probation outlined by the court. General conditions of probation usually include requirements that the offender not leave the state without permission, not use or possess controlled substances, submit to random drug tests, obey the law, notify the court in the event of a new job or residence, not associate with those with criminal records, etc. Individual offenders may have specific conditions on their probation that are directly tied to the charging offense. For example, sex offenders may be required to register as a sex offender, maintain a residence outside of certain areas, or participate in specific therapeutic programs. The conditions of probation are designed to restrict the movements and behaviors of offenders while under court-ordered supervision for the entirety of a specified term that, if successfully completed, will allow them to have no further obligation to the court and no longer be subject to incarceration for the charging offense.

A primary responsibility of the probation officer is the completion of the pre-sentence investigation (PSI) report. The PSI is used for a variety of purposes, including as a judicial tool in making a sentencing decision. The PSI presents an ethical consideration when we consider the extent to which it should be considered in the sentencing and placement of offenders.[4] The PSI contains offender-specific information and is designed to provide a detailed account of who the offender is in "the real world" outside of the offense for which they are charged. At the point of sentencing, the PSI is among the few, if not the only, pieces of information used by the judge in making a sentencing decision, as many offenders have already pled guilty, leaving the appropriate punishment as the only factor that is yet to be determined. Given the limited interaction of the judge and defendant prior to sentencing, the information contained in the PSI weighs heavily in a judge's sentencing decision, with judges accepting the probation officer's recommendation for probation in 85% of cases and for prison in 66% of cases.[5] As such, it is imperative that the probation officer preparing the report ensure that the information contained in the report is complete and accurate. The report may include information regarding the offender's prior criminal record, education, employment history, medical information, and counseling or substance abuse treatment records. After sentencing, the PSI is used at a number of other decision points that will impact the future of the offender for decisions ranging from placement in a correctional facility to evaluation by the parole board to consideration by judges in the event of a new offense.

The recommendation of the probation officer is an important component of the PSI and demonstrates the significance of their input. Specifically, the officer completing the PSI submits a statement to the court based on his or her personal opinion and evaluation of the offender after his or her investigation. The officer's opinion, then, is a highly valued and influential component in the sentencing process, as the probation officer is an officer of the court and generally has a working relationship with the judge. This recommendation should be an objective account of the offender's history and evaluation of risk to the community. However, other factors may influence the recommendation, including a prior relationship or prior knowledge of the offender. For example, an offender who was previously on probation within the same agency may have had a bad run-in with the probation officer but was largely compliant with the conditions of the previous probated sentence. Given that much of this evaluation may be based on personal experience and observation, the extent to which the PSI should be a consideration in sentencing the offender is important, and begs the question as to whether or not factors beyond the offense for which the offender is being sentenced should be considered in making a sentencing decision.

The completion of the PSI is indicative of the discretion the probation officer has in the completion of more managerial tasks associated with working his or her caseload. Daily tasks may include making sentencing and placement recommendations, determining when to suggest revocation, determining whether to allow additional drug testing after a failed urinalysis, scheduling appointments, monitoring participation in programs, and using diversionary programs to supplement offender conditions of probation and individual needs. Managing organizational expectations while checking in with probationers on their caseloads requires effective time management and a focus on efficiency in handling cases; however, if we believe that offenders can change given a little extra help, then the role of the probation officer moves beyond supervision and monitoring to include more rehabilitative and therapeutic tasks.[6]

An increase in the number of violent and serious offenders on probation also influences an officer's ability to perform in a less managerial capacity. As incarceration rates have increased, prison overcrowding has resulted in a growing number of more serious offenders being placed on probation as the number of offenders under the supervision of a single officer has also increased. As a result, probation officers are supervising an increasing number of dangerous offenders without an equal adjustment to workload considerations[7] making it more difficult for probation officers to provide individualized supervision to offenders on their caseload. Additionally, the probation population has begun to represent the prison population more closely with regard to offense type, making the job of probation officers more closely aligned with parole officers than even before.[8]

PAROLE

While probation comprises supervised release as a sentence in lieu of incarceration, parole is a period of conditional supervised release in the community following a prison term.[9] Many of the managerial tasks of parole officers overlap with those of probation officers; however, their caseload differs in that parolees have already been incarcerated and are in the process of re-entering the community. Parole is based on the idea that most offenders can benefit from a period of transition back into the community prior to the completion of their sentences. Parole was developed in response to a growing belief that individuals serving time in correctional facilities should be entitled to early release under direct supervision where offenders would have an opportunity to reenter society gradually and demonstrate changes in their behavior. Today it also serves as motivation for good behavior among incarcerated individuals hoping to secure early release, a way to open up additional space in correctional facilities while still supervising released offenders, and a method of improving public safety by reducing the incidence and impact of crime committed by parolees.[10]

Similar to probation officers, parole officers' daily tasks center on the monitoring and supervision of the offenders on their caseload, in that they monitor offenders by maintaining information on each of their cases, supervise those who are released, and assist parolees in obtaining education and/or vocational training as needed. As part of their caseload management, parole officers also conduct investigations regarding parole violations and may take a more active role in assisting parolees in securing work in order to aid in their successful completion of parole. Parole officers keep in regular contact with parolees through face-to-face visits, phone calls, and home visits. They also administer drug tests and ensure the offender is following the general and specific conditions of their parole release as defined by the paroling agency.

Parole considerations should include balancing the needs of the offender as well as the welfare of the victim. Victim participation in the parole process is an important consideration with regard to the treatment of the offender. From sentencing to parole decisions, the victim's voice increasingly has a place in judicial decisions affecting the offender's life. While it can be argued that the offender committed a crime impacting the victim and therefore the victim has the right to be heard, the alternate consideration would be on the extent to which the victim's experience should be a continued part of the judicial process. Rather, what should the role of the victim be in the parole decision? If the paroling decision is determined based on the original offense and takes into consideration risk to the community at the point of parole, if the offender's behavior while incarcerated demonstrates a modification in behavior from entrance to prison, should the victim's experience still factor into the determination to grant parole? If parole serves as a supervised release from prison during which time the offender is to demonstrate further their behavioral modifications, allowing the offender to prove him or herself should be of primary interest—as opposed to further punishment.

ETHICAL CONSIDERATIONS

There may be some differences in terms of the daily operations of parole and probation officers; however, their primary duties are very similar. As such, the ethical considerations with regard to treatment of offenders and interactions with offenders on their caseloads overlap. Several of these considerations are discussed in the following section.

Caseloads

Caseload and workload are important considerations in the ethical treatment of offenders under court-ordered supervision. Caseload describes the number of offenders under an officer's supervision, while workload can be considered the amount of time spent on each case. Determining appropriate caseload size has been at the center of debate for a number of years, as the reality is that there is no one-size-fits-all solution. Rather, the APPA provides ratios for recommended caseloads based on the risk level of the offenders under their supervision. Specifically, they suggest caseloads of: intensive-supervision offenders of 20 to1; moderate to high-risk offenders, 50 to 1; and low-risk offenders, 100 to 1.[11] Supervisory officers, however, continue to face larger caseloads demanding varying levels of attention. Larger caseloads mean less time is spent on any one individual case. New probationers and parolees may require more attention than those established on a supervisory officer's caseload. As the officer and offender get to know each other and what to expect from each other, more attention will be necessary. Additionally, as offenders present differing needs or potential risks to themselves or the community, the supervising officer will devote more time to those cases, potentially at expense to other cases on their caseload. For example, a recent news story examining parole officers in New Jersey revealed that the officers failed to maintain regular contact with sex offenders and other convicted felons who required monthly supervision.[12] There were 15,000 parolees being monitored by roughly 300 parole officers working a caseload of approximately 50 parolees each. The New Jersey parole department argued that their attempts to connect with parolees in their own environments, as opposed to scheduled meetings in their offices, were focused on getting a real sense of how the parolee was living. Maintaining the appropriate number of contacts with parolees on their caseload, ranging from twice a month to once every six months, forced a transition from quality of interactions to the quantity of interactions between the parolee and parole officer. This situation is indicative of circumstances in which smaller caseloads will allow for more focused attention to individual offenders, and how larger caseloads make effective supervision of all parolees more difficult.

Conflicting Goals

Probation and parole officers often seek these positions because they believe they can change people's behavior. Most departments require their officers to have some type of a college degree and they expect them to utilize their education and experience in serving a variety of constituents, including the criminal justice system, the community, and the offenders under their supervision. The expectation of the criminal justice system is that the supervisory officer will monitor the offender's behavior while on supervised release to ensure compliance with court-ordered conditions of probation or parole and to initiate the revocation proceedings if an offender violates these conditions. Societal expectations are to ensure public safety by monitoring offender behavior, preventing future criminal acts by changing the behavior of the offender, and tracking/reporting potential risk to the community. Finally, offender expectations may include connecting them with appropriate services to meet their individual needs, advocating for their rights both within and outside of the system, facilitating change in their behavior, and directing them to educational and employment opportunities. While citizens have the right to be free from harm, offenders have the right to be treated fairly.[13] The inherent challenge in meeting each of these goals are the conflicting tasks associated with achieving them, as what is in the best interest of the community may not always equate with the best interest of the offender under supervision. Which of these objectives should take priority? Is it more important for the officer to meet the organizational demands of the criminal justice system and societal expectations? Or should the well-being and treatment of the offender be the focus of attention?

Treatment of Offenders

The treatment of offenders while under supervised release is another important ethical consideration for probation and parole officers. In any given situation, offender treatment should be based on what an "ordinary, reasonable, and prudent professional, with the same or similar training, would do under the same or similar circumstances."[14] Probation and parole officer behavior must be line with public standards and expectations for behavior as their position holds a level of public accountability. As discussed, they have an obligation to fulfill the expectations of the criminal justice system and society in ensuring public safety while treating the offender in a fair and just manner that facilitates behavioral change. In working toward these competing goals, the question turns to what we are trying to achieve by placing an offender on probation or parole. Rather, is the objective one of rehabilitation or one of retribution, deterrence, and incapacitation? The former would suggest that the supervisory officer's primary task should be the provision of services to facilitate change in the offender, while the latter suggests the importance of serving the criminal justice system and societal goals by focusing on supervision and management tasks. In making this determination, we must also consider what society owes the offender. If the assumption is that offenders engage in rational choices to engage in or refrain from criminal behavior, then offenders choose to commit crime and, therefore, the only consideration now facing the justice system is a determination of the debt the offender owes to society and how the offender will be controlled or supervised to prevent the commission of future criminal acts.[15]

Another ethical issue associated with the treatment of offenders presents itself in how probation and parole officers interact with offenders on their caseload. Supervisory officers are expected to model appropriate behavior for their clients for the duration of the supervisory period. While they have been convicted of a criminal offense, most offenders at least attempt to complete their supervisory period by following the rules and being released from supervision without going to jail or prison. However, there are times when the supervisory officer is faced with an unruly offender who may lie, become agitated, or get an attitude with the officer. The supervisory officer is expected to remain calm and in control of the situation as he or she should model appropriate behavior regardless of how the offender responds to a situation. The bad behavior of the probationer should not produce the same type of behavior from the probation or parole officer. Additionally, every offender comes with his or her own set of problems ranging from psychological issues, struggles with addiction, to difficulties obtaining employment, education, or family issues. The probation officer or parole officer is expected to demonstrate appropriate behavior while being all things to all people.[16]

The professionalization of the criminal justice system and its actors has increased the attention given to discretionary decision points throughout the system. Officers' discretion impacts how they handle their caseloads, as well as how they schedule their time and structure their activities. Probation and parole officers are forced to make difficult choices on a regular basis from making a sentencing recommendation to the decision whether or not to revoke someone's probation or parole. Questions they might ask themselves may include: What violations are worthy of filing with the court? Should a violation be filed for every technical violation? Would they make the same decision given similar circumstances for an offender they "liked" versus one they did not "like"? The nature of these decisions exemplifies some of the difficult decisions that probation officers must make on a daily basis. And while most supervisory officers behave in an ethical manner in all of their interactions with offenders on their caseload, the following concerns of a probationer dealing with what they perceive as unrealistic expectations of their probation officer are presented below:

> she's always telling me wherever I live isn't good enough...that it's a bad environment. I can't keep my job when I have to move all the time. I only get two weeks to find a place to live and get a job. I can't keep doing it. I can't meet her deadlines and she's going to get me in trouble. What do I have to do to get a new probation officer?[17]

What would be the best response from the probation or parole officer in this case given their discretionary decision-making authority over the offender? How should the supervising officer respond to the offender in future interactions once they are aware of his or her concerns? If the officer's job is to ensure compliance with the conditions of supervised release, to what extent is it his or her responsibility to assist the offender in achieving each of these goals?

Involvement with Offenders

Another ethical consideration in probation and parole that is similar to the treatment of offenders under direct supervision relates to the establishment of appropriate boundaries between the probation or parole officer and offenders on their caseload. Boundaries should establish appropriate and inappropriate contact, communication, treatment, and behavior. Boundary issues may occur when probation or parole officers relate to clients in more than one relationship, whether it be professional, social, or business.[18] The nature of the relationship between the offenders on their caseloads and the probation or parole officers is such that the supervising officers possess a certain level of control over the relationship. For example, the supervising officer makes the ultimate decision as to when and what information should be provided to the court regarding the performance of the offender on supervised released. As judicial decisions typically align with the recommendation of the supervising officer, the honest and ethical behavior of the probation or parole officer becomes that much more important. The nature of this relationship, however, sometimes lends itself to situations in which ethical decisions may be cloudier, resulting in long-term consequences for both the supervising officer as well as the offender.

One of these considerations presents itself in the crossing of professional and personal boundaries between the supervising officer and offender under his or her control. What is the relationship between the supervising officer and offenders on his or her caseload? How far should their relationship go? For example, if an offender suggests she is interested in spending time with her supervising officer outside of their scheduled meetings in a more personal setting, the officer, in holding the position of power, must determine the ethical response to this situation. While probation and parole officers should avoid becoming involved with offenders under their supervision even if there is not a specific rule against it, there have been a variety of cases in which a different decision was made. A recent example presents itself in the decision of a former

Linn County Parole and Probation officer in Oregon, Kari Henderson, to engage in a sexual relationship with a sex offender under her supervision. While she went on to marry and have a baby with the offender, prosecutors argued that the criminal justice system should provide people with fair and impartial treatment and that their personal relationship was improper as long as he was under her supervision. Prosecutors further argued that she "could have ended her relationship with the offender, ended her supervision of the parolee, or ended her employment as a probation officer.[19]" The officer ultimately pled guilty to first-degree custodial misconduct and first-degree official misconduct as she not only had a relationship with the offender but also failed to report his address accurately as he was living with her while under supervision. While it seems rather obvious that a sexual relationship between a probation or parole officer and an offender on his or her caseload would be inappropriate, there are other circumstances in which the boundaries or ethical decisions are less clear.

An ethical issue that may not be as clear is seen in the consideration to accept gifts from offenders or family members of offenders on one's caseload. There may be circumstances in which an offender approaches the officer with some type of gift in appreciation of his or her supervision of the offender; however, the decision to accept the gift may cross ethical boundaries. For example, the intent behind the gift may or may not be clear. Is the individual offering the gift because he or she wants something in return? Is the gift being presented by a new offender on the officer's caseload or is the offender nearing the end of supervision? Is the individual offering the gift in the hopes of receiving preferential treatment, such as if the offender were to fail a drug test in the future? Or is he or she genuinely appreciative of the officer's assistance? Even if the gift giver had no intention of seeking special treatment, it is still likely inappropriate to accept the gift as it may appear to be unethical from the outside. Rather, in any situation, the probation or parole officer should behave in a manner that appears to be appropriate regardless of the circumstances, if the receipt of the gift could be construed as inappropriate it is best to decline the offer.

Monetary Issues

Another ethical concern presents itself in the collection of a fee for being on probation. Collecting money either in the form of restitution or probation fees is generally left to the probation officer. The potential for abuse may present itself in the form of requesting or accepting monetary payment for concealing or altering information related to the conditions of probation, as was the case in the recent case of Joseph Ardell Wells. Wells was a private probation officer arrested in 2013 on charges of bribery, extortion, and official misconduct after promising to vouch for an offender to the judge after he failed a drug test if the offender paid him $250.[20] Similarly, a retired Grant County probation officer pled guilty to 21 counts of misconduct in public office in response to accusations of taking money orders from 21 different probation and parole clients and depositing 46 money orders into personal accounts for more than $3820.[21] While most probation officers would never consider abusing the system in this manner, a variety of factors may influence ethical considerations in these circumstances. For example, some officers may feel as though they are not adequately financially compensated for the amount and type of work that they do. While they may have seen their caseloads grow, combined with no changes to the organizational expectations of their positions, and with no increase in pay, they may view the collection of probation fees as an opportunity to supplement their income. The example below may be further indicative of a situation in which the supervising officer took advantage of the situation:

> My son was found to be in violation when he went to see his probation officer. He had taken money with him to the appointment. I went to pick up his car from the probation office and I also wanted to get his wallet. The probation officer said that my son took his money to along to jail. But my son said that the probation officer told him he was not allowed to have the money when he went through processing. He was supposed to give it to his probation officer and have it picked up by his family along with his car. So did the probation officer keep his money? Where do we file a complaint to get it back?[22]

If this is indeed an accurate assessment of the interaction, what changes should be made moving forward to avoid this type of scenario from occurring again?

Establishing and Maintaining Ethical Guidelines

Statutory guidelines provide the foundation for the treatment of incarcerated offenders; however, there are fewer legal guidelines for the treatment of those on probation or parole. While the court specifically identifies behaviors that a probationer or parolee may or may not engage in, outside of complying with departmental policy, there is more ambiguity with regard to appropriate behavior for probation and parole officers. The professionalization of the criminal justice system has seen the development of standards of conduct defining appropriate behavior of law enforcement, and similar standards have been developed by the American Probation and Parole Association (APPA). Agency guidelines have traditionally been the foundation for appropriate behavior of probation and parole officers; however, APPA has developed a Code of Ethics outlining appropriate standards of behavior for probation or parole officers. While individual agencies may vary in their specific codes of ethics, the principles established by APPA provide an ideal model under which correctional supervisors should operate and include the following:[23]

1. I will render professional service to the justice system and the community at large in effecting the social adjustment of the offender.
2. I will uphold the law with dignity, displaying an awareness of responsibility to offenders while recognizing the right of the public to be safeguarded from criminal activity.
3. I will strive to be objective in the performance of my duties, recognizing the inalienable right of all persons, appreciating the inherent worth of the individual, and respecting those confidences which can be reposed in me.
4. I will conduct my personal life with decorum, neither accepting nor granting favors in connection with my office.
5. I will cooperate with my co-workers and related agencies and will continually strive to improve my professional competence through the seeking and sharing of knowledge and understanding.
6. I will distinguish clearly, in public, between my statements and actions as an individual and as a representative of my profession.
7. I will encourage policy, procedures, and personnel practices which will enable others to conduct themselves in accordance with the values, goals, and objectives of the American Probation and Parole Association.
8. I recognize my office as a symbol of public faith and I accept it as a public trust to be held as long as I am true to the ethics of the American Probation and Parole Association.
9. I will constantly strive to achieve these objectives and ideals, dedicating myself to my chosen profession.

The adoption of these principles by probation and parole agencies and their implementation by individual officers will aid in the ethical treatment of offenders. They provide clarity as to how supervisory officers should treat offenders on their caseloads. As evidenced by the examples discussed in this chapter, probation and parole officers possess a great deal of power over the offenders on their caseloads and they have a responsibility to handle offender interactions in an ethical manner. Special care should be taken in their words and actions and they should always "bear in mind the importance of excluding . . . all sources of error or indefiniteness, and of keeping each prisoner's record truthful and free from prejudiced statements."[24]

Probation and parole are important components in the operation of the correctional component of the criminal justice system. While the number of offenders under these types of supervision has declined in the past several years, over 4.5 million offenders remain under some type of community supervision. The large population of offenders under supervised release warrants consideration of the ethical issues confronting probation and parole officers on a daily basis. While probation and parole are privileges, clearly established standards for treatment will ensure that supervising officers have the tools and skills necessary to meet the conflicting needs of the criminal justice system and the offender. Even with these tools at their disposal, probation and parole officers will continue to face situations requiring discretionary decision making that demand integrity even when no one else is looking. While the majority of probation and parole officers comply with departmental requirements in their supervisory capacity, ethical choices continually present themselves. Ethical conduct should be considered both from the intent of individual making the decision as well as the perception of the decision. If the outcome of a decision could be conceived as inappropriate, it is generally better to err on the side of caution and make the responsible decision.

REFERENCES AND FURTHER READING

Canton, R. (2009). Nonsense upon Stilts? Human Rights, the Ethics of Punishment and the Values of Probation. British Journal of Community Justice.

Carter, R. M., & Wilkins, L. (1970). Probation and Parole, Selected Readings. John Wiley and Sons.

Champion, D. J. (2005). Probation, Parole, and Community Corrections. Pearson/Prentice Hall.

Cluley, E. (2012). Probation Review: Effective Probation Services. Probation Journal, 275–277.

Cree, V. E. (1999). Sociology for Social Workers and Probations Officers. Routledge.

Keinig, J. (2006). Correctional Ethics. Ashgate.

Kleinig , J., & Smith, M. L. (Eds.). (2001). Discretion, Community and Correctional Ethics. Rowman & Littlefield Publishers.

Morris, N., & Tonry, M. H. (1991). Between Prison and Probation: Intermediate Punishments in a Rational Sentencing System. Oxford University Press.

Plastic Comb. (1993). Desktop Guide to Good Juvenile Probation Practice. Diane Pub Co.

Wooten, H. B. (1986). Reconstructing Probation. Criminal Justice, 7(4).

ENDNOTES

1. Maruschak, L. M., & Bonczar, T. P. (2014, April). Probation and parole in the United States, 2012. In *Bureau of Justice Statistics*. Retrieved September 9, 2014, from http://www.bjs.gov/content/pub/pdf/ppus12.pdf

2. Maruschak, L. M., & Bonczar, T. P. (2014, April). Probation and parole in the United States, 2012. In *Bureau of Justice Statistics*. Retrieved September 9, 2014, from http://www.bjs.gov/content/pub/pdf/ppus12.pdf

3. Maruschak, L. M., & Bonczar, T. P. (2014, April). Probation and parole in the United States, 2012. In *Bureau of Justice Statistics*. Retrieved September 9, 2014, from http://www.bjs.gov/content/pub/pdf/ppus12.pdf

4. Muraskin, R. (2001). Probation and parole officers: Ethical behavior. In R. Muraskin & M. Muraskin (Eds.), *Morality and the Law*. Upper Saddle River, NJ: Prentice Hall.

5. Latessa, E. (1993). *An Analysis of Pre-sentencing Investigation Recommendations and Judicial Outcome in Cuyahoga County Adult Probation Department*. Cincinnati: Department of Criminal Justice, University of Cincinnati.

6. Muraskin, R. (2001). Probation and parole Officers: Ethical behavior. In R. Muraskin & M. Muraskin (Eds.), *Morality and the Law*. Upper Saddle River, NJ: Prentice Hall.

7. Silverman, M. (1993). Ethical issues in the field of probation. *International Journal of Offender Therapy and Comparative Criminology* 37: 85–93.

8. Taxman, F. Shephardson, E., & Byrne, J. (2004). *Tools of the Trade: A Guide to Incorporating Science into Practice*. Washington, DC: National Institute of Corrections, U.S. Department of Justice, Office of Justice Programs.

9. Maruschak, L. M., & Bonczar, T. P. (2014, April). Probation and parole in the United States, 2012. In *Bureau of Justice Statistics*. Retrieved September 9, 2014, from http://www.bjs.gov/content/pub/pdf/ppus12.pdf

10. Muraskin, R. (2001). Probation and parole officers: Ethical behavior. In R. Muraskin & M. Muraskin (Eds.), *Morality and the Law*. Upper Saddle River, NJ: Prentice Hall.

11. http://www.appa-net.org/eweb/docs/APPA/stances/ip_CSPP.pdf

12. Hutchins, R. (2014, January 29). NJ parole officers not keeping regular tabs on sex offenders, audit shows. In *NJ.com True Jersey*. Retrieved September 9, 2014, from http://www.nj.com/politics/index.ssf/2014/01/audit_parole_officers_not_keeping_regular_tabs_on_sex_offenders.html

13. Muraskin, R. (2001). Probation and parole officers: Ethical behavior. In R. Muraskin & M. Muraskin (Eds.), *Morality and the Law*. Upper Saddle River, NJ: Prentice Hall.

14. Reamer, F.G. (2000) The social work ethics audit: A risk-management strategy. *Social Work* 45: 355–366.

15. Braswell, M., McCarthy, B., & McCarthy, B.J. (1996). *Justice, crime, and ethics*. Cincinnati, OH: Anderson Publishing Co.

16. Souryal, S. S. (1992). *Ethics in Criminal Justice: In Search of the Truth*. Cincinnati, OH: Anderson Publishing Co.

17. How do you report abuse or misconduct of your probation officer? who can you go to or what can you do?. (2010). In *Avvo*. Retrieved September 9, 2014, from http://www.avvo.com/legal-answers/how-do-you-report-abuse-or-misconduct-of-your-prob-270090.html

18. Gutheil, T. G., & Brodsky, A. (2008). Self-disclosure. In Gutheil, T. G., & Brodsky, A. (Eds.), *Preventing Boundary Violations in Clinical Practice*, (pp. 104–128). New York: The Guilford Press.

19. Odegard, K. (2013, June 27). Former probation and parole officer guilty of misconduct. In *Albany Democrat Herald*. Retrieved September 9, 2014, from http://democratherald.com/news/local/former-parole-and-probation-officer-guilty-of-misconduct/article_03884034-df69-11e2-8917-0019bb2963f4.html

20. WTDTF Agents arrest probation officer on bribery, extortion & official misconduct charges (2013, September 30). In Shelby County District Attorney Newsroom. Retrieved September 15, 2014, from http://www.scdag.com/news/item/411-wtdtf-agents-arrest-probation-officer-on-bribery-extortion-official-misconduct-charges

21. Prestegard, S. (2014, January 22). Ex-probation officer pleads to misconduct charges. In SWNews 4U.com. Retrieved September 9, 2014, from http://www.swnews4u.com/archives/19180/

22. Forum Probation Officer Misconduct. (2011). In ExpertLaw. Retrieved September 9, 2014, from http://www.expertlaw.com/forums/showthread.php?t=116026

23. From https://www.appa-net.org/eweb/DynamicPage.aspx?WebCode=IA_CodeEthics, Copyright © American Probation and Parole Association. Reprinted by permission.

24. Documents of the Senate of the State of New York, Volume 2 http://books.google.com/books?id=GhVLAAAAMAAJ&pg=RA1-PA116&lpg=RA1-PA116&dq=sir+walter+crofton+quotes&source=bl&ots=rvSdyh7gxB&sig=jZLmQ2U4EUAZGP3ijhSl3BI9Wzs&hl=en&sa=X&ei=mmQUVPuAO4me8gHg9IDwAg&ved=0CD8Q6AEwBQ#v=onepage&q=sir%20walter%20crofton%20quotes&f=false

Ethical Issues and the Juvenile Justice System

CHAPTER 11

"Laws to make it easier to transfer youth to the adult criminal court system have little or no general deterrent effect, meaning they do not prevent youth from engaging in criminal behavior."

—*Office of Juvenile Justice Delinquency Prevention*

The philosophical underpinnings of the juvenile justice system are different than those of the adult criminal justice system. The criminal justice system, at least in its current form, is a punishment-based system where principles of utilitarianism and deontology are often used as the implicit or explicit ideology of policy formation. While tenets of these ethical philosophies are certainly present in the juvenile justice system and related policy, these philosophies are blended into a framework created to keep the best interest of the child as the guiding principle in decision making.

JUVENILE JUSTICE SYSTEM FOUNDATION

The founding principles on which the juvenile justice system was created at the end of the nineteenth century maintained that treating and rehabilitating youth was preferred over punishing them, and was necessary to divert juveniles from a path of further deviant behavior. Juveniles' needs were more important than the behavior that brought them into the juvenile justice system. The juvenile court adhered to an individualized treatment model, the juvenile court judge was charged with acting in the best interest of the juvenile, and proceedings and records were closed to the public. Due process and procedural safeguards afforded adults in the criminal justice system were not extended to juveniles involved in delinquent behavior. Based on this model, the juvenile court had a wide range of discretion in deciding the appropriate outcome for each juvenile.

Shortly after creation of the juvenile court, criticisms began to mount. Questions were raised regarding fairness, effectiveness, discriminatory practices, and lack of due process where juveniles could be detained, questioned, tried, and incarcerated without having access to a lawyer or even being notified of the charges against them.[1] Critics have charged both that the court was too lenient and too harsh.[2]

These criticisms led to U.S. Supreme Court intervention beginning in the 1960's, specifically with *Kent v the United States (1966)* and *In re Gault (1967)*, which limited the unfettered discretion afforded the juvenile court. However, the battle between decision making based on what is in the best interest of the juvenile and protecting society remains. Procedural safeguards and due process rights have been afforded juveniles that were not in place when the system was created. However, the extension of these protections to juveniles has also aided in creating a practical shift from decision making based on individual needs and the best interest of juvenile offenders to considering the seriousness of the offense, public safety, and appropriate punishment, as was evident in juvenile policy created during that 1980's and 1990's.

BOX 11.1

IN PRACTICE/CLOSER LOOK

Kent v. United States

383 U.S. 541

Kent v. United States (No. 104)

Argued: January 19, 1966

Decided: March 21, 1966

Syllabus

Petitioner was arrested at the age of 16 in connection with charges of housebreaking, robbery, and rape. As a juvenile, he was subject to the exclusive jurisdiction of the District of Columbia Juvenile Court unless that court, after "full investigation," should waive jurisdiction over him and remit him for trial to the United States District Court for the District of Columbia. Petitioner's counsel filed a motion in the Juvenile Court for a hearing on the question of waiver, and for access to the Juvenile Court's Social Service file which had been accumulated on petitioner during his probation for a prior offense. The Juvenile Court did not rule on these motions. It entered an order waiving jurisdiction, with the recitation that this was done after the required "full investigation." Petitioner was indicted in the District Court. He moved to dismiss the indictment on the ground that the Juvenile Court's waiver was invalid. The District Court overruled the motion, and petitioner was tried. He was convicted on six counts of housebreaking and robbery, but acquitted on two rape counts by reason of insanity. On appeal, petitioner raised, among other things, the validity of the Juvenile Court's waiver of jurisdiction; the United States Court of Appeals for the District of Columbia Circuit affirmed, finding the procedure leading to waiver and the waiver order itself valid.

Held: The Juvenile Court order waiving jurisdiction and remitting petitioner for trial in the District Court was invalid.

(a) The Juvenile Court's latitude in determining whether to waive jurisdiction is not complete. It assumes procedural regularity sufficient in the particular circumstances to satisfy the basic requirements of due process and fairness, as well as compliance with the statutory requirement of a "full investigation."

(b) The *parens patriae* philosophy of the Juvenile Court "is not an invitation to procedural arbitrariness."

(c) As the Court of Appeals for the District of Columbia Circuit has held, "the waiver of jurisdiction is a 'critically important' action determining vitally important statutory rights of the juvenile."

(d) The Juvenile Court Act requires "full investigation," and makes the Juvenile Court records available to persons having a "legitimate interest in the protection . . . of the child. . . ."

These provisions, "read in the context of constitutional principles relating to due process and the assistance of counsel," entitle a juvenile to a hearing, to access by his counsel to social records and probation or similar reports which presumably are considered by the Juvenile Court, and to a statement of the reasons for the Juvenile Court's decision sufficient to enable meaningful appellate review thereof.

(e) Since petitioner is now 21, and beyond the jurisdiction of the Juvenile Court, the order of the Court of Appeals and the judgment of the District Court are vacated, and the case is remanded to the District Court for a hearing *de novo*, consistent with this opinion, on whether waiver was appropriate when ordered by the Juvenile Court.

If that court finds that waiver was inappropriate, petitioner's conviction must be vacated. If, however, it finds that the waiver order was proper when originally made, the District Court may proceed, after consideration of such motions as counsel may make and such further proceedings, if any, as may be warranted, to enter an appropriate judgment.

119 U.S.App.D.C. 378, 343 F.2d 247, reversed and remanded.

Syllabus taken from Cornell University Law School, Legal Information Institute:

http://www.law.cornell.edu/supremecourt/text/383/541#writing-USSC_CR_0383_0541_ZS

BOX 11.2

IN PRACTICE/CLOSER LOOK

In re Gault

387 U.S. 1

In re Gault **(No. 116)**

Argued: December 6, 1966

Decided: May 15, 1967

99 Ariz. 181, 407 P.2d 760, reversed and remanded.

Syllabus

Appellants' 15-year-old son, Gerald Gault, was taken into custody as the result of a complaint that he had made lewd telephone calls. After hearings before a juvenile court judge, Gerald was ordered committed to the State Industrial School as a juvenile delinquent until he should reach majority. Appellants brought a habeas corpus action in the state courts to challenge the constitutionality of the Arizona Juvenile Code and the procedure actually used in Gerald's case, on the ground of denial of various procedural due process rights. The State Supreme Court affirmed dismissal of the writ. Agreeing that the constitutional guarantee of due process applies to proceedings in which juveniles are charged as delinquents, the court held that the Arizona Juvenile Code impliedly includes the requirements of due process in delinquency proceedings, and that such due process requirements were not offended by the procedure leading to Gerald's commitment.

Held:

1. *Kent v. United States*, 383 U.S. 541, 562 (1966), held "that the [waiver] hearing must measure up to the essentials of due process and fair treatment." This view is reiterated, here

(Continued)

BOX 11.2 (Continued)

in connection with a juvenile court adjudication of "delinquency," as a requirement which is part of the Due Process Clause of the Fourteenth Amendment of our Constitution. The holding in this case relates only to the adjudicatory stage of the juvenile process, where commitment to a state institution may follow. When proceedings may result in incarceration in an institution of **[p2]** confinement, "it would be extraordinary if our Constitution did not require the procedural regularity and exercise of care implied in the phrase 'due process.'" Pp. 12–31.

2. Due process requires, in such proceedings, that adequate written notice be afforded the child and his parents or guardian. Such notice must inform them "of the specific issues that they must meet," and must be given "at the earliest practicable time, and, in any event, sufficiently in advance of the hearing to permit preparation." Notice here was neither timely nor adequately specific, nor was there waiver of the right to constitutionally adequate notice. Pp. 31–34.

3. In such proceedings, the child and his parents must be advised of their right to be represented by counsel and, if they are unable to afford counsel, that counsel will be appointed to represent the child. Mrs. Gault's statement at the habeas corpus hearing that she had known she could employ counsel, is not "an 'intentional relinquishment or abandonment' of a fully known right." Pp. 34–42.

4. The constitutional privilege against self-incrimination is applicable in such proceedings:

an admission by the juvenile may [not] be used against him in the absence of clear and unequivocal evidence that the admission was made with knowledge that he was not obliged to speak, and would not be penalized for remaining silent.

[T]he availability of the privilege does not turn upon the type of proceeding in which its protection is invoked, but upon the nature of the statement or admission and the exposure which it invites. . . . [J]uvenile proceedings to determine "delinquency," which may lead to commitment to a state institution, must be regarded as "criminal" for purposes of the privilege against self-incrimination.

Furthermore, experience has shown that "admissions and confessions by juveniles require special caution" as to their reliability and voluntariness, and "[i]t would indeed be surprising if the privilege against self-incrimination were available to hardened criminals, but not to children."

[S]pecial problems may arise with respect to waiver of the privilege by or on behalf of children, and . . . there may well be some differences in technique—but not in principle—depending upon the age of the child and the presence and competence of parents. . . . If counsel was not present for some permissible reason when an admission was obtained, the greatest care must be taken to assure that the admission was voluntary. . . .

Gerald's admissions did not **[p3]** measure up to these standards, and could not properly be used as a basis for the judgment against him. Pp. 44–56.

5. Absent a valid confession, a juvenile in such proceedings must be afforded the rights of confrontation and sworn testimony of witnesses available for cross-examination. Pp. 56–57.

6. Other questions raised by appellants, including the absence of provision for appellate review of a delinquency adjudication, and a transcript of the proceedings, are not ruled upon. Pp. 57–58.

Syllabus taken from Cornell University Law School, Legal Information Institute:

http://www.law.cornell.edu/supremecourt/text/387/1

As stated in the Uniform Juvenile Court Act, the purpose of the juvenile justice system is "to provide for the care, protection, and wholesome moral, mental, and physical development of children coming with its provisions" (sec. 1).[3] The extensive scope of purpose, the founding philosophy of the court, and the desire for juvenile accountability has resulted in a system that is neither social welfare nor social control. As such, discretionary decision making and ethical considerations are different in the juvenile justice system in comparison to the adult system. This chapter will review some of these differences and highlight areas where ethical considerations are of greatest importance.

JUVENILE DELINQUENCY – WHO IS A JUVENILE? WHAT IS DELINQUENCY? WHY DOES IT MATTER?

It is important to remember that, while there are federal guidelines for who is considered to fall within the jurisdiction of the juvenile court and what is considered a delinquent act, each state creates its own policy. Each state decides the age range of juvenile court jurisdiction, which typically falls between ages 10 and 18. However, some states have legislated juvenile court jurisdiction for children as young as 6 and as old at 19. Ethical considerations of how to process a ten year old are often very different than considering a juvenile who is 18. Decision makers in the juvenile justice system may be tasked with difficult decision making when considering appropriate options for juveniles while taking into account age-based diminished culpability, environmental influences, and the severity of the delinquent act. (See *Consider the Outcome/Case Study/Case Example 11.3* for more discussion).

BOX 11.3

CONSIDER THE OUTCOME/CASE STUDY/CASE EXAMPLE

Robert "Yummy" Sandifer was small for his age and loved cookies and his two dogs, a bloodhound and a Chihuahua. Family members describe him as "bright," "sweet," and "liked to work with cars." Yummy was the third child of eight born in a rough neighborhood in Chicago to parents who were in and out of jail. At the age of 3, Yummy and his siblings were removed from an abusive home which included being burned with cigarettes, whippings with an electrical cord, and neglect—neighbors report Yummy and his siblings were left in the care of his 5 1/2 year old brother. The children were placed with their grandmother who was also raising a number of other children and grandchildren, reports range from 19-40 children were in her house at one time.

By age 8, Yummy was involved with the Black Disciples gang. By 11, he had committed 30 crimes, including stealing, fighting, motor vehicle theft, and armed robbery. Yummy's infamous crimes, though, are the attempted murder of a 15-year-old alleged rival gang member, aggravated assault of another 16 year old, and murder of a 14-year-old bystander. Considering the mitigating factors (age, background of abuse, neighborhood influence) and aggravating factors (delinquent history, gang involvement, seriousness of crime) in Yummy's case, how should the juvenile justice court proceed?

For more information on Yummy's case:

http://www.people.com/people/archive/article/0,,20103912,00.html

http://www.starnewsonline.com/article/20071218/YOUTH/71214002

Juvenile delinquency includes committing offenses that are not considered crimes as an adult. These offenses are referred to as status offenses and include truancy, running away, and curfew violations. The Juvenile Justice and Delinquency Prevention Act of 1974 deemed these offenses should be processed differently than other delinquent acts and mandated that states deinstitutionalize status offenses. In effect, the Act requires states to find alternatives to placing juveniles in detention for committing status offenses. In practice, deinstitutionalization of status offenders (DSO) has led to the unintended consequence of net-widening.[4]

Net-widening is the process of increasing labeling and stigmatization by bringing juveniles to the attention of the juvenile justice system who otherwise would have not been involved with it. Prior to DSO, juveniles who committed status offenses were largely disregarded by police or were handled without being formally processed. DSO created an official category for status offenders and encouraged the juvenile justice system to provide social services for these offenders. Thus, juvenile justice actors had an alternative to offender processing and instead of unofficial adjustments or diversion, status offenders were more likely to be officially processed through the system to receive social services. This increased the labeling of juveniles as delinquent and increased contact with the juvenile justice system.

DISCRETION IN DECISION MAKING

As previously discussed, the overriding concern of the juvenile justice system has been: what is in the juvenile's best interest? Although this is the fundamental guideline that created and shaped the system, many factors weigh on juvenile justice outcomes including public safety, attitudes of the decision maker, characteristics of the juvenile, as well as agency considerations such as program availability and detention space. Considering the best outcome for each juvenile, as well as other factors, can only be achieved when decision makers have discretion as to how to respond to each juvenile as an individual case. Various juvenile justice actors are deemed decision makers at points throughout the system (see Table 11.1).

The advantages of authority discretion in the juvenile justice system rest in the philosophy of individual treatment for each juvenile. Authorities have the ability to take legal and extra-legal factors into consideration while making decisions concerning juvenile offenders. Mitigating and aggravating factors may result in a justice outcome for one juvenile that is very different from another. On the other hand, the disadvantages of discretion by authorities result in what may appear to be unequal treatment. When juveniles commit similar offenses and receive very different outcomes, questions are raised (See Case Example 11.2).

TABLE 11.1   Juvenile Justice Processing and Primary Decision Maker(s)

Decision-making point	Decision maker
Referral	Police, School, Parent, Probation Officer
Arrest/Taking into Custody	Police
Diversion	Police, Probation Officer, Prosecutor, Judge
Detention	Probation Officer, Judge
Filing a Petition	Probation Officer
Prosecution	Prosecutor
Waiver	Prosecutor, Judge
Adjudication	Judge
Disposition	Judge

What extra-legal factors should be considered in decision making? In an effort to maintain a system of individualized responses, extra-legal factors such as family financial resources, family structure, and residential mobility are often considered in juvenile justice decision making. For example, a juvenile whose family has the resources to pay for drug treatment might be more likely to receive probation and family-funded private treatment, whereas a juvenile whose family does not have the same resources may be ordered to a state correctional facility that can offer drug treatment programming. Decision makers often give less punitive dispositions to juveniles living with two parents instead of one. Juveniles from families that frequently change residences may be more likely to be placed in detention than those who have a stable residence. On a case-by-case basis, decision makers may be acting in what they deem the best interest of each juvenile, cumulatively, however, taking extra-legal factors such as family status into consideration in decision making often disproportionately affects minority youth.

Police

Discretion in policing is a normal, necessary part of daily activities. Police officers are often viewed as having the greatest amount of discretion as, in comparison to other actors in the justice system, there are more of them and they encounter more citizens on a daily basis. Discretionary decision making is involved in almost every citizen encounter. In addition to being the gatekeepers of the justice system, making initial decisions about how to handle and dispose of incidents, police officer interaction with juveniles can be a formative or reinforcing experience.

Research examining characteristics of arrested juveniles is conflicting. Some research indicates characteristics such as age, race/ethnicity, or gender increase or decrease the likelihood of formal processing resulting from police encounters. However, recent researchers indicate the relationship is more complicated. A juvenile's behavior or demeanor toward law enforcement helps shape the officer's decision to arrest[5,6,7,8,9] more than individual characteristics. Myers (2004) found that among legal factors such as seriousness of offense, evidence, presence of a weapon, and prior history, verbal or behavioral disrespect increases the likelihood of arrest.[10] Conversely, juveniles who show what is deemed as "proper respect" toward officers, have had few, if any, previous encounters with police, and whose parents are perceived as being cooperative, are more likely to receive unofficial dispositions from police encounters.[11]

Therefore, in neighborhoods that have experienced negative interactions with police or view police as agents of control, attitudes from citizens toward police are less likely to be positive. "In minority communities where police-community relations have typically been impaired, it is perhaps to be expected that citizens will have a negative and distrustful view of the police."[12] Further, juveniles may be more likely to experience frustration resulting from real or perceived unfair treatment[13] which would affect their interactions with law enforcement. These formative experiences help shape attitudes of juveniles toward police and future outcomes of police encounters.

Prosecutor

Although police officers have a wide range of discretion regarding juveniles who are officially brought into contact with the juvenile justice system, the prosecutor makes the decision regarding which juveniles will be processed by the juvenile court. The juvenile justice prosecutor determines what cases will go to court, many waiver decisions (see prosecutorial waiver discussion), the nature of the petition, and often also impacts the disposition because rarely will a juvenile court judge impose a more severe punishment than the prosecutor requests.[14] There are legitimate concerns helping to dictate prosecutorial decision making, such as evidentiary requirements and probable cause, but, as with prosecutorial discretion in adult cases, illegitimate factors such as political or personal reasons may also be included.

In addition to formal processing, juvenile court prosecutors may impose unofficial probation. This is a process whereby the prosecutor gives the juvenile, and the juvenile's family, an option of

> ### BOX 11.4
>
> ## CLOSER LOOK/IN PRACTICE
>
> TAPS Academy
>
> The Teen And Police Service (TAPS) Academy represents a new chapter of community policing. By creating partnerships with at-risk teens and police, this union can proactively address some of the most pressing conditions in the community. TAPS Academy uses a three-pronged approach—empowering youth, enhancing communities, and engaging law enforcement—in order to move to the next phase of community policing, actively engaging one of the least participative groups in the community: at-risk teens.
>
> Empowering Youth
>
> TAPS Academy is an 11-week program primarily designed for at-risk youth. During this 11-week cohort, students partner with mentor officers to discuss issues such as: bullying, anger management, avoidance of gang life, drug usage, conflict management, and many other youth and law enforcement focused topics. Through these interactive sessions, students gain knowledge and skills to manage situations and make positive decisions in their daily lives.
>
> Enhancing Communities
>
> One of the primary purposes of this program is to strengthen communities by encouraging at-risk youth and law enforcement to work together. Within the 11-week program, students and officers engage in two community services projects. Students are given the tools to help them become better citizens in their schools and communities. Youth and their families are encouraged to participate in their communities and make them better places to live and work.
>
> Engaging Law Enforcement
>
> Social distance between at-risk youth and law enforcement has continued to rise over the past few decades. TAPS Academy works to break that cycle by engaging law enforcement personnel and youth before an issue escalates. TAPS creates an environment where law enforcement and youth learn from each other, build relationships, and discuss better ways to manage adverse situations. This program forges a path for these traditionally opposing groups to build a solid foundation of trust and mutual respect.
>
> For more information about TAPS Academy, visit http://tapsacademy.org/

proceeding to court or admitting to the offense and behaving according to guidelines set out by the prosecutor. If the juvenile successfully completes the requirements as determined by the prosecutor, formal processing will be avoided. The advantages to unofficial probation are that it saves time and money for the prosecutor's office, reduces the court's caseload, and, if the juvenile is guilty, decreases the likelihood of juvenile court stigmatization. The disadvantages include punishment without a trial or fact finding hearing and the concern over the voluntary nature of the arrangement. Does the juvenile consider agreeing to unofficial probation as voluntary when the other option, as explained by the prosecutor, is likely to result in a severe disposition?

Judge

The juvenile court judge holds more power and discretion than in the adult system. Juvenile court judges have greater responsibility than to act as an impartial referee between adversarial sides. Due to the philosophy of the juvenile justice system, the juvenile court judge is directly involved with the outcome of each case that is presented. Judges continually must make decisions that ensure public

---

BOX 11.5

CONSIDER THE OUTCOME/CASE STUDY/CASE EXAMPLE

A 14-year-old boy jumps out of a car and punches a man in the face. The back of the man's head hits the pavement resulting in his death two days later. The juvenile is represented by a public defender. The judge in this case adjudicates the juvenile delinquent and orders a disposition of ten years in a state juvenile correctional facility.

A 16-year-old boy, after having reportedly stolen two cases of beer, hits and kills four people, and injures several others, while driving under the influence of alcohol and drugs. His blood alcohol level is three times the legal limit for an adult and he was driving 70 mph in a 40-mph zone. The juvenile is represented by a private attorney and a psychiatrist is hired who testifies that, due to the family's wealth, the juvenile does not understand the consequences of his actions. The judge in this case adjudicates the juvenile delinquent and orders a disposition of ten years probation and alcohol rehabilitation.

Both cases were adjudicated by the same judge. The 14-year-old boy was African American and his family had few financial resources. The 16-year-old boy was Caucasian and his family paid for his treatment in a state hospital. The case of the 16-year-old boy has caused controversy due to the lenient sentence in light of the harm caused, as well as the appearance of justice inequality based on family financial means. The judge claims that she made a decision in both cases based on the information as presented by each juvenile's lawyer and the best outcome for each juvenile.

Do you think that the outcomes are fair?

How does discretionary decision making impact the outcomes of these cases?

---

safety and, at the same time, promote the best interest of the juvenile, while considering contact with the system, treatment options, and likely success. Individualized outcomes, taking into account all these factors, allow for a wide range of discretion. This discretionary decision making includes adjudication and disposition of juvenile delinquents as well as abuse and dependency determinations of children in need of care and services.

In addition to legal facts of each case, as with other actors in the juvenile justice system, personal attitudes and opinions, experience, and characteristics of the juvenile impact each final decision. A decision that is final, unless overturned on appeal, and has serious consequences on the life of each juvenile. This final decision is often based on a judge's intuition instead of a structured assessment or more objective criteria.[15] Although a juvenile judge's discretion has been limited by prosecutorial and statutory waiver laws, as well as unofficial dispositions imposed by police officers and prosecutors, they remain the most powerful actors in the juvenile justice system.

JUVENILE SEX OFFENDERS

Laws related to juvenile sex offending have become increasingly punitive.[16] The Sex Offender Registration and Notification Act (SORNA), a part of the Adam Walsh Child Protection Act signed into law in 2006, mandates that juveniles at least 14 years of age who commit certain offenses are required to register as sex offenders for 25 years to life (Title 1 of the Adam Walsh Child Protection and Safety Act of 2006). Such laws are based on emotional decisions born out of a few tragic, high-profile cases perpetrated by violent adult sex offenders and predicated on the assumption that all sex offenders are dangerous recidivists. The purpose of registries is to increase public safety and reduce sexual violence by providing closer scrutiny of sex offenders.[17]

Research impacting the creation of these laws is dated, inconclusive, and based on adults. Empirical evidence regarding predicting, preventing, or correcting juvenile sex offending is limited; however, recent investigations call into question the validity and efficiency of how juvenile sex offenders are treated, specifically in regards to mandatory sex offense registries. Recent findings indicate that sexually offending juveniles are no more likely to commit adult sex offenses than non-sex offending juveniles,[18] whether they are registered or not,[19] and registrations do a poor job at lowering the risk of further juvenile sex offending.[20]

The notion that juvenile sex offender registries are an effective way to prevent sex offending recidivism and protect the public is not supported by research. Specifically, Zimring, Piquero, and Jennings (2007) concluded that targeting juvenile sex offenders will miss more than 90% of those who commit sex crimes as adults and will misidentify 90% of juveniles who will never commit another sex offense. The authors put it this way, "it would be just as efficient to create a 'potential sex offender registry' composed solely of young men with juvenile contacts for auto theft" (p. 530).[21]

Because of these, and similar, findings, there is evidence to suggest that decision makers may take actions to avoid registration requirements that inadvertently disqualify offenders from treatment.[22] The negative impacts of these laws have grave consequences for juveniles and may be doing more harm than good. On the one hand, juveniles, who are not likely to sexually reoffend, are increasingly stigmatized through registration notifications. On the other hand, in an effort to avoid registration stigmatization, sexually offending juveniles are failing to get treatment that may prevent further victimization.

JUVENILE LIFE WITHOUT PAROLE

Roper v Simmons (2005) ended death sentences for juveniles. The U.S. Supreme Court reasoned that standards of decency are fluid and evolving and there was consistent evidence that the standards of decency in the United States had changed since the ruling in *Stanford v Kentucky* (1989) confirmed the constitutionality of the death penalty for 16 and 17-year-old offenders. Additionally, the court cited differences between juveniles and adults that demonstrate that juvenile offenders cannot be considered as the worst offenders, deserving of death as a penalty. Those differences include "susceptibility to immature and irresponsible behavior," lack of control making it difficult to "escape negative influences," and the changing nature of the adolescent personality does not support a conclusion that juvenile capital offenders possess an "irretrievable depraved character." Further, in *Roper*, the U.S. Supreme Court reasoned that the penological justifications for the death penalty, retribution and deterrence, did not apply to juvenile offenders due to their diminished culpability.

BOX 11.6

IN PRACTICE/CLOSER LOOK

ROPER V. SIMMONS (03-633) 543 U.S. 551 (2005) 112 S. W. 3d 397, affirmed.

SUPREME COURT OF THE UNITED STATES

ROPER, SUPERINTENDENT, POTOSI CORRECTIONAL CENTER *v.* SIMMONS CERTIORARI TO THE SUPREME COURT OF MISSOURI

No. 03-633. Argued October 13, 2004–Decided March 1, 2005

At age 17, respondent Simmons planned and committed a capital murder. After he had turned 18, he was sentenced to death. His direct appeal and subsequent petitions for state and federal postconviction relief were rejected. This Court then held, in *Atkins v. Virginia*, 536 U.S. 304, that the Eighth Amendment, applicable to the States through the Fourteenth Amendment, prohibits the execution of a mentally retarded person. Simmons filed a new petition for state postconviction relief, arguing that *Atkins'* reasoning established that the Constitution prohibits the execution of a juvenile who was under 18 when he committed his crime. The Missouri Supreme Court agreed and set aside Simmons' death sentence in favor of life imprisonment without eligibility for release. It held that, although *Stanford v. Kentucky*, 492 U.S. 361, rejected the proposition that the Constitution bars capital punishment for juvenile offenders younger than 18, a national consensus has developed against the execution of those offenders since *Stanford*.

Held: The Eighth and Fourteenth Amendments forbid imposition of the death penalty on offenders who were under the age of 18 when their crimes were committed. Pp. 6–25.

(a) The Eighth Amendment's prohibition against "cruel and unusual punishments" must be interpreted according to its text, by considering history, tradition, and precedent, and with due regard for its purpose and function in the constitutional design. To implement this framework this Court has established the propriety and affirmed the necessity of referring to "the evolving standards of decency that mark the progress of a maturing society" to determine which punishments are so disproportionate as to be "cruel and unusual." *Trop v. Dulles*, 356 U.S. 86, 100–101. In 1988, in *Thompson v. Oklahoma*, 487 U.S. 815, 818–838, a plurality determined that national standards of decency did not permit the execution of any offender under age 16 at the time of the crime. The next year, in *Stanford*, a 5-to-4 Court referred to contemporary standards of decency, but concluded the Eighth and Fourteenth Amendments did not proscribe the execution of offenders over 15 but under 18 because 22 of 37 death penalty States permitted that penalty for 16-year-old offenders, and 25 permitted it for 17-year-olds, thereby indicating there was no national consensus. 492 U.S., at 370–371. A plurality also "emphatically reject[ed]" the suggestion that the Court should bring its own judgment to bear on the acceptability of the juvenile death penalty. *Id.*, at 377–378. That same day the Court held, in *Penry v. Lynaugh*, 492 U.S. 302, 334, that the Eighth Amendment did not mandate a categorical exemption from the death penalty for mentally retarded persons because only two States had enacted laws banning such executions. Three Terms ago in *Atkins*, however, the Court held that standards of decency had evolved since *Penry* and now demonstrated that the execution of the mentally retarded is cruel and unusual punishment. The *Atkins* Court noted that objective indicia of society's standards, as expressed in pertinent legislative enactments and state practice, demonstrated that such executions had become so truly unusual that it was fair to say that a national consensus has developed against them. 536 U.S., at 314–315. The Court also returned to the rule, established in decisions predating *Stanford*, that the Constitution contemplates that the Court's own judgment be brought to bear on the question of the acceptability of the death penalty. *Id.*, at 312. After observing that mental retardation diminishes personal culpability even if the offender can distinguish right from wrong, *id.*, at 318, and that mentally retarded offenders' impairments make it less defensible to impose the death penalty as retribution for past crimes or as a real deterrent to future crimes, *id.*, at 319–320, the Court ruled that the death penalty constitutes an excessive sanction for the entire category of mentally retarded offenders, and that the Eighth Amendment places a substantive restriction on the State's power to take such an offender's life, *id.*, at 321. Just as the *Atkins* Court reconsidered the issue decided in *Penry*, the Court now reconsiders the issue decided in *Stanford*. Pp. 6–10.

(b) Both objective indicia of consensus, as expressed in particular by the enactments of legislatures that have addressed the question, and the Court's own determination in the exercise of its independent judgment, demonstrate that the death penalty is a disproportionate punishment for juveniles. Pp. 10–21.

(Continued)

BOX 11.6 (Continued)

(1) As in *Atkins*, the objective indicia of national consensus here—the rejection of the juvenile death penalty in the majority of States; the infrequency of its use even where it remains on the books; and the consistency in the trend toward abolition of the practice—provide sufficient evidence that today society views juveniles, in the words *Atkins* used respecting the mentally retarded, as "categorically less culpable than the average criminal," 536 U.S., at 316. The evidence of such consensus is similar, and in some respects parallel, to the evidence in *Atkins*: 30 States prohibit the juvenile death penalty, including 12 that have rejected it altogether and 18 that maintain it but, by express provision or judicial interpretation, exclude juveniles from its reach. Moreover, even in the 20 States without a formal prohibition, the execution of juveniles is infrequent. Although, by contrast to *Atkins*, the rate of change in reducing the incidence of the juvenile death penalty, or in taking specific steps to abolish it, has been less dramatic, the difference between this case and *Atkins* in that respect is counterbalanced by the consistent direction of the change toward abolition. Indeed, the slower pace here may be explained by the simple fact that the impropriety of executing juveniles between 16 and 18 years old gained wide recognition earlier than the impropriety of executing the mentally retarded. Pp. 10–13.

(2) Rejection of the imposition of the death penalty on juvenile offenders under 18 is required by the Eighth Amendment. Capital punishment must be limited to those offenders who commit "a narrow category of the most serious crimes" and whose extreme culpability makes them "the most deserving of execution." *Atkins*, 536 U.S. at 319. Three general differences between juveniles under 18 and adults demonstrate that juvenile offenders cannot with reliability be classified among the worst offenders. Juveniles' susceptibility to immature and irresponsible behavior means "their irresponsible conduct is not as morally reprehensible as that of an adult." *Thompson v. Oklahoma*, 487 U.S. 815, 835. Their own vulnerability and comparative lack of control over their immediate surroundings mean juveniles have a greater claim than adults to be forgiven for failing to escape negative influences in their whole environment. See *Stanford, supra*, at 395. The reality that juveniles still struggle to define their identity means it is less supportable to conclude that even a heinous crime committed by a juvenile is evidence of irretrievably depraved character. The *Thompson* plurality recognized the import of these characteristics with respect to juveniles under 16. 487 U.S., at 833–838. The same reasoning applies to all juvenile offenders under 18. Once juveniles' diminished culpability is recognized, it is evident that neither of the two penological justifications for the death penalty—retribution and deterrence of capital crimes by prospective offenders, *e.g.*, *Atkins*, 536 U.S., at 319–provides adequate justification for imposing that penalty on juveniles. Although the Court cannot deny or overlook the brutal crimes too many juvenile offenders have committed, it disagrees with petitioner's contention that, given the Court's own insistence on individualized consideration in capital sentencing, it is arbitrary and unnecessary to adopt a categorical rule barring imposition of the death penalty on an offender under 18. An unacceptable likelihood exists that the brutality or cold-blooded nature of any particular crime would overpower mitigating arguments based on youth as a matter of course, even where the juvenile offender's objective immaturity, vulnerability, and lack of true depravity should require a sentence less severe than death. When a juvenile commits a heinous crime, the State can exact forfeiture of some of the most basic liberties, but the State cannot extinguish his life and his potential to attain a mature understanding of his own humanity. While drawing the line at 18 is subject to the objections always raised against categorical rules, that is the point where society draws the line for many purposes between childhood and adulthood and the age at which the line for death eligibility ought to rest. *Stanford* should be deemed no longer controlling on this issue. Pp. 14–21.

(c) The overwhelming weight of international opinion against the juvenile death penalty is not controlling here, but provides respected and significant confirmation for the Court's determination that the penalty is disproportionate punishment for offenders under 18. See, *e.g.*, *Thompson, supra*, at 830–831, and n. 31. The United States is the only country in the world that continues to give official sanction to the juvenile penalty. It does not lessen fidelity to the Constitution or pride in its origins to acknowledge that the express affirmation of certain fundamental rights by other nations and peoples underscores the centrality of those same rights within our own heritage of freedom. Pp. 21–25.

112 S. W. 3d 397, affirmed.

Syllabus taken from Cornell University Law School, Legal Information Institute:

http://www.law.cornell.edu/supct/html/03-633.ZS.html

In *Graham v Florida* (2010), using similar reasoning as in *Roper* regarding capacity to change and juvenile culpability, the U.S. Supreme Court eliminated juvenile life without parole for juveniles who committed non-homicide cases. In 2012, two cases of 14-year-old homicide offenders came before the Supreme Court in *Miller v Alabama* and *Jackson v Hobbs*. The Supreme Court fell short of banning juvenile life without parole but struck down the use of state sentencing schemes that mandated juvenile life without parole for homicide offenses. In deciding disposition of capital cases, judges must consider age and other mitigating factors that diminish juvenile culpability.

BOX 11.7

CLOSER LOOK/IN PRACTICE

Miller v. Alabama

Holding: The Eighth Amendment prohibits a sentencing scheme that requires life in prison without the possibility of parole for juvenile homicide offenders.

Plain English Summary: In a series of decisions dating back to 1988, the Supreme Court has repeatedly ruled that youths under age 18 who commit crimes must not necessarily receive as severe a punishment as adults who committed the same kind of crimes. Among other rulings, the Court has forbidden the death penalty for minors who commit murders, and it has barred a sentence of life in prison without a chance of release for minors who commit crimes in which the victim is not killed. In this new ruling, the Court avoiding imposing such a flat ban on life without parole for a minor who commits murder, but it did rule out such a sentence as a mandatory requirement in all such cases. It said, though, that it does not expect very many youths under age 18 to get such a sentence that essentially would require them to stay in prison until they die.

Judgment: Reversed and remanded, 5-4, in an opinion by Justice Kagan on June 25, 2012. Justice Breyer filed a concurring opinion, in which Justice Sotomayor joined. Chief Justice Roberts filed a dissenting opinion, in which Justices Scalia, Thomas, and Alito joined. Justice Thomas filed a dissenting opinion, in which Justice Scalia joined. Justice Alito filed a dissenting opinion, in which Justice Scalia joined.

Taken from Supreme Court of the United States Blog:

http://www.scotusblog.com/miller-v-alabama/

While the Supreme Court has made it clear that the most severe sentences of death and juvenile life without parole are not supported by penological aims of deterrence and retribution, common characteristics of the approximately 2,500 juveniles that are sentenced to life without parole pose questions of equality and fairness. Juveniles sentenced to life without parole share common socio-economic disadvantages, educational failures, and abuse. Almost 80% report witnessing violence in their homes, over 50% witnessed weekly violence in their neighborhoods. Almost 80% of girls sentenced to juvenile life without parole had a history of physical and/or sexual abuse. A third of juvenile lifers were raised in public housing and almost one-fifth reported not living with a close relative before incarceration such as being homeless or living in a group home or detention facility. Educationally, 40% of juveniles sentenced to life without parole were in special education classes, over half were not attending school when the offense occurred, and 85% had been expelled or suspended at some time during their academic careers.[23]

How should we handle juveniles, often young juveniles, who have committed very serious crimes? The U.S. Supreme Court has issued a warning in *Miller* and *Jackson* to states that the use of juvenile life without parole should be reserved only when it is deemed a "proportional" penalty for a crime that "reflects irreparable corruption." States must grapple with creating proportional sentences that reflect the seriousness of the offense, protect the public, and make allowances for the mistakes of youth.

WAIVERS

The primary goal of waivers is "to punish more severely violent juvenile offenders through longer terms of incarceration. Evidently, the criminal court presents the most efficient forum for achieving this goal" (p. 343).[24] Perceived failure of the juvenile justice system and increased due process opened the door for legislators to capitalize on the public panic of the violent crime wave of the 1980's and early 1990's. Among the measures taken to get tough on juvenile offending was the revision of state juvenile waiver laws to allow juveniles to be tried as adults. In addition to discretionary or judicial waivers, many states also began to allow for presumptive and mandatory waivers and statutory exclusion laws. These revisions expanded the types of offenses and offenders eligible to be waived to the criminal justice system, included lowering the minimum age for waivers, increasing waiver-eligible offenses, and expanding prosecutorial discretion while reducing judicial decision making.[25]

Judicial waivers have been a part of juvenile justice processing since the advent of the juvenile court. Judicial waivers give juvenile court judges the authority to waive juvenile court jurisdiction and transfer the case to criminal court. Most jurisdictions allow judicial waivers based on the court's assessment of a youth's amenability to treatment or his/her potential dangerousness. Judges commonly use age, treatment prognosis, seriousness of offense, and history of delinquency in transfer decisions. Criticisms of judicial waivers claim that it permits the judge too much discretion and allows for disparity and inconsistency in justice outcomes.[26] Although criticized for their subjectivity, judicial waivers have due process protections as extended in *Kent v. United States (1966)* and are the only waivers that can be appealed.

Some states have statutory exclusion laws that exclude certain offenses from juvenile court jurisdiction. In these states, juveniles who meet age, offense, and prior record qualifications are remanded to the jurisdiction of the criminal court. For example, in Maryland, a 16-year-old juvenile alleged to have committed second-degree murder would be the automatic jurisdiction of the criminal court (HB 1122 – Ch. 416, 2012 Laws of Maryland). The goal of these laws is to ensure decisions regarding public safety and crime control are made by elected officials who are responsible for keeping their communities safe.[27] However, this is contrary to traditional juvenile court consideration of criminal sophistication, diminished capacity, maturity, or amenability of treatment; these laws are based on legal factors alone. Instead of making policy decisions based on the best interest of the juvenile, legislators have been criticized for using policy making in the best interest of their own political gain.[28]

For certain offenses and offenders, jurisdiction is shared by both the juvenile and criminal courts and the prosecutor has discretion to file such cases in either court; these are concurrent jurisdiction laws or prosecutorial waivers. "No hearing is held to determine which court is appropriate, and there may be no formal standards for deciding between them. The decision is entrusted entirely to the prosecutor" (p. 1).[29] In contrast to judicial waivers, prosecutors are not obligated to consider the best interests of the juvenile. Critics of prosecutorial transfers point to the possible political influence on juvenile transfers made by locally elected officials. They note that prosecutors can be pressured by "get tough" sentiment and transfer policy can vary geographically.[30] Additionally, prosecutors may be less apt to adhere to rehabilitative goals of the juvenile justice system.[31]

The efficacy of juvenile transfers can be based on the guiding principles of their use: deterrence, public safety, and retribution. The overriding philosophy of juvenile transfer laws is general and specific deterrence.[32] Research suggests, however, that transfer policies have little effect on deterrence. Time series analyses examining juvenile delinquency before and after implementation of punitive transfer policies show that these policies do not have a deterrent effect.[33,34,35] Research is also not supportive of waivers successfully reducing recidivism or protecting public safety. Bishop, Frazier, Lanza-Kaduce, and Winner matched juveniles transferred to the criminal system with juveniles handled in the juvenile system on offense seriousness, delinquent history, age, gender, and race to compare recidivism rates. They found the probability of re-arrest was greater, time to failure was shorter, and the subsequent offenses were more serious for the juveniles processed through the criminal justice system.[36]

In light of these findings, Sellers and Arrigo (2009) examined statutory exclusion and prosecutorial transfer laws from an ethical perspective. They concluded that the reasoning used by states and courts to support these types of waivers was in line with consequentialism (supporting the greater public good) and, to a lesser extent, deontology (a duty toward citizenry and juvenile responsibility) but not virtue ethics. The outcome, based on this ethical guidance, has been a process that fails to take into consideration the scientific research that supports developmental immaturity. This failure has led to a process that focuses on the nature of the offense over juvenile competency, neglects the extent that developmental immaturity is, "to a certain extent, the cause of violent crime and, correspondingly, how such causes affect the juvenile's legal decision-making abilities," fails to realize the impact of developmental immaturity on the juvenile's ability to participate in his or her own defense, and that reduces the likelihood of rehabilitation and pushes the juvenile toward becoming a "hardened career criminal" (p. 476).[37]

DISPROPORTIONATE MINORITY CONTACT

One of the most important issues facing the juvenile justice system is disproportionate minority contact (DMC), the overrepresentation of minority youth within the juvenile justice system. DMC has been addressed by social scientists as well as the federal government. Amendments made in 1988 (see 2002 amendment, to the Juvenile Justice and Delinquency Prevention (JJDP) Act of 1974) in part require that states investigate and address racial disparities. Additionally, the Office of Juvenile Justice and Delinquency Prevention (OJJDP), established in 1980, created the Disproportionate Minority Confinement, later renamed Disproportionate Minority Contact, (DMC) initiative in 1991 to assist states in meeting requirements to identify and reduce DMC.

Although there have been targeted measures taken at the state and national level to address and reduce DMC for more than two decades, minority juveniles continue to be referred, detained, placed, and waived to the criminal court at a higher rate than their representation in the general population.[38] This overrepresentation holds for each offense category. Conversely, a disparity exists where White juveniles are referred, detained, placed, and waived to the criminal court at a lower rate than their representation in the general population for all offenses. One factor that makes DMC analysis difficult, especially at the federal level, is that ethnicity is not included as a separate category; specifically, Hispanics are categorized by their race, which is typically white.

BOX 11.8

CLOSER LOOK/IN PRACTICE

JUVENILE JUSTICE AND DELINQUENCY PREVENTION as amended, Pub. L. No. 93-415 (1974)

JUVENILE JUSTICE AND DELINQUENCY PREVENTION ACT OF 2002

SUBCHAPTER II–PROGRAMS AND OFFICES PART B–FEDERAL ASSISTANCE FOR STATE AND LOCAL PROGRAMS [Title II]

42 U.S.C. 5633 [Sec. 223.] State plans

(a) Requirements

(22) address juvenile delinquency prevention efforts and system improvement efforts designed to reduce, without establishing or requiring numerical standards or quotas, the disproportionate number of juvenile members of minority groups, who come into contact with the juvenile justice system;

Although race is not officially designated as a mitigating or aggravating factor in juvenile justice decision making, other factors that are used to determine the degree of contact a juvenile has with the system are indirectly connected with race. Financial factors, parental status, employment, and school status are just some extra-legal factors that influence decision making. Juveniles who are negatively affected by these factors may appear to be a higher risk than others. Minority juveniles are overrepresented in each of these areas. While a decision maker does not specifically use the youth's race as a factor for a more punitive sentence, indirectly these factors often result in the same conclusion.

Traditionally, the cause of DMC is debated on differential involvement or differential treatment. The differential involvement perspective generally states that when legal factors, such as offense seriousness and criminal history, are considered, DMC is reduced. The resulting conclusion, from this perspective, is that minority youth commit a disproportionate amount of crime, and serious crime, and therefore are disproportionately represented in the juvenile justice system. Conversely, differential treatment perspective states that even when legal factors are controlled, race effects remain, indicating that the juvenile justice system treats minority youth differently. Further, differential treatment can be more subtle through cumulative effects of extra-legal factors affecting minority juvenile offenders. While extra legal factors may not be relevant to the current decision, if the juvenile has prior history, how can we account for the factors that played a part in previous decisions?

Regardless of the reasons, DMC continues to exist at unacceptable levels in many jurisdictions. Taking all research into consideration, there appears to be support for both differential involvement and differential treatment. Further, it seems equally apparent that DMC cannot be erased entirely at the system level[39] and also reflects differential offending patterns which point to deeper social problems. The highest rates of DMC are often found in urban neighborhoods, which are disproportionately home to youth who exhibit many of the oft-cited risk factors for juvenile delinquency, including, but not limited to, increased poverty, increased mobility, and decreased parental monitoring. The issue of DMC deserves a continued discussion and efforts aimed at solving the deeply rooted causes of racial inequality evident in the juvenile justice system.

Philosophies governing the creation of the juvenile justice system have not been obviated by the shift toward punitive policy in the 1980's through early 2000's. Diminished capacity, culpability, and room to reform remain the guiding characteristics when considering juvenile offenders. Developmental psychology and neuroscience support these fundamental characteristics in research findings that identify significant differences in juveniles' response to threats, assessment of risks, appreciation of long-term consequences, self-control, and judgment in comparison with adults.[40]

Many jurisdictions are moving toward a balanced approach of holding individuals responsible for their actions, addressing risk factors that increase the likelihood of delinquent involvement through treatment, and implementing preventative policy aimed at improving the lives of juveniles. Over a quarter of a century ago, it was recommended that the reduction of juvenile offending involve a long-term commitment to improving inner-city neighborhoods, providing adequate health care, improving living conditions of poor children, preventing child abuse, strengthening families, and reducing the number of unemployed youth.[41] Ethically and practically, these solutions cannot be the sole responsibility of the juvenile justice system. A holistic approach to juvenile offending that includes resources from local, state, and federal levels of government, as well as private business and community organizations, will go further than the juvenile justice court can achieve alone.

ENDNOTES

1. McCord, J., Widom, C.S., & Crowell, N.A. (Eds.). (2001). *Juvenile Crime Juvenile Justice: Panel on Juvenile Crime, Prevention, Treatment, and Control.* Washington, DC: National Academy Press.

2. Bernard, T.J., & Kurlychek, M.C. (2010). *The Cycle of Juvenile Justice.* Oxford: Oxford University Press.

3. National Conference of Commissioners on Uniform State Laws. (1968). *Uniform Juvenile Court Act.* Philadelphia: Author.

4. Champion, D.J. (2007). *The Juvenile Justice System: Delinquency, Processing, and the Law*, 5th ed. Upper Saddle River, NJ: Pearson.

5. Allen, T.T. (2005). Taking a juvenile into custody: Situational factors that influence police officers' decisions. *Journal of Sociology and Social Welfare* 32, 121–29.

6. Black, D.J., & Reiss, A. (1970). Police control of juveniles. *American Sociological Review* 35, 63–77.

7. Lundman, R. (1996). Extralegal variables and arrest. *Journal of Research in Crime and Delinquency* 33, 349–53.

8. Skolnick, J., & Fyfe, J. (1993). *Above the Law: Police and the Use of Force.* New York: Free Press.

9. Worden, R.E., & Shepard, R.L. (1996). Demeanor, crime, and police behavior: A reexamination of the police services study data. *Criminology* 34, 83–105.

10. Myers, S.M. (2004). Police encounters with juvenile suspects: Explaining the use of authority and provision of support, executive summary report. Washington, DC: U.S. Department of Justice.

11. Allen, T.T. (2005). Taking a juvenile into custody: Situational factors that influence police officers' decisions. *Journal of Sociology and Social Welfare* 32, 121–29.

12. Cox, S.M., Allen, J.M., Hanser, R.D., & Conrad, J.J. (2011). *Juvenile Justice: A Guide to Theory, Policy, and Practice.* Thousand Oaks, CA: Sage.

13. Agnew, R. (1992). Foundation for a general strain theory of crime and delinquency. *Criminology* 30, 47–88.

14. Cox, S.M., Allen, J.M., Hanser, R.D., & Conrad, J.J. (2011). *Juvenile Justice: A Guide to Theory, Policy, and Practice.* Thousand Oaks, CA: Sage.

15. Mulvey, E.P., & Iselin, A.-M. R. (2008). Improving professional judgments of risk and amenability in juvenile justice. *Future of Children* 18, 35–57.

16. Caldwell, M.F., & Dickinson, C. (2009). Sex offender registration and recidivism risk in juvenile sexual offenders. *Behavior Sciences and the Law* 27, 941–56.

17. Caldwell, M.F., & Dickinson, C. (2009). Sex offender registration and recidivism risk in juvenile sexual offenders. *Behavior Sciences and the Law* 27, 941–56.

18. Zimring, F.E., Piquero, A.R., & Jennings, W.G. (2007). Sexual delinquency in Racine: Does early sex offending predict later sex offending in youth and young adulthood? *Criminology & Public Policy* 6, 507–534.

19. Letourneau, E.J., & Armstrong, K.S. (2008). Recidivism rates for registered and nonregistered juvenile sexual offenders. *Sexual Abuse: A Journal of Research and Treatment* 20, 393–408.

20. Caldwell, M.F., & Dickinson, C. (2009). Sex offender registration and recidivism risk in juvenile sexual offenders. *Behavior Sciences and the Law* 27, 941–56.

21. Zimring, F.E., Piquero, A.R., & Jennings, W.G. (2007). Sexual delinquency in Racine: Does early sex offending predict later sex offending in youth and young adulthood? *Criminology & Public Policy* 6, 507–534.

22. Calley, N.G. (2008). Juvenile sex offenders and sex offender legislation: Unintended consequences. *Federal Probation* 72, 37–41.

23. Nellis, A. (2012). *The Lives of Juvenile Lifers: Findings from a National Study*. Washington, DC: The Sentencing Project. http://sentencingproject.org/doc/publications/jj_The_Lives_of_Juvenile_Lifers.pdf

24. Fagan, J., & Deschenes, E.P. (1990). Determinants of judicial waiver decisions for violent juvenile offenders. *Journal of Criminal Law and Criminology* 81, 314–47.

25. Redding, R.E. (2008). *Juvenile Justice Transfer Laws: An Effective Deterrent to Delinquency?* Washington, DC: U.S. Department of Justice, Office of Justice Programs, Office of Juvenile Justice and Delinquency Prevention.

26. Mears, D.P. (2002). Sentencing guidelines and the transformation of juvenile justice in the 21st century. *Journal of Contemporary Criminal Justice* 18, 6–19.

27. Burrow, J. (2008). Reverse waiver and the effects of legal, statutory, and secondary legal factors on sentencing outcomes for juvenile offenders. *Crime and Delinquency* 54, 34–64.

28. Feld, B.C. (2004). Juvenile transfer. *Criminology and Public Policy* 3, 599–604.

29. Griffin, P., Addie, S., Adams, B., & Firestine, K. (2011). *Trying Juveniles as Adults: An Analysis of State Transfer Laws and Reporting*. Washington, DC: US Department of Justice, Office of Juvenile Justice and Delinquency Prevention.

30. Feld, B.C. (2004). Juvenile transfer. *Criminology and Public Policy* 3, 599–604.

31. Pagnanelli, E. (2007). Children as adults: The transfer of juveniles to adult courts and the potential impact of Roper v. Simmons. *The American Criminal Law Review* 44, 175–94.

32. Redding, R.E. (2008). *Juvenile Justice Transfer Laws: An Effective Deterrent to Delinquency?* Washington, DC: U.S. Department of Justice, Office of Justice Programs, Office of Juvenile Justice and Delinquency Prevention.

33. Jensen, E.L., & Metsger, L.K. (1994). A test of the deterrent effect of legislative waiver on violent juvenile crime. *Crime and Delinquenc,* 40, 96–104.

34. Steiner, B., & Wright, E. (2006). Assessing the relative effects of state direct file waiver laws on violent juvenile crime: Deterrence or irrelevance? *The Journal of Criminal Law and Criminology* 96, 1451–77.

35. Steiner, B., Hemmens, C., & Bell, V. (2006). Legislative waiver reconsidered: General deterrent effects of statutory exclusion laws enacted post-1979. *Justice Quarterly* 23, 34–59.

36. Bishop, D.M., Frazier, D.E., Lanza-Kaduce, L., & Winner, L. (1996). The transfer of juveniles to criminal court: Does it make a difference? *Crime and Delinquency* 42, 171–91.

37. Sellers, B.G., & Arrigo, B.A. (2009). Adolescent transfer, developmental maturity, and adjudicative competence: An ethical and justice policy inquiry. *Criminology* 99, 435–87.

38. Puzzanchera, C., Sladky, A., & Kang, W. (n.d.). *Easy Access to Juvenile Populations: 1990–2008*. Washington, DC: US Department of Justice, Office of Juvenile Justice and Delinquency Prevention. Online: www.ojjdp.ncjrs.gov/ojstatbb/ezapop/

39. Kempf-Leonard, K. (2007). Minority youths and juvenile justice: Disproportionate minority contact after nearly 20 years of reform efforts. *Youth Violence and Juvenile Justice* 5, 71–87.

40. Bishop, D.M. (2004). Injustice and irrationality in contemporary youth policy. *Criminology and Public Policy* 3, 633–44.

41. Schwartz, I. (1986, June 19). *Testimony before the House Subcommittee on Human Resources.* In *Oversight hearing on the Juvenile Justice and Delinquency Prevention Act: Hearing before the Subcommittee on Human Resources of the Committee on Education and Labor, House of Representatives, Ninety-ninth Congress, Second session.* Washington, DC: GPO.

Racial Discrimination in the Criminal Justice System[1]

CHAPTER 12

> "We pledge ourselves to liberate all our people from the continuing bondage of poverty, deprivation, suffering, gender, and other discrimination."
>
> —*Nelson Mandela*

For a brief moment, as she stood silently at the podium at the funeral of Jesse "Duke" Smith, a young black teen killed in a retaliatory drive-by shooting in Chicago's horrific cycle of on-and-off violence, Ameena Matthews looked burdened. She exhaled and shook her head, pausing, almost in disbelief that the crowd of grieving young men and women attending the funeral had worn the red colors associated with "Duke" Smith's gang. Yet her background—as daughter to notorious El Rukn gang leader Jeff Fort, as a one-time gang member herself, as spectator to Englewood, Chicago's violent past—betrayed any sense of extreme desperation, as though she had been through many moments of disbelief before. "My brothers . . . ," she pleaded, "whatever it is that's going on . . . cease the fire, call a truce," and with the wisdom of years and experience ahead of the teenage crowd assembled in front of her, tried to reason with the often unreasonable, and tried to heal wounds that struggle to heal (PBS, 2012).

The Interrupters, a documentary film chronicling Matthews's and other Cease Fire Chicago volunteers' efforts to stop violence among Chicago's young urban youth, led to increased public discussion (and scrutiny) of programs such as Cease Fire's which act as alternatives to traditional methods of grappling with youth and gang violence in America. In effect, the film made a celebrity out of Matthews and other volunteers, portraying them as energetic, personable, and caring pillars of the Chicago community struggling against violence's insurmountable odds. But within a year, the City of Chicago had abandoned the Cease Fire program, as the promising but often-controversial outreach effort was replaced with more traditional police investigation tactics (Childress, 2013). The unhealed wounds seemed to stay unhealed once again.

What Matthews and the Cease Fire volunteers, the Chicago Police who replaced them in their anti-violence effort, and countless other police, criminal justice professionals, activists, and ordinary citizens across the United States are engaged in is an effort to heal wounds that have festered since the very first African became an African American, whenever that event may have been, and wherever it took place. Our national identity has been fatefully intertwined with the identities of individuals whose ancestors arrived before us, from places like Italy and Germany and Japan and China, but also the kingdoms of Mali, and Dahomey, and Guinea, to use the names of less modern nation-states. Race is intertwined with our national identity by design; but racial discrimination need not be.

The histories of African-American communities have long intersected with the criminal justice system at points across a long trajectory, from the earliest days of slavery in the Colonial Era to the contemporary issues of the modern struggle for equality. The criminal justice apparatus (courts, corrections, and policing) are a forum for examining the process of healing wounds—of becoming more American, perhaps, but not forgetting injustices and wrongs perpetrated, and negotiating the pain that lingers, and advancing beyond the self-preservation impulses that seem to pit different ethnic groups against each other in the United States. No chapter, no book, no lesson or course could adequately address all of the issues pertaining to the history of racial discrimination in the American criminal justice system. But this chapter intends to examine racial discrimination in the American criminal justice system by examining a metaphor, by examining *wounds*, how they were perpetrated in our national past, and how wounds may be *healed*, and how the healing process has occurred alongside further wounding. The ebb and flow of wounding and healing of our national character, our "body" if you will, is the subject of this examination of racial discrimination.

Wounds may be self-perpetrated, or may occur from some outside force—as in many instances of racial discrimination and upset (perhaps the murder of "Duke" Smith was one). But the long history of racial injustices thrust upon African-American citizens can be portrayed as a wounding to a body, and of an ever-present and procedural manner by which these wounds are healed and the body restored. Consider the impulse of reading a chapter about racial discrimination in the American criminal justice system, and how such a reading may generate fear, expectation, pride, and many other emotions captured in the long story of Black America. The legacy of racial discrimination over hundreds of years or more, and the impact of that legacy on criminal justice as a field of study, is intertwined with and indicated by flashpoints, of opportunities and events where wounds occurred, and where healing took place.

The manner by which events, statistics, and examples of "wounding" and "healing" have been chosen for discussion here involved assessing which specific events tell the greater story of racial discrimination as a process, and how that process becomes embedded within the social history of the nation, generating change and the impetus to heal. Some wounds are in the form of statistics, some are in the form of events; many instances of healing are reform movements, new policies, and opportunities to revise the story of discrimination. The impression of change generated by this metaphor is that African-American racial discrimination is intertwined with the criminal justice apparatus as an influential force for two-way legitimacy: Black America has often needed the positive reinforcement of the criminal justice system to support its legitimacy, and the criminal justice system often fails to be seen as legitimate to the public as it has discriminated. The issue of legitimacy is at the heart of this discussion.

WOUNDS OF DISCRIMINATION

The Trial of Roy Bryant and John William Milam, Sumner, Mississippi, September 1955

Although the death of Chicago teenager Emmitt Till can serve as the critical backdrop from which many potential flashpoints of racial discrimination can be drawn, the trial of the two persons accused of his murder resonates deepest as a reflection of the severity of the principles by which Jim Crow existed, and the opportunities for change that occurred. Till, 14 years of age and a visitor to sharecropper Mississippi from streetwise Chicago, did not comprehend the inappropriateness of accosting a white woman, a transgression that resulted in his being abducted from the home of his great-uncle, Mose Wright, and murdered. The story of Emmitt Till's abduction and murder still resonates with the American public over 50 years later; Jim Crow was reinforced by popular culture, economic dislocation, geographic isolation, and disfranchisement (Litwack, 1997). But at the trial of the two men charged with Emmitt Till's murder, Roy Bryant and John William Milam, startling events took place which served as the foundation for generations of outcry and redemption. For example, the audacity of Wright himself in identifying Bryant as Till's abductor by pointing at him, and giving verbal indication to the court by saying "there he is," represents a watershed moment in the self-confidence of African Americans in trusting the integrity of the criminal justice system (Whitfield, 1991). This unique event has been portrayed as an indication of a severe generational rift with regards to Black Americans and their refusal to be intimidated by violence, and as a singular ethical moment in the history of human oppression (Mitchell, 2007). Beito & Beito (2009) attest that, despite the knowledge that the two accused were guilty, the jury declined to punish either man with death or life imprisonment, exposing another inherent flaw in the court system that later served as a flashpoint for ethical reform. Despite the acquittal by an all-white jury, the trial stands as an early example of the manner by which African Americans were willing to invest attention into learning their citizenship rights to dismantle kangaroo-court systems that reinforced racial discrimination. The Bryant-Milam trial still reverberates in the legacy of later trials of note: the O.J. Simpson criminal trial in 1995, the Angela Davis trial in 1972, and the George Zimmerman trial in 2012. It stands as the primary example of a nation's mismanagement of the earliest legacy of slavery as the United States struggled to determine how best to function under new rules and in uncharted ethical waters.

MOVE and the Philadelphia Police Department, 1985

The troubled relationship between African-American citizens of Philadelphia, Pennsylvania, and their city government and police department has been well-documented in multiple incidents of mistrust and anger, from the Mumia Abu-Jamal case to the current attention to strengthening police tactics in the "flash mob" era championed by Mayor Michael Nutter (Anderson & Hevenor, 1990; Boyette & Boyette, 2013; Simon, 2011). Disbelief, misrepresentation, corruption, and anguish have characterized the long history of Philadelphia's criminal justice system, and is reflected in one profound event which sent shock waves throughout the Black community. Long a notorious and increasingly difficult thorn in the side of neighbors and police alike, the MOVE organization (a loosely-defined activist group with an ambiguous political agenda) was involved in an armed standoff with Philadelphia police in 1978, resulting in the death of one officer and subsequent arrest and conviction of several of the organization's members. By the mid-1980's, the relationship between the organization and the police had reached a boiling point, and when the police attempted to arrest several members of the group for various indictments at their townhome in West Philadelphia, another standoff occurred. This time, however, police dropped 2 bombs on the roof of the house, igniting a blaze that engulfed and destroyed 50 homes and killed 11 MOVE members (Anderson & Hevenor, 1990). Local and national outcry was swift in blaming police for inappropriate use of force. MOVE appeared as folk heroes to many African-American citizens who decried overreaching police tactics and coercion, similar to how the 1993 Branch Davidian siege at Waco, Texas, galvanized public opinion regardless of the esoteric and unpopular beliefs of the fringe group involved. But as to whether or not MOVE was simply a "radical chic" organization using their platform for opportunistic political attention or a legitimate group of revolutionaries bent on instigating armed confrontation, the event exposed significant divisions between the city government and the Philadelphia Police and the African-American community at large. It also acted as a rallying point for significant reform of police tactics and outreach in the pre-community policing era, and can be said to have led to increased calls for political representation as well as police workforce reform (Boyette & Boyette, 2013). The wound opened by the MOVE incident in Philadelphia was not restricted to the city's Black residents and exposed a deepening frustration with the evolution of police tactics in the United States.

Arthur McDuffie and the Outcry for Police Reform in Miami, 1980

The city of Miami, Florida, is somewhat unique among large American cities with respect to the populations of Black citizens and their relationship to the police department. The city is largely diffuse, physically spread among disparate neighborhoods, and reflective of multiple ethnicities that have immigrated to Miami over years of settlement. In 1979, Arthur McDuffie, a 33-year-old Black insurance salesman riding his motorcycle at high rates of speed, was pursued by several police vehicles and subsequently beaten to death as he fled on foot (Porter & Dunn, 1984). McDuffie was found to have had a suspended driver's license and an array of traffic citations, but largely was seen as a somewhat successful middle-class businessman whose beating took on a more significant tone in the post-Civil Rights Era. The officers, all of whom had prior records of multiple citizen complaints, were indicted for manslaughter and the trial moved to the city of Tampa for fear of civil unrest. But by the time the trial had begun in the spring of 1980, significant changes to the social fabric of the city of Miami had occurred: the growing Cuban population of the city had exploded with the Mariel Boatlift which persisted throughout the trial itself. When the officers were acquitted by an all-White-male jury in May, 1980, the pressure-cooker environment endemic to Miami's poor African-American population exploded into street violence. As in other cases of spontaneous civil unrest, the degree to which infringements upon the slim amount of political and economic power held by Miami's Black citizens translated into rage and perceptions of injustice are unclear. But it is significant that the riots that followed the McDuffie verdict occurred in tandem with an influx of over 100,000 Cubans to the city of Miami (Driscoll, 2005). The violence that tore through Miami's Liberty City and Overtown areas left ruins, but offered a greater outcry against police use of force and set the stage for an even larger event a decade later in Los Angeles with the Rodney King incident. In addition, the riots further wounded an already tenuous relationship between the police and the Black urban poor in Miami, a city with a complex patchwork of escalating racial upheaval. It was a critical bridge between the unrest of the civil rights years and the more stringent outrage of a subsequent era.

Sentencing Disparities Identified

The perception that capital punishment represented a pillar of racial discrimination in the United States was an intriguing discussion point from the post-Civil Rights Era. Yet in the absence of empirical evidence, the implication appeared presumptuous and rhetorical. After the establishment of the criminal justice research apparatus in the 1980's and its increasing focus on issues of social justice, research supporting the thesis that sentencing outcomes were a product of racial discrimination began to appear. Beginning in the field of sociology (Radelet, 1981) and extending to government monographs (US GAO, 1990), data demonstrated a number of salient outcomes pertaining to racial disparities in sentencing, particularly for capital punishment cases. Evidence pointing to racial disparity was widely noted across different geographic locations, cases, data sets, and using a variety of statistical controls (Baldus et al., 1998). But even more interestingly, and particularly wounding to the psyche of African Americans, was the evidence that the court perception of a defendant's "blackness" affected the severity of punishment. More pronounced stereotypically "Black" physical features of a defendant (i.e., larger lips or darker skin) resulted in a higher likelihood of a sentence of death (Eberhardt et al., 2004; Eberhardt et al., 2006). These and other studies led to greater public outcry against the perceived racism inherent in death sentencing and helped mobilize opposition to such sentences and a general demand for sentencing reform as mandatory minimum sentencing began to strain the psyche of African-American citizens.

The Prison-Industrial Complex and Mass Incarceration

Hand in hand with the focus on sentencing disparity was a concurrent outcry against the pervasiveness of the incapacitation function of correctional policy that began in the early 1990's. From disparate sources such as popular culture (Levitt, 1990), to the dual focus on the effect of prison proliferation on disadvantaged communities (Eason, 2010), to the racial injustices of sentencing fueling prison populations (Fulcher, 2012), empirical studies of racial discrimination in corrections policy began to examine the racial incapacitation effect. The prison-industrial complex began to be more defined, and appeared as a cooperative effort between business investment, private industry, and state control to use prisons as an outsource opportunity for exploitative labor and retributive justice (Herzing & Burch, 2003). A particular point in regards to the existence of a prison industrial apparatus was concern over disproportionate representation of African Americans in the War on Drugs policies which brought about stiff mandatory-minimum sentencing in the 1990's (Mitchell & Lynch, 2011). The prison-industrial complex had its original detractors in Angela Davis and other 1970's critics of criminal justice policy, but the steep rise in incarceration rates throughout the 1990's, especially for nonviolent drug offenses, allowed African-American communities to reflect on the damage being done to their communities by incarceration policy. Adding to that mix was the steep crime drop of the 1990's which can be partially attributed to the incapacitation dimensions of corrections policy (Levvitt, 1990).

A 1998 *Howard Law Journal* editorial goes as far as to suggest that the prison-industrial complex represented a new form of slavery for African Americans based upon disproportionate and exploitatively punitive policies comparative to the Black Codes of the Reconstruction Era (Howard Law Journal, 1998). A more subtle wound is effected when the GEO Group, a multinational corporation profiting from prison construction, proposes purchasing naming rights to a college football stadium (an idea that was abandoned in 2013 due to public outcry) (Kirkham, 2013). But no greater evidence of the wounds brought by incarceration on African-American communities exists than incarceration policy's effect on the physical structure of communities themselves by removing massive numbers of African-American males from positions of family authority, as potential leaders in their communities, as potential husbands and fathers, and as the cornerstone of modern Black America (Smith & Hattery, 2010). It is easy to draw parallels between the incapacitation effect of current United States incarceration policy and the prison-industrial complex, and the legacy of African slavery that ravaged African civilizations by extracting men for slave labor from their communities in the years of colonial rule in Africa. At the very least, the legitimacy of the criminal justice system's role in rehabilitating offenders is questioned in light of these controversies.

Each of these examples of wounds on the psyche of Black America, brought by the system which purports to protect the well-being and lives of all American citizens, are difficult to defend given the long past of exploitation, institutional and legal discrimination, and unkept promises. Self-inflicted wounds nonwithstanding, it is apparent that attempts to resolve these difficult and debilitating challenges have consumed Black America and its politics, family dynamic, motivation for social progress, and psychological attention for generations. As the criminal justice apparatus slowly rectifies past wrongs, it appears as though the process of healing is continuous.

HEALING THE WOUNDS OF DISCRIMINATION

Recruitment and Training for Diversity in Criminal Justice

The city of Austin, Texas, is a likely forum for one of the more innovative police training programs of recent years, given its seat as the state capitol and being home to the state's flagship public university. Austin can be said to garner a degree of community diversity and understanding that creates programs like the Community Immersion Project, created in 2004 to strengthen community policing efforts and establish a bond between new police recruits and the communities they would be serving. The program, which has been replicated in other forms in multiple other police departments since 2004, places police recruits into community subgroups (African-American citizens, Latino or Hispanic, handicapped, deaf citizens, homeless, and others) in order to sensitize recruits to the specific policing needs of these communities. In many ways, concrete changes in cadet attitudes about the groups has occurred, leading to increased community involvement by police and impressionable cooperation on the part of the subgroups in acting as community stakeholders (Adickes, 2009). The Austin Community Immersion program is but one method used since the advent of the community policing era to grapple with the concern that policing, a historically White male profession, failed to recruit individuals into roles where the community itself needed representation. The issue of recruiting for diversity (among African Americans but also with other community subgroups) is seen as supportive of transparency, police legitimacy among the community, and as a concrete effort to implement the community-policing model by altering the character of police organizations (Irlbeck, 2008; Orrick, 2008).

Observing Police Behavior and Constructing Police Legitimacy

Police empirical scholarship, for an extended period of time in the 1990's, was heavily focused on the phenomenon of racial profiling. Critical analyses of police traffic stop behavior illustrated the degree to which police struggled with balancing a need for fighting crime using statistical data and the need to respect and treat community members with equity (Smith & Petrocelli, 2001). In the 2010's, these concerns have not dissipated, but have instead formed the foundation for what might be called the "police legitimacy movement," a comprehensive focus on the purpose of police policies that prohibit discrimination, as opposed to the mechanics of the policies themselves (Mentel, 2012; Tyler, 2004). Police legitimacy scholarship has cast light on the methodologies employed by police departments in conducting their own internal assessments of racial bias, even leading to the examination and development of technologies and tools which augment existing recordkeeping to provide real-time analysis (Barnum, & Perfetti, 2010). The phenomenon of concern over legitimacy—over whether or not police strategies, tactics, programs, and organizational character are seen as lawful and binding with communities—links to procedural justice movements in that it underscores community transparency, participation in decision making, and involvement in creating and enhancing trust (PERF, 2014). A recent program in the New Orleans Police Department illustrates the stake African-American communities can now play in helping to steer the course of police policy so that it better represents their unique community need (PERF, 2014).

Government Oversight and Investigation into Police Civil Rights Violations

In much the same way that civil lawsuits act as a check-and-balance mechanism for police tactics and policy, civil rights investigations and consent decrees, while embarrassing and hurtful to police and community morale, have been able to unearth fundamental causes of racial discrimination rooted in police organizations and assist in adopting new policies and procedures to avert future crises. A 2013 PERF report illustrates multiple large urban police departments which have endured such processes (many of which can take nearly a decade to conclude) in order to establish legitimacy with the public (PERF, 2013). These are not frivolous events and can be all-encompassing to the police leadership, structure, and workforce, and can label a community or department over time in negative ways. But the manner by which some departments treat civil rights investigations as opportunities for growth and partnership underscores the degree to which African-American communities wield a great deal of political power in driving police reform. The term "constitutional policing" is an outgrowth of these events, a way to ensure that all community subgroups are treated with fairness and equity under the law.

NOBLE: Plugging a Leadership Void

A police chief, leader, or executive is not merely a symbolic figurehead in a police organization. The chief sets the stage for the organization's overall mission, directs the personnel landscape and recruitment, negotiates budgets, and determines the overall public tone of the organization by acting as its public face. When the public face of that organization is an individual who is a representative of that jurisdiction's character and population, symbolic leadership may produce feelings of legitimacy and authority (Holdaway & O'Neill, 2004). The organization NOBLE (National Organization of Black Law Enforcement Executives) is an organization committed to training, executive development, and advancement of African-American police leaders. It is but one example of current efforts to fill a long-standing organizational void in police leadership.

Dismantling the Prison-Industrial Complex

In her book *The New Jim Crow*, Alexander (2012) lays partial blame for the problem of mass incarceration at the foot of civil rights leadership. In a stunning indictment of corrections policy as well as efforts to heal the wounds of incapacitation's effect on Black communities, Alexander states that an inherent classism prevents some civil rights advocates from being as ethically determined to dismantle the machinery of mass incarceration as they are in turning their attention towards more high-profile civil rights campaigns. Alexander has outlined a larger problem with regard to incarceration policy and its effect on African-American communities: if there is no comprehensive vision for reforming the system itself because persons who are incarcerated are "forgotten" and are seen as expendable, then the incapacitation state and its associated business interests will continue to proceed unabated. When we collectively despise convicted criminals as a society, how can any group spend time or resources caring about the symbolism of race-based incarceration efforts which damage communities long-term?

Alexander makes an interesting point about the fight against racial inequality by critiquing affirmative action programs, which she believes stunt growth and concern for the racial effects of criminal justice race-based inequality (Alexander, 2012). She implies that, in order for our society to come to terms definitively with the racial discrimination inherent in criminal justice policy, interest in reform must be stimulated by self-empowerment. Therefore, when the discussion of the negative impacts of incapacitation ensues, a greater fear about the implications of inequality is exposed. This thesis is supported by myriad efforts to address the incarceration epidemic, most notably the push for restorative justice embedded within community corrections (VERA, 2013). Programs like the Cease Fire Chicago movement are a by-product of the approach to reimagining the role of corrections in modern society. Originating in the high-crime years of 1980's America, mass incarceration implied a zero-tolerance, "fed up" mentality on the part of citizens, voters, and communities. What Alexander seems to be saying is that the time has come for people to be more "fed up" with the policies which place people behind bars for nonviolent crime and summarily destroy communities, and less angry at the acts of the supposed criminals which ensure their incarceration. When many of these acts are nonviolent, it creates an entirely new corrections apparatus that can create new ethical principles based on fairness, equity, legitimacy, and the desire to rehabilitate offenders.

The End of "Black America"?

Underscoring Alexander's frustration with civil rights leadership which has either subconsciously or intentionally turned their backs on the urban poor who find themselves victims of incarceration policy is the belief that, at least statistically, the "Black community" as it has been commonly known has changed dramatically. Fundamental differences between different segments of African Americans have shed light on the fragmented social, economic, and political nature of Black America. Out of either convenience, or misunderstanding, or simplicity of analysis, the myth that African Americans are more similar than they are disparate has persisted and endangers a more comprehensive understanding of what exactly constitutes a population subgroup at all. Robinson's *Dis-Integration* (2010) raises the possibility that four distinct groups of African Americans represent different backgrounds, goals, income levels, lifestyles, political attitudes, and attitudes toward what constitutes "civil rights." It is therefore difficult to construct simplistic one-size-fits-all solutions for the mythical universal "Black community" if in fact multiple types of communities exist.

Robinson has articulated a growing concern over simplistic designations in social science analysis, policy evaluation, and in movements for political empowerment. By raising the possibility that south-central Los Angeles, for example, is an entirely different form of "Black community" than the Atlanta suburbs, where large swaths of middle and upper-class Black families reside, Robinson renders discussions of universal solutions to the issues reflected above suspect. In keeping with our metaphor, perhaps certain African-American communities are wounded differently by different events and exposed truths than others. This would support Alexander's assertion that certain African Americans simply do not care about the massive Black incarceration rate *simply because the prisoners are Black too*.

This is an intriguing and promising theoretical development in social science research, and a consideration that has important implications for the study of criminal justice as well as how we frame arguments of racial discrimination. Is it possible that some subset of "Black America" is affected disproportionately by the wounds we have outlined than others, leading to different strategies and programs for healing? Let us consider examples we have raised so far in this section. Arthur McDuffie was relatively middle-class and a successful businessman, yet his death and the trial of police officers that followed led to dissatisfaction and unrest with a significantly lower-class population in Miami than he occupied. Mass incarceration as examined by Alexander is a relatively class-based phenomenon, yet the mechanisms of civil rights leadership and change that can effect a transformation in policy are largely reliant on the media-driven and well-funded core of establishment civil rights organizations. NOBLE, one of the most important indications of the ascendancy of Black Americans to positions of power in policing in America, is composed of leadership drawn from varieties of police agencies, from large jurisdictions to small, and rural to urban. Finally, Austin's community immersion program would probably not be nearly as effective "immersing" police recruits in middle-class Black neighborhoods in order to sensitize future police officers to the unique needs of Austin's Black community. It appears that multiple ways of seeing community problems brought about by Robinson's interesting thesis can expand horizons and develop future policy by better defining who is affected by discrimination, and who responds.

THE HEALING PROCESS REVISITED

It is often a cliché to refer continually to the 1960's civil rights struggle in an effort to determine how African-American communities in America have struggled with the legacies of racial discrimination. However, the time period immediately after the civil rights years, from the late 1960's to 1970's, best represents the hidden phase of the civil rights struggle because of the explicit focus on political and economic empowerment that took place during that time. An important documentary film focusing on this era, *The Black Power Mixtape*, contains period interviews with 1970's civil rights activists as they tried to bring the civil rights movement home and use its lessons to reshape criminal justice policy through a new form of legal struggle in the 1970's. This forgotten era, in which the fringe elements such as the Black Panther Party coexisted and consorted with the mainstream of American politics as exemplified by the first Black mayoral candidates, is a critical venue to study the importance of healing the wounds of discrimination. In the 1970's, activists such as Angela Davis, Huey Newton, and Bobby Seale and their messages were battered and wounded by the criminal justice apparatus which pursued them; however, this apparatus had suddenly been changed by the small victories of urban renewal and the Black political empowerment movement. An interview with Angela Davis herself in the documentary demonstrates the extreme difficulties of making sense of the legacies of the civil rights struggle in this environment. As Davis answers a reporter's questions about her supposed advocacy of violence, which at the time appear in contrast to mainstream acceptance, she looks down frustratingly, away from the camera, as she realizes the impossibility of relating her perspective on violence ingrained from her youth experiences with the discrimination and chaos brought by Jim Crow (*The Black Power Mixtape*, 2011). The long pause given by her inability to find the words to relate the meaning and metaphor of violence, and her statement that people who criticize Black activists for advocating violence "have absolutely no idea what Black people have gone through," is a moment of reflection on the various ways in which the criminal justice system wounds those who often struggle to find ways to heal (*The Black Power Mixtape*, 2011).

Just as Ameena Matthews struggled with the disbelief of seeing "Duke" Smith's friends and peers arrive at his funeral in gang colors, so too did Angela Davis struggle with the challenge of relating the extreme violence endured by African Americans during the Jim Crow era to a reporter. Both poignant moments on film demonstrate the manner by which generations of African Americans have struggled within and without in an effort to reshape the societal and political foundation which allowed for discrimination and institutionalized racism. It is a slow and deliberate path that has been walked by a great many generations, yet continues to be a pathway of healing toward new understandings.

REFERENCES AND FURTHER READING

Adickes, J. (2009). The Community Immersion Program: Building relationships. *FBI Law Enforcement Bulletin*, 16-20.

Alexander, M. (2012). *The New Jim Crow: Mass Incarceration in the Age of Colorblindness*. New York, NY: The New Press.

Anderson, J., & Hevenor, H. (1990). *Burning Down the House: MOVE and the Tragedy of Philadelphia*. New York, NY: Norton Publishers.

Baldus, D.C., Woodworth, G., Zuckerman, D., Weiner, N.A., & Broffitt, B. (1998). Racial discrimination and the death penalty in the post-Furman era: An empirical and legal overview, with recent findings from Philadelphia. *Cornell Law Review, 83*, 1638-1770.

Barnum, C. & Perfetti, R.L. (2010). Race-sensitive choices by police officers in traffic stop encounters. *Police Quarterly, 13* (2), 180-208.

Beito, D. & Beito, L. (2009). *Black Maverick: T. R. M. Howard's Fight for Civil Rights and Economic Power*. Chicago, IL: University of Illinois Press.

Boyette, M. & Boyette, R. (2013). *Let It Burn: MOVE, the Philadelphia Police Department, and the Confrontation that Changed a City*. Philadelphia, PA: Quadrant Books.

Childress, S. (2013, October 17). Chicago drops Cease Fire from anti-violence strategy. *PBS Frontline*. Retrieved April 22, 2014, from http://www.pbs.org/wgbh/pages/frontline/social-issues/interrupters/chicago-drops-ceasefire-from-anti-violence-strategy/

Driscoll, A. (2005, May 15). The McDuffie riots 25 years later. *Miami Herald*. Retrieved May 1, 2014, from http://www.housingissues.org/floridacdc/articles/050515-1.html

Eason, J. (2010). Mapping prison proliferation: Region, rurality, race, and disadvantage in prison placement. *Social Science Research, 39*, 1015–1028.

Eberhardt, J.L., Goff, P.A., Purdie, V.J., & Davies, P.G. (2004). Seeing black: Race, crime, and visual processing. *Journal of Personality and Social Psychology, 87*, 876–893.

Eberhardt, J.L., Davies, P.G., Purdie-Vaughns, V.J., & Johnson, S.L. (2006). Looking deathworthy: Perceived stereotypicality of black defendants predicts capital-sentencing outcomes. *Psychological Science, 17*(5), 383–386.

Fulcher, P.A. (2012). Hustle & flow: Prison privatization fueling the prison industrial complex. *Washburn Law Journal, 51*(3), 589–617.

Herzing, R. & Burch, M. (2003). Challenging the prison-industrial complex. *USA Today, 132*, pp. 22.

Holdaway, S. & O'Neill, M. (2004). The development of black police associations: Changing articulations of race within the police. *British Journal of Criminology, 44*(6), 854–865.

Howard University Law Journal (1998). The prison industrial complex: A modern justification for African enslavement? (Editorial). *Howard Law Journal, 41*(2), 349–381.

Irlbeck, D. (2008). Latino police officers: Patterns of ethnic self-identity and Latino community attachment. *Police Quarterly, 11*(4), 468–495.

Kirkham, C. (2013, April 2). GEO Group stadium deal is off; Private prison company cites "ongoing distraction" after protests. *Huffington Post*. Retrieved May 22, 2014 from http://www.huffingtonpost.com/2013/04/02/geo-group-stadium-private-prison_n_2999133.html

Levitt, S.D. (2004). Understanding why crime fell in the 1990s: Four factors that explain the decline and six that do not. *Journal of Economic Perspectives, 18*(1), 163–190.

Litwack, L. F. (1999). *Trouble in Mind: Black Southerners in the Age of Jim Crow*. New York, NY: Vintage Books.

Mentel, Z. (2012, August). *Racial Reconciliation, Truth-telling, and Police Legitimacy*. Washington, DC: United States Department of Justice, Office of Community Oriented Policing Services.

Mitchell, J. (2007, February 19). Re-examining Emmitt Till case could help separate fact, fiction. *USA Today*. Retrieved May 2, 2014 from http://usatoday30.usatoday.com/news/nation/2007-02-18-till-legends_x.htm

Mitchell, O. & M.J. Lynch (2011). Criminal justice, race, and the War on Drugs. In N. Parsons-Pollard (Ed.), *Disproportionate Minority Contact: Current Issues and Policies* (pp. 139–155). Durham, NC: Carolina Academic Press.

Orrick, W.D. (2008). *Recruitment, Retention, and Turnover of Police Personnel: Reliable, Practical, and Effective Solutions*. Springfield, IL: Charles C. Thomas Publishers.

Police Executive Research Forum (PERF) (2013, July). *Civil Rights Investigations of Local Police: Lessons Learned*. Washington, DC: Police Executive Research Forum. Retrieved April 2, 2014 from http://www.policeforum.org/assets/docs/Critical_Issues_Series/civil%20rights%20investigations%20of%20local%20police%20-%20lessons%20learned%202013.pdf

Police Executive Research Forum (PERF) (2014, March). *Legitimacy and Procedural Justice: The New Orleans Case Study*. Washington, DC.: Police Executive Research Forum. Retrieved April 2, 2014 from http://www.policeforum.org/assets/docs/Free_Online_Documents/Leadership/legitimacy%20and%20procedural%20justice%20-%20the%20new%20orleans%20case%20study.pdf

Porter, B. & Dunn, M. (1984). *The Miami Riot of 1980: Crossing the Bounds*. Lanham, MD: Lexington Books.

Public Broadcasting Service (PBS) (2012). *Frontline: The Interrupters*. Film, retrieved April 24, 2014 at http://www.pbs.org/wgbh/pages/frontline/interrupters/

Radelet, M.L. (1981). Racial characteristics and the imposition of the death penalty. *American Sociological Review, 46*, 918–927.

Simon, D. (2011, August 7). Mayor blasts violent flash mobs. *Philadelphia Inquirer*. Retrieved June1,2014fromhttp://articles.philly.com/2011-08-07/news/29861647_1_young-people-flash-mobs-immaculate-conception

Smith, E. & Hattery, A.J. (2010). African American men and the prison industrial complex. *Western Journal of Black Studies, 34*(4), 387–398.

Smith, M.R. & Petrocelli, M. (2001). Racial profiling? A multivariate analysis of police traffic stop data. *Police Quarterly, 4*(1), 4–27.

The Black Power Mixtape. (2011). New York, NY: Louverture Films.

Tyler, T.R. (2004). Enhancing police legitimacy. *The Annals of the American Academy of Political and Social Science, 593*(84), 84–99.

United States General Accounting Office (GAO). (1990). *Death Penalty Sentencing: Research Indicates a Pattern of Racial Disparities*. Washington, DC: US General Accounting Office.

VERA Institute of Justice. (2013, July). *The Potential of Community Corrections to Improve Safety and Reduce Incarceration*. New York, NY: Vera Institute of Justice.

Whitfield, S.J. (1991). *A Death in the Delta: The Story of Emmitt Till*. Baltimore, MD: Johns Hopkins University Press.

ENDNOTE

1. The authors of this book acknowledge that racial discrimination can come in many forms and toward many different types of groups of people. For the purpose of this section, we are going to focus on discrimination against African Americans in the criminal justice system. The concepts outlined can easily be applied to discrimination against other racial and ethnic groups.

The Ethics of Criminal Justice Policy Making

CHAPTER 13

> "Laws are like cobwebs, which may catch small flies, but let
> wasps and hornets break through"
>
> —*Jonathan Swift*

By now you are aware of what ethics are—what we ought to do or ought not to do in any given situation. What is good or bad, right or wrong, or just or unjust and how we apply ethics to our decision making. The amorphous "we" and "our" can refer to each individual's ethics and decision making but it can also apply to groups or societies. In this chapter, we examine the ethics of criminal justice policy making. While individuals contribute to public opinion that often drives public policy, the issues examined here concern the decision making of groups or governments.

Thus, public policy can be defined as governmental action or inaction. Ethical guidelines for public policy, then, are the principles that help governments decide what they ought to do and ought not to do. The main ethical questions posed to policy makers when devising or altering a policy are: 1) what is a policy trying to achieve, or what is the goal? and, 2) what means ought to be taken to realize the goal?

Generally, policy makers view these questions from a deontological or consequentialist approach. A deontological approach views the policy and goal as upholding certain agreed-upon principles. Problems with this approach are that it is not always clear *what* principles ought to be valued and, further, *who* decides which principles are to be valued? A consequentialist approach views the policy based on the consequences resulting from it. Critics of this perspective point out that not all consequences of a policy can be known when the policy is created; it may take years before all consequences are evident; and debate regarding the weighting of consequences.

Although there are problems with either approach to ethical policy making, governments cannot opt out of policy creation and implementation. Even if a government chooses to do very little in the way of policy making, this is still considered a policy—a policy of not making policies.[1] Therefore, it is instructive to understand how criminal justice policies are created and why.

POLICY CREATION AND ADOPTION

Morality

Morality policies have various definitions and may include certain characteristics such as conflict of basic moral values and lack of compromise,[2] at least one side views the issue as one of morality or sin,[3] and that issues are framed by deontological reasoning of right and wrong.[4] Morality policies are based on basic moral values such as freedom, justice, fairness, and security[5] and not on other interests, like economic interests.[6] They are motivated by public opinion or policy makers' beliefs about what public opinion is on a subject.[7] Oft-cited morality policy includes laws pertaining to abortion, homosexuality, capital punishment, prostitution, gambling, alcohol and drugs, and pornography.

BOX 13.1

IN PRACTICE/A CLOSER LOOK

Civil Commitment for Addiction

Criminal Justice Policy Coalition

The Massachusetts Correctional Institution (MCI) Framingham has an increasing number of women in custody who have not been charged with nor convicted of a crime. These women are alcoholics and drug addicts who have been determined by the civil court to be a danger to themselves and/or others due to their addiction and so they have been involuntarily committed for detox and treatment.

The practice of women being detained at Framingham has been going on for some time, but the number of women and the length of time they spend there is increasing. Men and women can be ordered to go into treatment under Massachusetts General Law chapter 123, section 35. Women get sent to MCI Framingham when there is no room available in other detox facilities. Following a civil procedure that needs not involve any criminal charges (many cases are accompanied by criminal charges), they can be committed for up to 30 days. Any police officer, physician, spouse, blood relative, guardian, or court official can begin the civil procedure.

Once women are committed, the Institute for Health and Recovery (IHR) in Cambridge places them. The objective is to keep women out of prison, but if there is no room available anywhere else, women may be placed there for a few days until a spot opens up at another facility. In the last several months, there has been a reduction of about 50 percent statewide in the number of detox beds available so that accounts for the sizable increase of women being placed at MCI.

Addapted from cjpc.org at http://www.cjpc.org/Issues_CivilCommitment.htm

---

Morality policies are based on basic moral values. Therefore, public opinion, and consequently policy makers' proposals, are based on moral beliefs and not empirical evidence or objective information. Further, public opinion regarding morality policies is more likely to be influenced by religious leaders.[8]

Morality policies are simple and lack compromise. Public opinion and policy makers' responses are predicated on right and wrong and rarely are there acceptable levels in the middle. The more morality-based a policy is, the less likely that a compromise is possible. These policies are most likely to be associated with issues firmly rooted in religious beliefs. Because, as previously discussed, outside information is not likely to change one's opinion, morality policies are technically simple. Less information is needed to make a decision regarding morality policy than some more complex issues.[9]

Thus, morality policy is deontological. Consequences of morality policy are of little importance. Principles determine policy choices and upholding principles is an end in itself. A deontological supporter of morality policy concerning abortion would reason, "abortion is murder, and murder is wrong, even if lifting restrictions on it would lead to fewer risky back-alley abortions and unwanted children".[10]

UTILITY

Criminal justice policy based on utility evaluates how good or bad an expected outcome is at achieving the goals of the policy. This type of policy making is less about the principles of what is good and bad or right and wrong in themselves but what good and bad consequences will be achieved through the policy—the policy has utility if the good outcomes outweigh the bad outcomes. Thus, intrinsic value is less important than the goodness of outcomes. Primary utilitarian criminal justice policy areas are crime prevention, deterrence, and incapacitation—all based on the outcome of reducing crime and victimization.

Criminal justice policy based in utility is consequentialist. As such, criticisms of policy based primarily on utility are similar to consequentialist criticisms and include the lack of basic principles like justice and fairness in pursuit of best consequences. Equality, culpability, individual rights, and desert may not factor as prominently in utilitarian policy making compared to morality or deontological policy making.

BOX 13.2

IN PRACTICE/CLOSER LOOK

DA: Death penalty not practical in Colorado

On December 16, 2012, Stan Garnett, the District Attorney for Boulder County, Colorado, wrote an article discussing his views of the death penalty as the Colorado legislature was about to consider repealing it.

Garnett stated that he was not against the death penalty and as an elected official, he would continue to review every case and consult with a victim's family to determine whether that punishment would be sought.

Garnett listed the issues that he has with the death penalty as a punishment, the first being the cost. Prosecution costs for a death penalty case in the trial court can run in excess of one million dollars. This doesn't include the costs of the judiciary and the defense counsel, and those costs are typically paid with taxpayer monies in a death penalty case. Garnett stated that his entire operating budget for the year is 4.6 million dollars, and with that budget, they prosecute 1,900 felonies per year (in 2012, there were 50 felony jury trials including six homicides). Garnett's argument is that a first-degree murder conviction grants a sentence of automatic life with no parole in a high-security prison with no chance of escape. Thus, the public is safe from the perpetrator.

The second issue is time. It takes at least many months more to reach a verdict for a death penalty case. A death penalty case can take years before there is a verdict in the trial court. A verdict of life without parole is mandated immediately and a victim's family can then move on with their

(Continued)

BOX 13.2 (Continued)

lives. The convicted defendant fades into oblivion once put behind bars forever. Defendants who are fighting the death penalty remain in the media and often have people supporting commutation, which can be an assault to family members who are trying to cope with their loss.

Garnett's last issue is the randomness. He stated that the majority of murders could potentially be death penalty cases. In Boulder County, despite the fact that there have certainly been horrific murders, there has never been a death verdict in nearly 140 years since statehood. However, in Arapahoe/Douglas County, there are several pending death penalty cases for murders that aren't much different from ones that have occurred in Boulder County. Why seek a penalty for only a small percentage of the cases where it could be sought? How and why does geography and other factors influence the decision whether to seek the death penalty?

Garnett asked that these issues be considered as the public discussion of the death penalty begins.

Source: Adapted from dailycamera.com at http://www.dailycamera.com/ci_22194910/da-death-penalty-not-practical-colorado

---

Privatization

How do we evaluate the utility of a policy? Utilitarian evaluations are based the costs and benefits of implementing the policy and the likely outcomes. Costs and benefits extend beyond a simple adding and subtracting of monetary sums. Costs and benefits also include the social outcomes of a policy. However, economic considerations are often a large consideration of the cost-benefit analysis.

In 2010, the price of corrections to taxpayers was $39 billion.[11] Policies that led to increased sanctioning for more behaviors and incarceration for longer periods have resulted in large expenses for all levels of government. Meeting these demands as efficiently as possible opened the door for private industry in criminal corrections. Private corrections companies make claims that they can offer corrections services at a lower cost than state and federal governments have been able to do. These promises are reflected in statements made by private prison companies like Corrections Corporation of America (CCA).

BOX 13.3

IN PRACTICE/A CLOSER LOOK

Corrections Corporation of America – CCA

CCA was founded in 1983. It is the first company of its kind to have a public-private partnership in corrections. The goal was to combine strict governmental regulations and accountability with the business sector's cost savings and innovative ideas.

CCA is responsible for every aspect of its prisons, jails, detention centers and residential reentry centers including design, construction, management, and operation of the facilities. They work with the Federal Bureau of Prisons, Immigration and Customs Enforcement, the U.S. Marshals Service, and numerous states and counties nationwide.

The main goals for CCA are to protect public safety, employ qualified people, prepare inmates for reentry into society, contribute to communities, and bring new methods of security to corrections in a way that is fiscally responsible.

Adapted from cca.com at http://www.cca.com/about-cca

A number of ethical issues have been raised in connection with privatizing corrections. "Outsourcing decisions over matters with drastic and irreversible implications for inmates' lives to profit-seeking businesses with an interest in minimizing expenditures and maximizing punishment is immoral and incompatible with fundamental notions of justice."[12] Private companies are profit driven. To maximize profitability, private prisons should operate at capacity with low costs. To operate at capacity, every prison bed should be filled. This creates an incentive for private corrections groups to lobby politicians to maintain punitive responses to crime. Cost-cutting measures, when compared to state and federal prison systems, have included hiring less-qualified staff, requiring fewer hours of training, and offering lower wages and benefits, which results in high employee turnover which has been linked to increased violence and danger.[13] Other reduction strategies include lower quality of inmate services like healthcare and nutrition, as well as cutting prison programming aimed at rehabilitation.

State and federal governments strive to increase public safety through decreasing crime. Inmate programming services such as substance abuse treatment, mental health therapy, and education and vocational training aim at offering forms of rehabilitation to increase the chances that an offender will not recidivate and return to prison. Private corrections companies have a disincentive to rehabilitate offenders. Indeed, private companies maintain a financial interest at ensuring offenders recidivate. Offering quality rehabilitative services is expensive and reduces the likelihood that "clients" will return.

Incarceration is a public responsibility as a legitimate function of governmental power which is coercive in nature. Delegating this power or authority of punishment to a private entity raises ethical concerns about the legitimacy of the punishment. In addition to the ethical questions of legitimacy of private punishment, there are legal questions as well. It has been argued that delegating discretionary governmental functions to private entities violates individual due process.[14]

When all factors are considered, there is no evidence that private correctional facilities are more cost effective. In some instances, the direct costs for private corrections companies exceed those for state-run prisons.[15] Additionally, indirect costs such as increasing recidivism and legal costs associated with litigation surrounding the safety of private facilities further calls into question the economic efficacy of private corrections.

EVIDENCE

Evidence-based policy is the creation or adoption of policy based on research determining the policy's efficacy toward the issue for which it was created. The goal of the policy could be either deontological or consequentialist in nature, but the policy itself is justified by the evidence supporting its likely success instead of on moral rightness or anticipated consequences.

There is a long history of research affecting policy making. Tarde, Lombroso, Garofalo, and Ferri are among just some of the European researchers who helped to shape criminal justice policy in the 20th century. In the United States, academics out of the Chicago School in the 1920's–1940's, including Burgess, Park, Mead, Reckless, Sutherland, Thrasher, Addams, Shaw, and McKay, among others, engaged in policy debate, sentencing reform, and social activism. Additionally, Clarke and Felson are noted for their work in crime prevention; Skogan, Sherman, Weisburd, and Wilson are common names when discussing policing scholars; and Norris, Clear, Petersilia, Glaser, and Gottfredson have influenced corrections policy. This list is evidence that scholarly research can, and does, influence policy creation. But, research evidence influences policy "in some places, at some times, and on some subjects."[16] Place, time, and subject usually must align for research evidence to be utilized for policy purposes. The following indicates the intricacy of the relationship:

- Communication between policy makers and researchers is complicated. Researchers often do not speak a language that makes their evidence easily understood and applicable to policy makers.
- Research knowledge must be repeatedly filtered before impacting policy-making decisions. Rarely is there a direct line between the researcher and the policy maker. Often the

knowledge is shuffled through various parties, all with different agendas or desires, before it reaches the policy maker.

- Policy makers must be receptive to change or research influence. Various factors impact the likelihood that a policy maker may include or discard research, including personal ideology, social pressure, cost, and desire for change.

This complicated process helps to explain why policies and initiatives have remained after evidence suggests they are ineffective or harmful. Further, governments are often so committed, ideologically and monetarily, to policies that they do not want the policies evaluated for effectiveness nor do they want to know if research has negatively assessed the policy.[17] Therefore, policy backers will fail to fund research evaluating the policy or refuse to accept independent findings. Some of the more infamous policies that have not been supported by empirical evidence to be crime deterrents or preventatives but remained, or continue to remain, in effect include Drug Abuse Resistance Education (DARE), scared straight programming, three strikes laws, sex offender registries, and mandatory minimum sentencing laws.

Regardless of the likelihood that policies which have no evidentiary support will be changed, evaluating their effectiveness remains an important step in the discussion of ethical policy making. As with some of the examples above, some policies remain impervious to evidence contradicting the goals on which these policies were created. For example, there is no credible evidence that supports the use of capital punishment as a deterrent or for economic utility. Therefore, those policies without research support to their effectiveness must be debated on moral grounds, which is what most likely motivates supporters and opponents.[18] By acknowledging the lack of evidence supporting such policies, the discussion regarding their use can be grounded in the fundamental basis of the policy and not be argued on points that research has not proven to be accurate.

In sum, "evidence, although not irrelevant, is but one of many influences on policy making and often not a major one. Political considerations, public opinion, conventional wisdom, ideology, resource concerns, entrenched bureaucracies, and interest groups are always at least as important and often more important."[19] However, if evidence is to make an impact on policy making, a better understanding of why some policies are more likely to spread than others increases the likelihood that evidence-based policy will supplant ineffective or harmful policy.[20]

BOX 13.4

IN PRACTICE/CLOSER LOOK

Evidenced-Based Public Policy Options to Reduce Future Prison Construction, Criminal Justice Costs, and Crime Rates

Steve Aos, Marna Miller, and Elizabeth Drake
Washington State Institute for Public Policy

Under current long-term forecasts, Washington State faces the need to construct several new prisons in the next two decades. Since new prisons are costly, the 2005 Washington Legislature directed the Washington State Institute for Public Policy to project whether there are "evidence-based" options that can reduce the future need for prison beds, save money for state and local taxpayers, and contribute to lower crime rates.

We conducted a systematic review of all research evidence we could locate to identify what works, if anything, to reduce crime. We found and analyzed 571 rigorous comparison-group evaluations of adult corrections, juvenile corrections, and prevention programs, most of which were conducted in the United States. We then estimated the benefits and costs of many of these evidence-based options. Finally, we projected the degree to which alternative "portfolios" of these programs could affect future prison construction needs, criminal justice costs, and crime rates in Washington.

We find that some evidence-based programs can reduce crime, but others cannot. Per dollar of spending, several of the successful programs produce favorable returns on investment. Public policies incorporating these options can yield positive outcomes for Washington. We project the long-run effects of three example portfolios of evidence-based options: a "current level" option as well as "moderate" and "aggressive" implementation portfolios. We find that if Washington successfully implements a moderate-to-aggressive portfolio of evidence-based options, a significant level of future prison construction can be avoided, taxpayers can save about two billion dollars, and crime rates can be reduced.

http://www.wsipp.wa.gov/ReportFile/952/Wsipp_Evidence-Based-Public-Policy-Options-to-Reduce-Future-Prison-Construction-Criminal-Justice-Costs-and-Crime-Rates_Full-Report.pdf

POLICY DIFFUSION

Policies are often created or adopted without rigorous inquiry regarding the ethical underpinnings or likely outcomes of the policy. Although criminal justice policy making is underresearched,[21] often policies are created or adopted for financial, geographic, political, and/or emotional reasons. Policy is likely to spread to neighboring states that learn from and compete with each other.[22] A policy may be adopted in a neighboring state because of the positive outcome it had in another state[23] or to maintain competitive advantage.[24] Neighboring states also tend to share similar political ideologies.[25] Liberal or conservative ideologies among populations would support similar types of policy adoption.

Media coverage also impacts how policies are spread and why some policies are created. The public generally has limited experience and knowledge with the criminal justice system. Therefore, we rely on mass media to inform us of crime and policy related to crime.[26,27] Traditionally, television news and programming and print outlets were the primary sources of information about crime and the ways in which the public perception of crime was shaped. Now, public perception is influenced by online sources and social media as well. This has allowed the public to gain a broader perspective of the reality of crime. However, research indicates that the public gravitates toward sensational stories, regardless of media outlet, that tend to confirm their preconceived notions about the nature of crime.[28]

In a national survey, 81% of respondents claim that they identify crime as a social problem based on the extent of media coverage.[29] However, media outlets consistently highlight a very small portion of all crime that occurs. Taking all crime into consideration, violent crime constitutes a relatively small amount of crime. However, news media, reality shows, crime dramatizations, and even social media, concentrate on violent crime, and usually the more violent, the more random, the more coverage. Subsequently, the general public perceives that this type of crime happens at a higher rate, is more likely to affect them, and should receive more policy attention than would be justified by the actual occurrence of these types of crime.

Media coverage of crime, particularly violent crime, can also lead to a moral panic. Moral panics can be defined as the emergence of a condition, event, or group of persons that becomes defined as a threat to the values and interests of society. The condition, event, or group is presented in a stereotypical fashion by the media and "experts" who encourage the public to take moral positions, make judgments, and suggest how the issue should be handled.[30] While moral panics often begin with a real issue or problem, the media's role in exacerbating the problem can cause the public to perceive the issue as more serious than it is. Moral panics have been used to explain the inclusion of emotionally based policies in terrorism and sex offender laws. Moral panics fueled by media sensationalism have also resulted in policies that have had discriminatory outcomes like drug laws resulting from the War on Drugs.

The quality of information gained through media outlets makes it challenging for the public to have an informed and balanced view of crime. Researchers have found that knowledge of criminal punishment policy, relying on media coverage for information, results in the least accurate knowledge. Respondents who were media-reliant for criminal justice information were the least accurate of those surveyed, when tested on their knowledge of correctional policy.[31]

A skewed public perception of crime, then, impacts which public policies are supported.[32] When the public's fear of crime increases, pressure is placed on policy makers to "do something." Further, the public likely gravitates toward officials who have a more punitive ideology toward crime and are more likely to react in a quick and harsh manner. This has resulted in a political agenda that has increasingly supported retributive responses to crime, including longer sentences for more types of behavior.[33]

SEX OFFENDER POLICY

Sex offender policy is often considered to be an example of how a moral panic develops into public policy. A few heinous and tragic but "statistically unusual" stranger abduction and sexual assault crimes by adults against children[34] (for example, see crimes related to Adam Walsh, Megan Kanka, Polly Klaas, and Jessica Lunsford), particularly in the 1990's, resulted in a media storm of coverage and bolstered public fear of sexual predators. From these emotionally charged cases, federal sex offender registration and notification laws were created. Box 13.5 - In Practice/Closer Look provides an overview of current federal guidelines.

BOX 13.5

CLOSER LOOK

Sorna

SORNA refers to the Sex Offender Registration and Notification Act which is Title I of the Adam Walsh Child Protection and Safety Act of 2006 (Public Law 109–248). SORNA provides a comprehensive set of minimum standards for sex offender registration and notification in the United States. SORNA aims to close potential gaps and loopholes that existed under prior law and generally strengthens the nationwide network of sex offender registration and notification programs. Additionally, SORNA:

- Extends the jurisdictions in which registration is required beyond the 50 states, the District of Columbia, and the principal U.S. territories, to include also federally recognized Indian tribes.

- Incorporates a more comprehensive group of sex offenders and sex offenses for which registration is required.

- Requires registered sex offenders to register and keep their registration current in each jurisdiction in which they reside, work, or go to school.

- Requires sex offenders to provide more extensive registration information.

- Requires sex offenders to make periodic in-person appearances to verify and update their registration information.
- Expands the amount of information available to the public regarding registered sex offenders.
- Makes changes in the required minimum duration of registration for sex offenders.

For state specific information, visit http://ojp.gov/smart/sorna.htm

To allay public concern and create a sense of security, policy changes were undertaken concerning sanctioning of sex offenders in three main areas—sentencing, civil commitment, and community management. Many states implemented mandatory minimum sentences for sex offenders as well as imposed long prison sentences on offenders who failed to adhere to registry and notification requirements. Approximately twenty states and the federal government have laws allowing for civil commitment of sex offenders.[35] These laws provide a mechanism to commit certain sex offenders to secure treatment facilities for an indefinite period of time after they have served their incarcerations. Critics have raised a number of constitutional challenges to civil commitments including double jeopardy, ex-post facto, and violations of due process. However, the U.S. Supreme Court has upheld the constitutionality of civil commitments. See In Practice/Closer Look 13.6.

BOX 13.6

IN PRACTICE/CLOSER LOOK

Supreme Court of the United States

Syllabus

Kansas v. Hendricks
certiorari to the supreme court of Kansas
No. 95-1649. Argued December 10, 1996 – Decided June 23, 1997

Kansas' Sexually Violent Predator Act establishes procedures for the civil commitment of persons who, due to a "mental abnormality" or a "personality disorder," are likely to engage in "predatory acts of sexual violence." Kansas filed a petition under the Act in state court to commit respondent (and cross petitioner) Hendricks, who had a long history of sexually molesting children and was scheduled for release from prison. The court reserved ruling on Hendricks' challenge to the Act's constitutionality, but granted his request for a jury trial. After Hendricks testified that he agreed with the state physician's diagnosis that he suffers from pedophilia and is not cured and that he continues to harbor sexual desires for children that he cannot control when he gets "stressed out," the jury determined that he was a sexually violent predator. Finding that pedophilia qualifies as a mental abnormality under the Act, the court ordered him committed. On appeal, the State Supreme Court invalidated the Act on the ground that the precommitment condition of a "mental abnormality" did not satisfy what it perceived to be the "substantive" due process requirement that involuntary civil commitment must be predicated on a "mental illness" finding. It did not address Hendricks' *ex post-facto* and double jeopardy claims.

(Continued)

BOX 13.6 (Continued)

Held:

1. The Act's definition of "mental abnormality" satisfies "substantive" due process requirements. An individual's constitutionally protected liberty interest in avoiding physical restraint may be overridden even in the civil context. *Jacobson v. Massachusetts*, 197 U.S. 11, 26. This Court has consistently upheld involuntary commitment statutes that detain people who are unable to control their behavior and thereby pose a danger to the public health and safety, provided the confinement takes place pursuant to proper procedures and evidentiary standards. *Foucha v. Louisiana*, 504 U.S. 71, 80. The Act unambiguously requires a precommitment finding of dangerousness either to one's self or to others, and links that finding to a determination that the person suffers from a "mental abnormality" or "personality disorder." Generally, this Court has sustained a commitment statute if it couples proof of dangerousness with proof of some additional factor, such as a "mental illness" or "mental abnormality," see, *e.g., Heller v. Doe*, 509 U.S. 312, 314–315, for these additional requirements serve to limit confinement to those who suffer from a volitional impairment rendering them dangerous beyond their control. The Act sets forth comparable criteria with its precommitment requirement of "mental abnormality" or "personality disorder." Contrary to Hendricks' argument, this Court has never required States to adopt any particular nomenclature in drafting civil commitment statutes and leaves to the States the task of defining terms of a medical nature that have legal significance. Cf. *Jones v. United States*, 463 U.S. 354, 365, n. 13. The legislature is therefore not required to use the specific term "mental illness" and is free to adopt any similar term. Pp. 8–13.

2. The Act does not violate the Constitution's double jeopardy prohibition or its ban on *ex post-facto* lawmaking. Pp. 13–24.

   (a) The Act does not establish criminal proceedings, and involuntary confinement under it is not punishment. The categorization of a particular proceeding as civil or criminal is a question of statutory construction. *Allen v. Illinois*, 478 U.S. 364, 368. Nothing on the face of the Act suggests that the Kansas Legislature sought to create anything other than a civil commitment scheme. That manifest intent will be rejected only if Hendricks provides the clearest proof that the scheme is so punitive in purpose or effect as to negate Kansas' intention to deem it civil. *United States v. Ward*, 448 U.S. 242, 248–249. He has failed to satisfy this heavy burden. Commitment under the Act does not implicate either of the two primary objectives of criminal punishment: retribution or deterrence. Its purpose is not retributive: It does not affix culpability for prior criminal conduct, but uses such conduct solely for evidentiary purposes; it does not make criminal conviction a prerequisite for commitment; and it lacks a scienter requirement, an important element in distinguishing criminal and civil statutes. Nor can the Act be said to act as a deterrent, since persons with a mental abnormality or personality disorder are unlikely to be deterred by the threat of confinement. The conditions surrounding confinement—essentially the same as conditions for any civilly committed patient—do not suggest a punitive purpose. Although the commitment scheme here involves an affirmative restraint, such restraint of the dangerously mentally ill has been historically regarded as a legitimate nonpunitive objective. Cf. *United States v. Salerno*, 481 U.S. 739, 747. The confinement's potentially indefinite duration is linked, not to any punitive objective, but to the purpose of holding a person until his mental abnormality no longer causes him to be a threat to others. He is thus permitted immediate release upon a showing that he is no longer dangerous, and the longest he can be detained pursuant to a single judicial proceeding is one year. The State's use of procedural safeguards applicable in criminal trials does not itself turn the proceedings into criminal prosecutions. *Allen, supra*, at 372. Finally, the Act is not necessarily punitive if it fails to offer treatment where treatment for a condition is not possible, or if treatment, though possible, is merely an ancillary, rather than an overriding, state concern. The conclusion that the Act is nonpunitive removes an essential prerequisite for both Hendricks' double jeopardy and *ex post-facto* claims. Pp. 13–21.

(b) Hendricks' confinement does not amount to a second prosecution and punishment for the offense for which he was convicted. Because the Act is civil in nature, its commitment proceedings do not constitute a second prosecution. Cf. *Jones, supra*. As this commitment is not tantamount to punishment, the detention does not violate the Double Jeopardy Clause, even though it follows a prison term. *Baxstrom v. Herold*, 383 U.S. 107. Hendricks' argument that, even if the Act survives the "multiple punishments" test, it fails the "same elements" test of *Blockburger v. United States*, 284 U.S. 299, is rejected, since that test does not apply outside of the successive prosecution context. Pp. 22–23.

(c) Hendricks' *ex post-facto* claim is similarly flawed. The *Ex Post-Facto* Clause pertains exclusively to penal statutes. *California Dept. of Corrections v. Morales*, 514 U.S. 499, 505. Since the Act is not punishment, its application does not raise *ex post-facto* concerns. Moreover, the Act clearly does not have retroactive effect. It does not criminalize conduct legal before its enactment or deprive Hendricks of any defense that was available to him at the time of his crimes. Pp. 23–24. 259 Kan. 246, 912 P. 2d 129, reversed. Thomas, J., delivered the opinion of the Court, in which Rehnquist, C. J., and O'Connor, Scalia, and Kennedy, JJ., joined. Kennedy, J., filed a concurring opinion. Breyer, J., filed a dissenting opinion, in which Stevens and Souter, JJ., joined, and in which Ginsburg, J., joined as to Parts II and III.

Community management of sex offenders is conducted through registration (law enforcement can track offenders), community notification (inform neighbors for self-protection), and residency restrictions (increase safety by restricting where offenders can live).[36] Community management includes, depending on the state and county, that sex offenders, for at least ten years and up to life, not live within 2,000 feet of schools, be within 500 feet of parks or movie theaters, enter public libraries, drive buses or taxis, photograph or film minors, use social networking websites, advertise their status on drivers' licenses or social networking sites, and must wear GPS bracelets at their own expense, notify local police when they are in any county more than ten days, provide notice to neighbors within a quarter-mile radius, and pay annual registry fees.[37]

BOX 13.7

CLOSER LOOK

20 Year Anniversary of Washington's Community Protection Act

King County, Washington Prosecuting Attorney Comments on the Community Protection Act

Daniel T. Satterberg, Prosecuting Attorney for King County, Washington, observed the 20-year anniversary in January 2010 of Washington's Community Protection Act by writing his opinion of it.

Satterberg was in favor of the Legislature passing a law to protect Washington's law enforcement officers. At the time Satterberg wrote this, there had been recent attacks of violence that targeted the State's law enforcement officers. He called to mind the Community Protection Act that had been passed two decades before as a model of how a law can achieve positive results.

(Continued)

BOX 13.7 (Continued)

The Community Protection Act was created in 1990 due to two extremely violent sex crimes that outraged citizens and caused the entire state to take action. The first victim was Diane Ballasiotes, who was a young woman who had been abducted and murdered in a parking garage. Her attacker was a dangerous psychopath who had walked away from work release. Shortly after that crime occurred, a Tacoma boy who was riding his bike around the neighborhood was abducted, sexually assaulted and mutilated by a convicted sex offender who had just been released from prison. The boy was just seven years old. His attacker had a long history of sexually assaulting other children. Those who knew him in prison stated that it was only a matter of time before he would attack another child.

These two horrific crimes sparked public outrage that demanded a reform in how the state of Washington handled violent sex offenders. The Governor's Task Force on Community Protection was created, with King County Prosecuting Attorney Norm Maleng leading the task force. It was charged with revamping the approach to sex crimes, aid to victims, and community security. The mothers of the two victims in the aforementioned cases served on the task force.

The Community Protection Act was unanimously passed into law in 1990 and it proved to give the kind of protection that made the state of Washington a model for the entire country when it came to addressing sexual violence and sexual predators. Many other states used Washington as a model for creating their own laws. The Community Protection Act increased sentences for all sex offenses, enacted registration requirements and community notification requirements for sex offenders as well as crafting the first civil commitment laws for sexually violent predators.

At the time Satterberg wrote his opinion 20 years after the Community Protection Act was passed, he stressed that there would again be a need for reform in light of the violence against the law enforcement officers and he stressed that the success of the Community Protection Task Force proved that such a change to protect officers would have positive outcomes, and indeed, the victims and their families deserved a review of the justice system and had a right to expect that the safety of the community would improve with their efforts.

It has been argued that the totality of these responses affecting most sex offenders based on the actions of a few have resulted in violations of constitutional rights through the denial of due process, proportionality, and privacy and cruel and unusual punishment. Further, although there have been incidents of other violent crimes that have led to public outrage, including murder, these classes of offenders are not required to adhere to similar regulations. However, it is argued that public rejection of sex offenders is greater[38] and these offenders are viewed differently than other types of offenders.[39]

When considering the phrases "sexual predator" and "sex offender," the first images that often come to mind are adult "monsters"—most likely male—who stalk children from parks and schools. These images have been reinforced through media reports of child abduction and registries that target these types of offenders garner the most public support.[40] While this type of offending makes up a small percentage of the overall sexual offending behavior, it is the most feared by parents and despised by society. In reality, the overwhelming majority of child offending is perpetrated by someone related to the child and the offense is most likely carried out in the offender's home[41]—incidents current sex offender requirements would not prevent. Also, there has been a widespread belief that sex offenders do not respond to rehabilitative therapy and will repeatedly offend. However, research continues to reveal that most sex offenders are not recidivists[42] and offender therapy can be effective.[43]

Rarely does any criminal justice policy adhere to only one set of ethical guidelines. Often, policies are influenced by morality, utility, and empirical evidence based on desired goals and outcomes. One of the most difficult challenges facing criminal justice policy makers is the interdisciplinary nature of any justice policy. Criminal behavior does not occur in a vacuum. Policies responding to such behavior cannot neglect the totality of inputs that assist in creating the behavior. Criminologists and criminal justicians must be aware of the intentions of a policy and not only the consequences it will likely have on the justice system, but also on related systems including mental health, economic, public health, housing, and education. The issues that arise from analyzing the impact a policy may have on any and all of these areas are complex.

ENDNOTES

1. Boston, J., Bradstock, A., & Eng, D. (Eds.). (2010). *Public Policy: Why Ethics Matter*. Canberra, Australia: ANU E Press. Pgs 1–5, Ch. Introduction.

2. Mooney, C.Z. (2001). The public clash of private values. In C.Z. Mooney, (Ed), *The Public Clash of Private Values: The Politics of Morality Policy* (pp. 3–20). Chatham, NJ: Chatham House.

3. Haider-Markel, D.P., & Meier, K.J. (1996). The politics of gay and lesbian rights: Expanding the scope of conflict. *Journal of Politics, 58*(2), 332–49.

4. Mucciaroni, G. (2011). Are debates about 'morality policy' really about morality? Framing opposition to gay and lesbian rights. *Policy Studies Journal, 39*(2), 187–216.

5. Mucciaroni, G. (2011). Are debates about 'morality policy' really about morality? Framing opposition to gay and lesbian rights. *Policy Studies Journal, 39*(2), 187–216.

6. Mooney, C.Z & Schuldt, R.G. (2008). Does morality policy Exist? Testing a basic assumption. *The Policy Studies Journal, 36*(2), 199–218.

7. Camobreco, J.F., & Barnello, M.A. (2008). Democratic responsiveness and policy shock: The case of state abortion policy. *State Politics and Policy Quarterly, 8*, 48–65.

8. Mooney, C.Z & Schuldt, R.G. (2008). Does morality policy Exist? Testing a basic assumption. *The Policy Studies Journal, 36*(2), 199–218.

9. Mooney, C.Z & Schuldt, R.G. (2008). Does morality policy Exist? Testing a basic assumption. *The Policy Studies Journal, 36*(2), 199–218.

10. Mooney, C.Z & Schuldt, R.G. (2008). Does morality policy Exist? Testing a basic assumption. *The Policy Studies Journal, 36*(2), 199–218.

11. Mooney, C.Z & Schuldt, R.G. (2008). Does morality policy Exist? Testing a basic assumption. *The Policy Studies Journal, 36*(2), 199–218.

12. Mucciaroni, G. (2011). Are debates about 'morality policy' really about morality? Framing opposition to gay and lesbian rights." *Policy Studies Journal, 39*(2). 187–216. Quote p. 191.

13. Henrichson, C., & Delaney, R. (2012). *The Price of Prisons: What Incarceration Costs Taxpayers*. Vera Institute of Justice. http://www.vera.org/sites/default/files/resources/downloads/price-of-prisons-updated-version-021914.pdf

14. Anderson, L. (2009). Kicking the national habit: The legal and policy arguments for abolishing private prison contracts. *Public Contract Law Journal, 39*(1), 119–139.

15. Oppel, Jr., R.A. (May 18, 2011). Private prisons found to offer little in savings. *The New York Times*. http://www.nytimes.com/2011/05/19/us/19prisons.html?pagewanted=all&_r=0

16. Tonry, M. (2010). Public criminology and evidence-based policy. *Criminology and Public Policy, 9*(4), 783–797. p. 793.

17. Tonry, M. (2010). Public criminology and evidence-based policy. *Criminology and Public Policy, 9*(4), 783–797.

18. Tonry, M. (2010). Public criminology and evidence-based policy. *Criminology and Public Policy, 9*(4), 783–797.

19. Tonry, M. (2010). Public criminology and evidence-based policy. *Criminology and Public Policy, 9*(4), 783–797. p. 787.

20. Bergin, T. (2011). How and why do criminal justice public policies spread throughout the U.S. states? A critical review of the diffusion literature. *Criminal Justice Policy Review, 22*(4), 403–421.

21. Ismaili, K. (2006). Contextualizing the criminal justice policy-making process. *Criminal Justice Policy Review, 17,* 255–269.

22. Walker, J. L. (1969). The diffusion of innovations among the American states. *American Political Science Review, 63,* 880–899.

23. Boehmke, F. J. & Witmer, R. (2004). Disentangling diffusion: The effects of social learning and economic competition on state policy innovation and expansion. *Political Research Quarterly, 57*(1), 39–51.

24. Allard, S. W. (2004). Competitive pressures and the emergence of mothers' aid programs in the United States. *The Policy Studies Journal, 32,* 521–544.

25. Nicholson-Crotty, S. (2009). The politics of diffusion: Public policy in the American states. *The Journal of Politics, 71*(1), 192–205.

26. Callanan, V. J. (2012). Media consumption, perceptions of crime risk and fear of crime: Examining race/ethnic differences. *Sociological Perspectives, 55,* 93–115.

27. Kort-Butler, L. A., & Hartshorn, K. J. S. (2011). Watching the detectives: Crime programming, fear of crime, and attitudes about the criminal justice system. *The Sociological Quarterly, 52,* 36–55.

28. Thompson, A.C. (2011). From sound bites to sound policy: Reclaiming the high ground in criminal justice policy-making. *Fordham Urban Law Journal, 38,* 775–820.

29. Beale, Sara S. (2006). The news media's influence on criminal justice policy: How market-driven news promotes punitiveness. *William and Mary Law Review, 48,* 397–441.

30. Cohen, S. (1972). *Folk Devils and Moral Panics: The Creation of the Mods and Rockers.* London: MacGibbon & Kee.

31. Pickett, J.T., Mancin, C., Mears, D.P., & Gertz, M. (2014). Public (mis)understanding of crime policy: The effects of criminal justice experience and media reliance. *Criminal Justice Policy Review,* DOI: 10.1177/0887403414526228

32. Thompson, A.C. (2011). From sound bites to sound policy: Reclaiming the high ground in criminal justice policy-making. *Fordham Urban Law Journal, 38,* 775–820.

33. Beale, S.S. (2003). Still tough on crime? Prospects for restorative justice in the United States. *Utah Law Review,* 413–427.

34. Lancaster, R.N. (February 20, 2013). Panic leads to bad policy on sex offenders. *The New York Times.* http://www.nytimes.com/roomfordebate/2013/02/20/too-many-restrictions-on-sex-offenders-or-too-few/panic-leads-to-bad-policy-on-sex-offenders

35. Association for the Treatment of Sexual Abusers. (2010). Civil Commitment of Sexually Violent Predators. http://www.atsa.com/civil-commitment-sexually-violent-predators

36. Maguire, M. & Singer, J.K. (2011). A false sense of security: Moral panic driven sex offender legislation. *Critical Criminology, 19,* 301–312.

37. Miller, E. (2014). Let the burden fit the crime. *The Yale Law Journal, 123,* 1607–1625.

38. Winnick, T.A. (2008). Another layer of ignominy: Beliefs about public views of sex offenders. *Sociological Focus, 41,* 53–70.

39. Craun, S.W., Kernsmith, P.D., & Butler, N.K. (2011). "Anything can be a danger to the public": Desire to extend registries beyond sex offenses. *Criminal Justice Policy Review, 22*(3), 375–391.

40. Kernsmith, P., Craun, S. W., & Foster, J. (2009). Public attitudes towards sexual offenders and sex offender registration. *Journal of Child Sexual Abuse, 18,* 290–301.

41. Maguire, M. & Singer, J.K. (2011). A false sense of security: Moral panic driven sex offender legislation. *Critical Criminology, 19,* 301–312.

42. Lanagan, P.A., Schmitt, E.L., & DuRose, M.R. (2003). Recidivism from Sex Offenders Released from Prison in 1994. US Dept of Justice: Bureau of Justice Statistics. NCJ 198281 http://www.bjs.gov/content/pub/pdf/rsorp94.pdf

43. Yates, P. (2013). Treatment of sex offenders: Research, best practices, and emerging models. *International Journal of Behavioral Consultation and Therapy, 8,* 89–95.

Ethics and International Terrorism

CHAPTER 14

"Never give in—never, never, never, never, in nothing great or small, large or petty, never give in except to convictions of honor and good sense. Never yield to force; never yield to the apparently overwhelming might of the enemy."

—*Winston Churchill*

"This mass terrorism is the new evil in our world today. It is perpetrated by fanatics who are utterly indifferent to the sanctity of human life . . . [We] will not rest until this evil is driven from our world."

—*Tony Blair*

The attack on the United States on September 11, 2001 by the Islamist terrorist group *Al-Qaeda* has had a profound impact on international relations. The event known as *9/11*, which resulted in the deaths of nearly 3,000 people,[1] became the catalyst for the Bush Administration's "war on terror" and subsequent U.S. military invasions and wars in Afghanistan and Iraq as well as for the U.S. government's support of the Pakistani authority's counter-insurgency campaign.[2] This response to terrorism has had far-reaching human, social, and economic repercussions. The number of civilians killed directly as a consequence of war in Afghanistan, Iraq, and Pakistan between October 2001 and April 2014 is estimated at between 174,000 and 220,000.[3] As well as loss of life, the population of Iraq has been further impacted by high levels of migration as a result of the conflict. The Iraqi *Ministry of Displacement and Migration* has estimated that more than 30 percent of Iraq's professors, doctors, pharmacists, and engineers emigrated between 2003 and 2007.[4] According to a *United Nations High Commission for Refugees* report in September 2007, it was estimated that more than four million Iraqis were displaced internally and externally from their homes.[5] Although such displacement was occurring before 2003, it intensified dramatically after the U.S. invasion of Iraq in 2003 with 1.5 million Iraqis displaced in 2006–2007 alone.[6] It is, however, just in Afghanistan, Iraq, and Pakistan where the costs of the war on terror have been felt (which the United States Congress and the Executive Branch calls *overseas contingency operations*).[7] Economically the spending cost for these conflicts and on homeland security to the U.S. government from 2001 through to the fiscal year 2014 is approximately $4.4 trillion.[8]

Despite the enormous sums spent by the U.S. government on these wars, terrorist incidents within these regions of conflict have increased significantly in the ten years since 9/11 compared with the ten years before. According to the *Global Terrorism Database* there were almost 30,000 documented global terrorist incidents in the ten years from the day after 9/11.[9] This compares to just fewer than 25,000 in the ten years up to the day before September 11, 2001.[10] A breakdown of the data for terrorist incidents in this ten-year period after 9/11 shows that, out of a total of thirteen regions, terrorism actually *fell* in nine of them when compared with the number of incidents in the ten-year period prior.[11] Across these nine regions: Central America and Caribbean, East Asia, North America, Australasia and Oceania, South America, Central Asia, Sub-Saharan Africa, Eastern Europe, and Western Europe, there was a 64 percent reduction in terrorist incidents.[12] The four regions of Southeast Asia, Middle East and North Africa, USSR and the Newly Independent States, and South Asia saw terrorist incidents more than double in comparison.[13] These four regions accounted for 25,006 of the 29,706 terrorist incidents during this post 9/11 period.[14] The U.S. operations in the Middle East and South Asia appear to have done little to dent the level of terrorist organization in these regions. Indeed, ten years on from 9/11, eleven of the 20 most active terrorist groups in 2011 were linked to Al-Qaeda.[15]

The events of 9/11 also had a significant impact on the volume of academic work produced on the subject of terrorism. Silke, writing in 2008, states that "90 percent of the literature on terrorism had been written since 1969. If current trends continue, however, within two or three years we will certainly be able to say that over 90 percent of the entire literature on terrorism will have been written since 9/11."[16] In 2000 some 150 books on terrorism were published.[17] In 2001 the profound impact of 9/11 on academic discourse was apparent as this figure rose to 1,108, with most of these titles being published in the final three months of the year.[18] 2002 saw 1,767 titles published (equating to approximately 34 titles every week).[19] Silke states that terrorism "has become the defining issue of international politics in the first decade of the twenty-first century. It would be remarkable if such prominence was not matched by a significant increase in research interest in this area."[20]

Terrorism, as a subject of criminological discourse, is typically analyzed by asking such questions as: what is it? What is its extent? How do we explain it?

Although the purpose of such questions is to provide factual understanding of terrorism as a phenomenon, it remains an essentially contested concept, largely due to definitional disagreements, which ultimately underlies all subsequent analyses. However, despite this lack of analytic consensus a high degree of factuality can still emerge out of these discussions which may allow for academic objectivity. That is: terrorism can be defined; there is a measurable amount of terrorist incidents; and these have causes.

Terrorism as a philosophical subject is well-suited for a discussion of ethical matters. This is because there is much ethical contestation around the issues of who is defined a terrorist; the appropriateness of counter-terrorism strategies; and whether terrorist suspects are entitled to the same due process of law as other accused criminals. Ethics, or moral philosophy, attempts to understand the nature of moral knowledge, of how we ought to live, and what constitutes right conduct. Contemporary philosophers usually divide ethical theories into three general subject areas: meta-ethics, normative ethics, and applied ethics. Meta-ethics investigates the proper grounds for justifying moral claims, the nature of moral judgments (i.e., are moral standards universal or culturally relative), and the meaning of ethical terms or judgments such as "good," "bad," "right," and "wrong." Normative ethics, also known as prescriptive ethics, attempts to arrive at moral standards through ethical systems that prescribe how people ought to behave. This can involve outlining the duties we should follow, the good habits we should acquire, or the consequences of our actions for others. All ethical systems, such as Kant's duty ethics[21] and utilitarianism,[22] are normative. Normative ethics is often contrasted with descriptive ethics which refers to the attitudes of individuals or the code of conduct put forward by a group which describes how they do behave. Applied ethics is concerned with identifying the morally correct course of action one should take in addressing a problem. Applied ethics is the use of philosophical methods, the purpose of which is to address moral problems, practices, and policies in the realms of professions, technology, government, and various other fields of human life.

Criminal justice ethics can be viewed through both a narrow and a broad framework.[23] Within the narrow framework its focus is on the challenges generated by the institutions of criminal justice themselves, such as prison overcrowding and the place of police discretion. Also associated with the narrow framework is a focus on the challenges encountered by practitioners within the criminal justice system. This could be around problems of professional ethics, for example, an officer conscientiously objecting to particular police strategies. Within the broad framework, criminal justice ethics encompasses the following: ethical problems that emerge in relation to the foundations of the criminal justice system; the ethical limits of criminal law; moral issues that arise within the discourse on the nature and origins of criminality; and more general ethical concerns that have important "particularized expressions" within the criminal justice framework.[24]

The application of ethical analysis to the subject of international terrorism for the purpose of determining whether the "terrorist," counter-terrorism or judicial actions of agents, organizations, and institutions are morally justified is not without problem. Moral relativists such as Gilbert argue that no moral framework is objectively privileged over another.[25] That is, what can be morally right in one moral framework could be morally wrong in relation to a different one. Yet to achieve an objective measure of moral justification, the discussion needs to be framed within a metaphysic of moral objectivity or moral realism. The key problem here therefore is around the perennial question of whether moral facts exist. However, the purpose of this chapter is not to engage in the complexity of the moral realism, anti-realism, or quasi-realism debate[26] but instead to provide a means by which the reader will be able to assess within a normative ethical framework whether the actions of "terrorists" and those who oppose them, as well as those who seek to apply fundamental criminal justice principles, have any moral validity.

In this chapter, I will first examine the problem of defining terrorism and the distinction between domestic terrorism and international terrorism. I will then explore three foci of analysis whereby ethical considerations are applied to the area of international terrorism and criminal justice. These are *terrorist action*, specifically the question of whether a terrorist act can ever be morally justified; *counter-terrorism measures*, with a particular focus on enhanced interrogation techniques and torture; *justice system response*, in which I focus particularly on the ethical considerations around extrajudicial killings or assassinations and whether terrorist suspects receive the same due process of law and protection of rights as non-terrorist suspects. These discussions will be addressed through the use of consequentialist and deontological moral frameworks. Consequentialism is an ethical position that views morality as being based on producing the right kinds of outcomes. Deontology (sometimes referred to as non-consequentialism) is an ethical position that views morality as based on specific foundational principles, obligations, or duties. It should be recognized that there are a number of different types of consequentialist and deontological arguments. However, in this chapter I present a generalized position for both frameworks which captures this essential *outcomes* versus *duties* dichotomy. In conclusion I will present challenges to the consequentialist and deontological frameworks and argue that upholding a commitment to consistent duty-based ethical standards, despite the challenges, is an effective means by which states can counter international terrorism at an ideological level.

PROBLEM OF DEFINITION

There is no internationally agreed-upon legal definition of terrorism. Scholars have struggled with the difficulties of establishing a coherent definition for decades. For example Schmid and Jongman, writing in the 1980's, listed more than one hundred different definitions of terrorism.[27] Mythen and Walklate argue that the term "terrorism" is better understood as a "culturally constructed and historically variable category rather than an immutable objective descriptor."[28] Also, how terrorism is defined is often mediated through the perspective of the subject discipline from which the institutional actor chooses to understand this phenomenon. Thus Weston and Innes suggest that studies which emerge out of economics, for example, attend to different qualities than those from psychology or sociology.[29]

According to Williams[30] defining terrorism is complicated by two sources of ambiguity inherent within the concept itself. First, it is difficult to distinguish terrorism from similar activities. For example, there is some overlap with both conventional and guerrilla warfare in which specific acts are aimed at terrorizing the enemy. It can also be difficult to distinguish some forms of terrorism from more "conventional" criminal acts of violence. For example, the actions of the Norwegian Anders Breivik in 2011, in which he killed eight people via the detonation of a bomb he placed in a car outside government buildings in Oslo and then moved onto a workers youth league camp shooting and killing 69 individuals, could better be described as a "spree killing"[31] rather than an act of terrorism.[32] The second source of ambiguity is that political agendas often determine what and who becomes defined as "terrorism" and "terrorist." Acts of violence are seen in very different ways depending on the audience. Thus for some these are terrorist acts whilst for others these are the actions of freedom fighters.

Contemporary definitions of terrorism have been criticized for focusing too much on individuals and groups ("bottom-up") and not enough on forms of state repression ("top-down").[33] Cohen notes that there are nation states that resort to communicating an intimidatory message of violence against their own citizens, in pursuit of their own political objectives so as to spread fear. Therefore state terrorism should not be viewed separately from other forms of terrorism.[34]

Despite this, Innes and Levi show how the literature does educe the following themes that appear in the attempts to delineate the conceptual boundaries of terrorism:

- "political violence – there is widespread agreement that a necessary condition for defining an act as terrorist and thus distinguishing it from some other forms of violence is that it is conducted in pursuit of some political objective;

- communicative violence – accompanying the preceding point, almost all definitions acknowledge that terrorist acts are marked by a desire to communicate an intimidatory message beyond the immediate victims; and

- asymmetry of power – more contentiously perhaps, many contributions identify that terrorist violence tends to arise when a relatively powerless group identifies a need to mobilize a response to a more powerful adversary."[35]

One of the more contested recent debates in terrorism revolves around whether 9/11 attacks by Al-Qaeda constitute a new form of terrorism. Since 9/11 a number of academics, politicians, journalists, and security experts have concurred on the idea that the type of terrorism carried out by extreme Islamic fundamentalist groups such as Al-Qaeda and Lashkar-e-Taiba is qualitatively different from previous forms. This unprecedented type of terrorism has been variously called "postmodern," "super," or "new" terrorism.[36] Mythen and Walklate state that "new terrorism" constitutes an existential threat, a threat to our very existence, which necessitates the introduction of exceptional security measures. However, they argue that some of the characteristics which lead to this terrorism being viewed as "new" such as new tactics, technologies, strategies, and organizational structure are equally applicable to groups and individuals that have used or attempted to use political violence in the twentieth century.[37] For example, the Irish Republican Army (IRA) operated an organizational cell system,[38] and Samuel Byck attempted to hijack a passenger plane so as to fly it into the White House to kill President Nixon more than a quarter of a century before 9/11.[39]

A tight demarcation is typically made between international terrorism and domestic terrorism in legal, political, and academic literature.[40] For example the Memorial Institute for the Prevention of Terrorism defines international terrorist incidents as those "in which terrorists go abroad to strike their targets, select domestic targets associated with a foreign state, or create an international incident by attacking airline passengers, personnel or equipment."[41] The institute defines domestic incidents as ones "perpetrated by local nationals against a purely domestic target."[42] However, such strict demarcation between these two, often narrowly defined categories is, according to Saikia and Stepanova, increasingly becoming inaccurate.[43] Globalization means that political groups are able to internationalize much of their logistics, fundraising, propaganda, and planning activities. This also includes having bases far from their areas of operation. Thus Saikia and Stepanova argue that:

today it is more relevant to distinguish between *local/regional terrorism* employed to pursue an agenda confined to a particular armed conflict, national boarders or regional context and internationalized to some extent—and the truly *transnational terrorism* employed by networks pursuing unlimited goals in a transregional or even global context (Italics in original).[44]

This said it is important to recognize that a difference does exist between terrorist organizations whose primary goals are around national politics and those that have a much wider internationalized agenda.

DISCUSSION OF THE ETHICAL CONSIDERATIONS: THE TERRORIST ACT

The key question in any ethical assessment of terrorism is whether a terrorist act can ever be morally justified? A number of conditions have been proposed for a possible justification of terrorism.[45] These may include a subjugated minority group suffering serious systematic violence at the hands of a majority (such as in the recent conflicts in Kosovo and Aceh, Indonesia); citizens of a country occupied by a foreign military (as in Cyprus under the British in the 1950's); those lacking political power in relation to an oppressive state and its institutional apparatus (as was the case for Blacks in South Africa under Apartheid). Much of the discussion around the justification for the use of terrorism focuses on domestic or local context issues such as in the above. However, in an interview, the former Al-Qaeda leader Osama Bin Laden provides his justification for the type of international terrorism witnessed on 9/11:

> The American people should remember that they pay taxes to their government and that they voted for their president. Their government makes weapons and provides them to Israel, which they use to kill Palestinian Muslims. Given that the American Congress is a committee that represents the people, the fact that it agrees with the actions of the American government proves that America in its entirety is responsible for the atrocities that it is committing against Muslims.[46]

Bin Laden's statement is an attempt to reframe our understanding of "innocent victim" by arguing that these victims were not really innocent. However, his tenuous linking of "America in its entirety" to U.S. government policy can be criticized for its harsh conclusion that voting in U.S. elections and paying taxes to the government is a justification for all Americans to be maimed or killed.

Bin Laden's rather weak attempt to justify the killing of non-combatants by re-framing the classification of a non-combatant away from its often-associated notion of innocence (though some non-combatants are directly connected to the political harm of others) appears at one level to be a tacit acknowledgement that killing innocent people is morally wrong. Some terrorist attacks do target infrastructure and not people and at times use the threat of violence without carrying it out (though those that have done this such as the IRA have more than demonstrated previously their willingness to use force). However, it is the justification for the use of violence against the innocent that poses the ultimate moral challenge to those who resort to terrorism.

Consequentialism

A consequentialist view of terrorism needs to consider two related questions: what is the good that is being promoted? How useful is terrorism as a means of promoting it?[47] Fotion argues that for a terrorist act or policy to be justified it must demonstrate: a) that the end sought justifies the means; b) that the end will be achieved through the use of terrorism; and c) that terrorism is the least costly way to achieve this end—morally and otherwise.[48] Honderich argues that liberation-terrorism, terrorism used to get power for a people when nothing else will achieve this for them, is morally justified.[49] He goes on to argue that Palestinians have the moral right to use suicide bombings against Israeli civilians.[50] Suicide bombing, a tool used by a number of Islamist transnational terrorists, is often the primary effective weapon used to address the asymmetry of power between states and non-state actors. In employing such tactics Mackinnon and Fiala argue that some terrorists may be engaged in a consequentialist calculation whereby they perceive there is nothing wrong with targeting innocent civilians because they conclude that the only way to influence the current state of affairs is to resort to terrorism.[51] They go on to state that for one to draw a conclusion as to whether the end justifies the means, empirical studies would need to be undertaken to see whether international terrorist acts actually produce the desired outcomes. For example, research could be undertaken on whether the September 11 attacks changed the U.S. government's international behavior.

However, consequentialists like Fotion claim that the type of argument presented by Honderich and MacKinnon and Fiala is too permissive. He points out that arguments made by terrorists, that they had no other choice but to take innocent lives, are empirically false.[52] For him terrorists always have other choices. For example they can engage with their opponent's military structure. Saul specifically criticizes Honderich's assertion that the killing of Israeli civilians by Palestinian terrorists is permissible, by arguing that deliberately killing innocent people is a means disproportionate to the problems they seek to alleviate.[53] Another problem is that this end or "higher good" promoted by terrorists, that justifies the use of violence, is often defined in ideological terms, rather than based on the established preferences or interests of the people they claim to serve.[54] As Smilansky points out:

> The nationalistic and religious hatred lying behind IRA, Palestinian and al-Qaeda terrorism goes a long way towards explaining it. It is not so much substantive moral concerns—with massive danger to life, collective self-determination, personal freedom, basic cultural and religious rights, lack of alternatives or the like—that lie behind these instances of terrorism, but the ghosts of history, the depths of ill will and the temptations of power.[55]

Deontology

Typically the deontological position is one in which terrorism is considered morally wrong in itself, not because the consequences are bad on balance but because of what it is. However, Held argues that deontologists can morally justify a limited use of terrorism in some circumstances by appealing to deontological considerations of basic human rights and justice.[56] She argues that terrorism will be justified if it brought about a society where human rights of all citizens are respected. For example, if the rights of group A (e.g., the right to personal safety) is being violated by an oppressing group B and not being addressed under the current system of justice, whilst group B's right to personal safety is being protected under the law, then as a process of transition to achieve a better society Held argues it would be justified to equalize the violation of rights. That is, so as to elicit change to a proper situation it is morally permissible for the oppressed group to violate the rights of members of the oppressing group through the use of terrorism. In so doing it is hoped that this equalization of rights violation (in the above case the right to personal safety) would eventually lead to a cessation of such violation on both sides resulting in both groups' rights now being respected. As Held goes on to state:

> to fail to achieve a more just distribution of violations of rights (through the use of terrorism if that is the only means available) is to fail to recognize that those whose rights are already not fairly respected are individuals in their own right, not merely members of a group . . . whose rights can be ignored. . . . Arguments for achieving a just distribution of rights violations need not be arguments . . . that are more than incidentally about groups. They can be arguments about individuals' rights to basic fairness.[57]

However, as previously indicated, most deontological philosophers consider terrorism to be absolutely morally wrong. Gewirth argues that freedom and safety should be fundamental prerequisites of action, the protection of which generates a set of rights. Thus all innocent people have "an absolute right not to be made the intended victims of a homicidal project."[58] Bauhn argues that there is a moral difference between being directly and indirectly causally responsible for the action of others. We are morally responsible for what we directly deliberately cause but, except in certain special circumstances, not for those outcomes caused indirectly.[59] Primoratz criticises Held's argument for justifiable terrorism by stating that a citizen merely belonging to a relatively privileged group in society has not done anything to forfeit her life. In killing her so as to make the distribution of right to life violations in the entire population more just, then the terrorist is violating that person's individual right to life for reasons to do with the group she belongs. Such an act has nothing to do with any bad thing she has done or good she has failed to do but is purely carried out for the sake of the group.[60]

COUNTER-TERRORISM MEASURES

Counter-terrorism is a series of proactive policies which set out to eliminate terrorist groups and the environments in which they could thrive. Counter-terrorism agencies aim to proactively diminish the incidence of terrorist threats and attacks through the following counter-terrorism strategies:

> diplomacy (persuading others of the right of one's position), financial controls (undermining terrorists, criminal money making ventures, confiscating funds and dissuading or criminalizing individual donors), military force, intelligence (the constant collection and analysis of small, often seemingly unimportant pieces of information) and covert action; through legal (granting of powers to the authorities such that many of these actions are possible, e.g., extended stop and search, extra powers of detention, and the use of law to criminalize certain behaviors often associated with terrorism); repressive (use of asylum and refugee proceedings to detain suspected terrorists and to fingerprint others); conciliatory responses to terrorism; or through targeted and untargeted prevention.[61]

Counter-terrorism can be contrasted with anti-terrorism which refers to such situational crime prevention measures as target hardening (e.g., very high security measures at airports and airlines), surveillance through enhanced security (e.g., closed-circuit television, ports of entry controls) as well as other measures to deter or prevent attacks. The basic distinction between these two approaches is that counter-terrorism is an offensive or proactive strategy whereas anti-terrorism is a defensive or reactive strategy.[62]

Some of these counter-terrorism strategies are not without controversy. The strategy of covert surveillance has raised a number of ethical concerns. On privacy, Article 8 of the *European Union Convention on Human Rights* states "there shall be no interference by a public authority with the exercise of this right except such as is in accordance with the law and is necessary in a democratic society in the interests of national security, public safety or the economic well-being of the country, for the prevention of disorder or crime, for the protection of health or morals, or for the protection of the rights and freedoms of others."[63] In 2001 the U.S. government passed the USA PATRIOT Act.[64] Among other things the Act provides for enhanced tapping into e-mails, private records, and address books, the use of "roving wire-taps" for eavesdropping on telephone conversations, and access to private records.[65] In the United States this has caused controversy around whether National Security Agency counter-terrorism surveillance methods have violated U.S. citizens' human and fourth amendment rights[66] (The Fourth Amendment of the United States Constitution provides, "The right of the people to be secure in their persons, houses, papers, and effects, against unreasonable searches and seizures, shall not be violated, and no Warrants shall issue, but upon probable cause, supported by Oath or affirmation, and particularly describing the place to be searched, and the persons or things to be seized.").[67]

As well as concerns around privacy, other ethical considerations related to surveillance include its impact on an individual's autonomy, the motivation of those carrying it out, the means by which it is carried out, and the authority of those sanctioning and carrying it out. Consequentialists would argue that if large-scale surveillance by a state leads to security benefits for its citizens then this imposition is morally justified.[68] Deontologists are likely to reject any argument which implies that the rights of the few can be overridden by the interests of the many.[69]

Another contentious and arguably even more emotive issue is on the use of "enhanced interrogation techniques" and torture as counter-terrorism measures. Ethical considerations relate to whether these measures are ever justified (though some feel that the term "enhanced interrogation techniques" is merely a euphemism for torture).[70] Article 1 of the UN *Convention against Torture and other Cruel, Inhuman or Degrading Treatment* defines torture during interrogation as:

> Any act by which severe pain or suffering, whether physical or mental, is intentionally inflicted on a person for such purposes as obtaining from him or a third person information or a confession . . . when such pain or suffering is inflicted by or at the instigation of or with the consent or acquiescence of a public official or other person acting in an official capacity.[71]

Furthermore, Article 2 (2) of the Convention states that: "No exceptional circumstances whatsoever, whether a state of war or a threat of war, internal political instability or any other public emergency, may be invoked as a justification of torture."[72]

Commenting on research by Basoglu, Costanzo and Gerrity discuss how this work reveals seven types of torture: "sexual torture (e.g., rape, genital manipulation), physical torture (e.g., beating, burning), psychological manipulations (e.g., threats of torture, witnessing torture), humiliating treatment (e.g., forced nudity, feces in food), forced stress positions (e.g., forced standing for long periods, binding the body to restrict movement), sensory discomfort (e.g., extreme cold, blindfolding), and deprivation of basic needs (e.g., sleep, food)."[73]

Consequentialism

The application of consequentialism to counter-terrorism methods means asking whether such strategies leave the citizen more secure in the long term. Ginbar[74] outlines the consequentialist argument for torturing terrorists in what is called the "ticking bomb" scenario (the need to torture a known terrorist to find the location of a bomb). Consequentialists argue that the moral cost of the suffering of one terrorist under torture is justified when pitted against the suffering of many innocent civilians if the bomb detonates. U.S. federal judge, Richard Posner, states that those who doubt that torture is permissible when the stakes are high enough should not hold a position of responsibility.[75]

A number of nations have used "legalized torture" as a counter-terrorism measure to prevent terrorist attacks. In Israel the Landau model of "legalized torture," under which the interrogation of suspected terrorists was regulated between 1987 and 1999, with Supreme Court approval, detailed instructions to interrogators such as how to apply psychological "pressure" and a "moderate measure of physical pressure."[76] Methods included sleep deprivation, forced painful positions, and incommunicado detention.[77] This model was viewed as lawful under the "defense of necessity" provision in the penal law. However, it was subsequently replaced by a 1999 Israeli Supreme Court ruling which declared the Landau system as illegal, citing no legal justification for the "defense of necessity" provision as previously applied.[78] However, the Court ruled that the "defense of necessity" is available to interrogators who apply "physical methods" (the same as applied in the Landau model) in ticking bomb situations.[79] The United States introduced the "High Value Detainees" model after 9/11. This model is deemed to be one of "quasi-legalized torture."[80] Its initial legal basis consisted of executive orders, the classification of terrorist detainees as having no legal rights, a very narrow definition of torture, and a view that the Constitution granted the president as armed forces commander-in-chief unlimited powers, including the power to order torture.[81] The methods used included waterboarding, sleep and sensory deprivation, painful positions, and humiliation.[82] Neither Israel nor the United States have restricted torture to ticking bomb situations.

There have been a number of examples in which it is claimed the use of torture has led to good outcomes. Dershowitz, in advocating the efficacy of torture in foiling international terrorist incidents, offers the following story about a successful interrogation carried out by Philippine authorities in 1995 who:

> tortured a terrorist into disclosing information that may have foiled plots to assassinate the pope and to crash eleven commercial airliners carrying approximately four thousand passengers into the Pacific Ocean, as well as a plan to fly a private Cessna filled with explosives into CIA [Central Intelligence Agency] headquarters. For sixty-seven days, intelligence agents beat the suspect 'with a chair and a long piece of wood [breaking most of his ribs], forced water into his mouth, and crushed lighted cigarettes into his private parts'—a procedure that the Philippine intelligence service calls 'tactical interrogation.'[83]

In his book *Decision Points* former President George W. Bush states that the use of waterboarding on three suspects helped prevent attacks on Heathrow Airport and Canary Wharf in London, as well as against a number of U.S. targets both at home and abroad. He goes on to argue that "I knew an interrogation program this sensitive and controversial would one day become public. When it did, we would open ourselves up to criticism that America had compromised our moral values. I would have preferred that we get the information another way. But the choice between security and values was real."[84]

However, there are a number of objections from a consequentialist perspective to the use of torture. First, torture can be viewed as a slippery slope by which each act of torture potentially makes it easier to accept the use of torture in the future and could ultimately lead to legalized and institutionalized torture. Second, it is questionable as to how effective it is as it may lead to suspects providing false admissions just to stop the pain. Also, as the interrogator is never quite sure that they are getting the truth it is always likely to be in excess of what is necessary to elicit the information required. Third, there are legal implications, such as in the United Kingdom, by which it may not be possible to prosecute a suspect successfully if she or he has been tortured.[85] Fourth, carrying out torture could possibly lead to unhealthy psychological transformations in interrogators that damage their humanity, making them less sensitive to the pain of others.[86] Fifth, torture has the potential to damage the reputation and moral authority of the institution and state that sanctions it, leading to a strengthening of opposition against the torturer state.[87]

Research on the efficacy of such interrogation practices has generally concluded that torture is an ineffective tool in gathering intelligence. In his research, Schiemann found that information obtained from interrogational torture is highly likely to be unreliable, with this form of interrogation more likely to produce ambiguous and false information.[88] For example, Buckley points to the case of a person who was tortured by Philippine authorities and confessed to having taken part in the Oklahoma City bombing, about which he had no knowledge.[89] Costanzo and Gerrity not only found that torture elicited unreliable information, but it also led to a mental and emotional toll on victims *and* torturers, a loss of international stature and credibility for the state(s) involved, and led to a risk of retaliation against soldiers and civilians.[90] Indeed senior military personnel have argued that the fair treatment of prisoners means the enemy is more likely to surrender in combat.[91] As Conroy states: "not even a beaten enemy will surrender if he knows his captors will torture or kill him. He will resist and make his capture more costly. Fair treatment encourages the enemy to surrender."[92]

Deontology

The most familiar deontological position is that choices cannot be justified by their effects. Regardless of how "good" the consequences, some choices are morally forbidden. For these deontologists, "right" always has primacy over "good" regardless of the good that might be produced. Such moral absolutism is captured in Immanuel Kant's categorical imperative, second formulation, which states that we should treat people always "as an end and never simply as a means."[93] Although not an absolutist, the deontological philosopher W.D. Ross states that we also have a duty of nonmaleficence—a duty not to injure others.[94] A choice is morally right if it conforms to a moral norm and if the duties laid-out by Kant and Ross are to be adhered to it becomes clear why torture would be at odds with deontological principles.

However, what about the ticking bomb scenario? The situation in which the interrogators reasonably believe that torturing the terrorist will probably save thousands of innocent lives; they know that there is no other way to save those lives; the threat to life is imminent; the terrorist is known to be responsible for planning, transporting, and arming the device and will be morally responsible for the murder of thousands if it explodes. Kleinig presents the following arguments to suggest that, although a scenario may be presented hypothetically as in the above, it does not present itself in reality. He states:

- It suggests there is a known threat—not just a possibility or probability—but in practice such a high degree of certainty is unlikely to occur . . .

- There is a need for immediate action, because it is certain that the bomb will explode— again, is this degree of certainty likely to be common in practice?

- The magnitude of the danger is enormous, and so it is said to be permissible to apply torture, but . . . the moral status of any alternative decision is unclear. Similarly, there is no moral clarity about whether or not torture is justified, excusable, or regrettable in these circumstances.

- It is claimed that only the application of torture will secure the necessary information, but we cannot really be sure there are no other alternatives. Also torture ought not to be regarded as a kind of shortcut that is convenient in such circumstances . . .

- It would seem essential that the person we intend torturing be the maker of the threat. This is so because . . . the moral justification for torture seems much weaker if we encourage him to talk by, for example, torturing his child or his aging mother in front of him.

- It is said that the outcome of the torture will be the removal of the threat. It is assumed, then, that information gained from the torture will almost certainly dispel the danger, but can this be claimed with absolute certainty?[95]

But *what if* the "perfect storm" of the ticking bomb scenario did occur in reality? Harel and Sharon propose an argument in which deontologists can justify torture in such scenarios without compromising deontological principles.[96] They attempt to do this by providing a way by which deontology can distinguish between its categorical and conditional obligations as principles, and specific exceptions. Harel and Sharon state that this is possible because one may legitimately reject the identification of deontology with exceptionless rules. That is, deontological constraints do have exceptions.[97] They argue that the agents performing torture in extreme cases ought not to be guided by general rules or principles as to whether they are or are not breaking these rules, but should instead be carrying out such interrogation strictly as an act of necessity.[98] Therefore, in the ticking bomb scenario, it is not the principle according to which torture may or may not be permissible that should be at the forefront of an interrogator's reasoning, but the imperative to save lives. This allows for the practical necessity of torture in very extreme scenarios whilst maintaining the categorical nature of the prohibition on torture. For Harel and Sharon, this explains how torture can be categorically prohibited by international law yet be subject to a defense of necessity or duress under international criminal law.[99]

JUSTICE SYSTEM RESPONSE

The key question in this section is: can a system of justice guarantee justice for suspected terrorists? A number of issues emerge. First, there is the problem of classification: are suspected terrorists criminals or enemy combatants? Haynes outlines the legal definition of enemy combatant as:

an individual who, under the laws and customs of war, may be detained for the duration of an armed conflict. In the current conflict with al Qaida and the Taliban, the term includes a member, agent, or associate of al Qaida or the Taliban. In applying this definition, the United States government has acted consistently with the observation of the Supreme Court of the United States.[100]

There are two sub-categories in the general category of enemy combatant: lawful combatants and unlawful combatants. Lawful combatants are entitled to prisoner of war status and the full protections under the Third Geneva Convention. Unlawful combatants do not receive such status and protections.[101] The Bush Administration determined that Al-Qaeda members are unlawful combatants because "(among other reasons) they are members of a non-state actor terrorist group that does not receive the protections of the Third Geneva Convention."[102] Teson states that by their own admission terrorists are at war yet choose not to identify themselves as combatants, thus preventing the laws of war to operate normally. Thus they can claim combatant license to kill others (they regard to be at war with) yet claim civilian immunity when the army is looking for them.[103]

Feldman discusses the legitimate criminal justice response to this problem. He argues that in the case of international terrorism, such acts can plausibly be characterized as crime and war, because terrorism constitutes a kind of war crime,[104] thus undermining the binary character of the crime/war distinction. Feldman recognizes that generally criminals may not be killed by those pursuing them if they do not pose an immediate threat and instead may be punished after capture. In contrast, war adversaries may be killed by pursuers who are not obliged to show mercy—but they generally are not punished after capture. International terrorists therefore can be treated as war adversaries whilst being pursued, but as criminals after they are captured. Teson argues that the treatment of terrorism is *sui generis*: for it does not fall neatly into a law-enforcement domain or a just-war domain.[105] He therefore argues for a standard that "mediates between the law-enforcement and just-war positions by trying to address the main concerns of each. It rejects the law-enforcement view that terrorists are just like any other criminals, by allowing the targeted killing of a terrorist who threatens to kill innocents. It likewise rejects the just-war view that known terrorists are enemy combatants who can be killed on sight regardless of the threat they actually pose."[106] Second, there is the problem of whether suspected terrorists will get a fair trial (an essential right in all sovereign states respecting the rule of law). However, the rights such suspects have under the criminal law and the covert intelligence gathering techniques and strategies needed to bring them to justice may run into conflict. Wedgwood succinctly sums up this conflict when she states:

> states that criminal cases need more than circumstantial evidence. There needs to be much more than proof 'beyond a reasonable doubt'. Ordinarily, there needs to be brave eyewitnesses who will testify, despite the possibility of retaliation for their testimony. To compound that, the rules of evidence often result in important information never reaching the courtroom due to not having a search warrant when it was found. Even though the evidence is critical to the case, it cannot be used in court, along with—for example, the al Qaeda computer hard drives chock full of organizational data that a *Wall Street Journal* reporter found in a Kabul marketplace—might not be admissible, no matter how important they are. Statements made by combatants in custody might also be rejected if the fighters were denied access to counsel at the time. Any defense lawyer sent to the battlefield would advise captured combatants to stop talking, undermining chances of uncovering timely intelligence about al Qaeda's plans. And criminal law requires that sensitive methods of surveillance be disclosed when they yield information offered as evidence, even though such transparency may prevent intercepting telltale signs of future attacks.[107]

Despite this concern, evidence suggests that it is indeed possible for suspected terrorists to receive a similar level of justice to suspects of other crimes. A Center on Law and Security report charting convictions for jihadist terrorist threats against U.S. domestic targets prosecuted in U.S. federal courts from September 11, 2001 to September 11, 2011 found that "Aside from the rate of cases that go to trial, there appears to be no statistically significant difference in how effectively the justice system processes [jihadist] terrorism cases versus all federal criminal cases."[108]

Third, there are a number of extrajudicial issues in fighting the war on terror. For example, extrajudicial detention, the detention of suspects by a state without it laying formal charges against them (such as is the case for many of the high value detainees held in Guantanamo Bay by the United States). Extraordinary rendition, defined as "the transfer—without legal process—of a detainee to the custody of a foreign government for purposes of detention and interrogation."[109] The CIA have reportedly been involved in this practice, with 54 foreign governments participating in some way.[110] Extrajudicial or targeted killings, defined as "the extrajudicial intentional killing by the State of an identified person for a public purpose."[111] "Intentional" in this context means the state directly intends to kill the target.[112] One of the central moral problems with extrajudicial killings is that the state has a moral obligation not to take the life of a person without due process. This also includes foreign nationals who have a universally recognized right to life. According to Teson there are four conditions which justify a targeted killing during peacetime:

1. The targeted killing will save many lives, including many innocent lives.
2. The public purpose of the targeted killing is just.
3. The target of the killing is morally culpable, a villain.
4. There are no non-lethal alternatives available, such as diplomatic threats or capture.[113]

However, these four conditions would not be accepted as justifications by all moral philosophers.

It is important to examine two general objections to targeted killings before continuing with a consequentialist and deontological examination of this issue. These objections are an epistemic objection and objection from virtue.[114] The epistemic objection is one in which governments fighting terrorism must assess whether the conditions exist to permit a targeted killing. They must determine whether it is a wartime or peacetime setting; that they have the right person; that killing this person is necessary to avert a terrorist attack; and that the operation will have acceptable collateral costs.[115] Therefore a key ethical issue around the killing of Osama Bin Laden in 2011 is whether Abbottabad (Pakistan), where he was discovered, was a wartime or a peacetime setting. If it was a wartime setting, then Bin Laden was an enemy combatant and could be legitimately killed. If it was a peacetime setting, then he could only have been killed in order to avert a terrorist threat (and even then, only if he was given the chance to surrender). The objection from virtue assumes that liberal democratic governments have certain values and virtues for which they stand, such as being proportionate, engaging in lawful coercion and coercion under the rule of law. In considering the morality of targeted killings the state must weigh-up the goodness of the terrorist's death against the badness that could emerge from the undermining of the moral integrity of the government sanctioning the killing.[116]

Consequentialism

According to Rachels the consequentialist rationale for an extrajudicial targeted killing or assassination is justified if the following conditions are met:

1. The outcome of the assassination must be such in terms of the good achieved as to outweigh the act of destroying a human life.
2. The assassination must be the only or the least objectionable method of achieving the good results.
3. Out of all the possible actions available, it should represent 'the best overall balance of maximizing good and minimizing evil.'[117]

Moore states that there are two consequentialist balances to assess: first, does the practice of targeted killings produce net good consequences, and second, does some particular targeted killing produce net good consequences?[118] Each answer impacts the other. For example, the agent in the field pursuing terrorist suspects needs to consider the long-term consequences of his or her action (such as how this will contribute to the reputation of his or her country, and how his or her country will be perceived in relation to upholding international law, etc.). Similarly, state authorities sanctioning a policy of targeted killings should consider the fact that the policy could be imperfectly applied in the field and damage the reputation of the state the agent works for. However, consequentialists in favor of targeted killings will argue that the good achieved in killing terrorists, and by doing so ensuring the protection of the state and its allies, outweighs the negativity surrounding its reputation.

Although some consequentialist philosophers may argue that the trade-off of reputation for safety is a price worth paying, in reality both reputation and safety in the long-term could be undermined. For example, drone strikes,[119] a key method used in targeted killings by the CIA and instrumental in hindering Taliban operations by killing hundreds of low-level Taliban fighters and a number of their top commanders in Pakistan,[120] have had a number of unintended negative consequences. Between June 2004 through mid-September 2012 drone strikes have killed an estimated 471–881 civilians including 176 children.[121] Such strikes have soured U.S.-Pakistani relations to such an extent that a study by the Pew Research Center showed that 74% of Pakistanis in 2012 consider the United States an enemy.[122]

Deontology

According to Moore a deontological permission for targeted killings can be found from a retributivist standpoint whereby deontologists may justify a targeted killing from the categorical obligation to punish the guilty, particularly those, it has been argued, whose acts in the past have merited a sentence of death.[123] However, the typical deontological position, and the one most in keeping with Kantian deontology, is that extrajudicial killings can never be morally justified.

Deontological obligations (such as the duty not to kill innocent people) must be adhered to even if in doing so it does not produce the best consequences. An example of how a violation of the duty not to kill an innocent person led to a net good consequence is illustrated in the story of the capture of four Soviet diplomats in the 1980's by Middle Eastern terrorists who made certain demands on the Soviet Union accompanied by threats to kill the diplomats.[124] After the terrorists killed one of the diplomats to demonstrate how serious they were, the KGB,[125] knowing who they were but powerless to attack them, killed an innocent relative of one of the terrorists and threatened to kill every relative of the terrorists in the Middle East if the remaining three Soviet diplomats were not released unharmed. The terrorists released the diplomats and no further kidnappings of Soviet or Russian officials took place for 20 years in the Middle East.[126] For deontologists, the killing of the innocent relative is not morally justified despite the net good consequences. Khatchadourian argues that extrajudicial killings are never morally justified where the suspected terrorist's life is taken, and no due process of law has occurred so as to allow the suspect an opportunity to bring a defense against the alleged charges.[127]

At a philosophical level many of the issues around the legal status of terrorists, appropriate levels of coercion in eliciting information, covert surveillance, and targeted killings are difficult. Deciding upon the ethically right conduct is a constant duel between seeking the best overall consequences and adherence to fundamental duties. Consequentialism and deontology as moral frameworks to investigate these ethical issues are useful but not without their flaws.

Consequentialism has a number of practical and philosophical problems. First, it is often difficult to predict the medium and long-term future consequences of a decision. At a strategic level, an assessment of the possible outcomes is calculated by individuals who will make decisions based on their current understanding of the possible ramifications of these actions. Clearly the more informed an individual is the better placed he or she will be to make the correct decision. However, even for established counter-terrorism organizations, predicting the future is never easy and judgments made based on evaluations of past cause-and-effect results are not necessarily going to produce the same outcomes in the future. Second, an assessment of whether an act is good may vary at different points in time. For example, the immediate good outcome of eliciting information through torture or the extrajudicial killing by a state agent of a high-level terrorist operative may have more long-term negative consequences due to a public backlash, which in net terms far outweighs the "positives" of the state's original action. Third, there is an asymmetry of consequences for those engaged in the fight against international terrorism. The evidence suggests that the consequences for those fighting terrorism in the West, in terms of the risk of being a victim of terrorism, is significantly lower than for those living in parts of the Middle East, North Africa, and South Asia. Therefore it must be recognized that efforts to tackle international terrorism will have uneven consequences in terms of its negative impacts. Any consequentialist calculation must factor this in before deciding the morally correct outcome. Fourth, consequentialist decisions can at times be at odds with the law which will always be a restraining factor in a state's overtly expressed counter-terrorism practices.

The deontological system of assessing the morally correct course of action has also practical and philosophical problems. First, adherence to a set of principles may not be appropriate when fighting in an anomalous conflict as is the case in the fight against international terrorism. Such a conflict, which deviates from standard, normal, or expected rules of engagement, whereby innocent non-combatants are deemed appropriate targets by terrorists, often mean that governments are expected to play by the rules against adversaries who are *anomos* ("without law"). The ticking bomb scenario is an example of this and one that absolutist deontologists will always struggle to address adequately. Second, as obligations always trump outcomes in the absolutist deontological equation, notions that would "make sense" to many, such as torturing a known terrorist operative so as to elicit invaluable life-saving information, would be deemed immoral due to the violation of the principle of nonmaleficence ("first, do no harm"). Third, and a corollary of the second point, deontology does not address the problem of conflicting duties particularly well. For example, the principle of nonmaleficence is a right of both the terrorist and their potential innocent victim. Yet absolutist deontologists would not advocate the abrogation of this right for the terrorist (through torture) even though the terrorist is willing to see this right abrogated for an innocent victim (through terrorism).

The discussion of ethics as it relates to international terrorism and criminal justice is not just of relevance to the philosopher, criminologist, or legal expert. International terrorism challenges liberal democracies and the very principles upon which they are founded. In meeting this challenge liberal democratic governments must adhere to the laws and conventions for which they have signed up to defend and which also affirm the values for which they stand. Counter-terrorism and judicial practices must therefore conform to these duties as in effect such laws are deontological. It is therefore duties, not consequences, which should be the primary determinant of a state's actions, and a government's integrity in the fight against international terrorism and winning the war of ideas rests on its willingness and ability to see through its fundamental values—even when the bomb is ticking.

ENDNOTES

1. The National Consortium for the Study of Terrorism and Responses to Terrorism. (2011). *Background Report: 9/11, Ten Years* Later. http://www.start.umd.edu/sites/default/files/files/announcements/BackgroundReport_10YearsSince9_11.pdf

2. Belasco, A. (2011). *The Cost of Iraq, Afghanistan, and Other Global War on Terror Operations since 9/11*. Congressional Research Service http://fas.org/sgp/crs/natsec/RL33110.pdf

3. Summary: Direct War Death Toll in Iraq, Afghanistan and Pakistan since 2001 http://www.costsofwar.org/sites/default/files/Direct%20War%20Death%20Toll%20in%20Iraq,%20Afghanistan%20and%20Pakistan%20since%202001%20to%20April%202014%206%2026.pdf

4. Krieger, Z. Iraq's Universities Near Collapse. *Chronicle of Higher Education*, May 18, 2007 in Hugh Gusterson (n.d.) The University of War http://costsofwar.org/sites/default/files/articles/54/attachments/Gusterson%20Universities%20and%20the%20Costs%20of%20the%20Iraq%20Wars-3.pdf

5. UNHCR. Statistics of displaced Iraqis around the world: Global overview (September 24, 2007). http://www.unhcr.org/egi-bin/texis/vex/home/opendoc.pdf?tbl=SUBSITES&id=470387fc2 In O. Dewachi (Ed.) (2011). *Insecurity, Displacement and Public Health Impacts of the American*

Invasion of Iraq (p. 3) http://costsofwar.org/sites/default/files/articles/17/attachments/DewachiIraqiRefugees.pdf

6. Dewachi, O. (2011). *Insecurity, Displacement and Public Health Impacts of the American Invasion of Iraq.* p. 4 http://costsofwar.org/sites/default/files/articles/17/attachments/DewachiIraqiRefugees.pdf

7. Crawford, N.C. (2014). U.S. Costs of Wars Through 2014: $4.4 Trillion and Counting: Summary of Costs for the U.S. Wars in Iraq, Afghanistan and Pakistan p. 1 http://costsofwar.org/sites/default/files/articles/20/attachments/Costs%20of%20War%20Summary%20Crawford%20June%202014.pdf

8. Crawford, N.C. (2014). p. 2.

9. Global Terrorism Data Base: Global incidents from 09.12.2001–09.11.2011 http://www.start.umd.edu/gtd/search/Results.aspx?start_yearonly=&end_yearonly=&start_year=2001&start_month=9&start_day=12&end_year=2011&end_month=9&end_day=11&asmSelect0=&asmSelect1=&dtp2=all&success=yes&casualties_type=b&casualties_max=

10. Global Terrorism Data Base: Global incidents from 09.11.1991–09.10.2001 http://www.start.umd.edu/gtd/search/Results.aspx?start_yearonly=&end_yearonly=&start_year=1991&start_month=9&start_day=11&end_year=2001&end_month=9&end_day=10&asmSelect0=&asmSelect1=&dtp2=all&success=yes&casualties_type=b&casualties_max=

11. Global Terrorism Data Base: Incidents by Region 09.12.2001–09.11.2011 http://www.start.umd.edu/gtd/search/Results.aspx?charttype=bar&chart=regions&casualties_type=b&casualties_max=&start_year=2001&start_month=9&start_day=12&end_year=2011&end_month=9&end_day=11&dtp2=all Incidents by Region 09.11.1991-09.10.2001 http://www.start.umd.edu/gtd/search/Results.aspx?charttype=bar&chart=regions&casualties_type=b&casualties_max=&start_year=1991&start_month=9&start_day=11&end_year=2001&end_month=9&end_day=10&dtp2=all

12. Global Terrorism Data Base: Incidents by Region 09.12.2001–09.11.2011 and Incidents by Region 09.11.1991–09.10.2001.

13. Global Terrorism Data Base: Incidents by Region 09.12.2001–09.11.2011 and Incidents by Region 09.11.1991–09.10.2001.

14. Global Terrorism Data Base: Incidents by Region 09.12.2001–09.11.2011 and Incidents by Region 09.11.1991–09.10.2001.

15. The National Consortium for the Study of Terrorism and Responses to Terrorism. (2012). New data reveals al-Qaida-linked groups among most active terrorist groups in the world. The groups are: Taliban; al-Shabaab; Boko Haram; Tehrik-i-Taliban; al-Qaida in the Arabian Peninsula; al-Qaida in Iraq; al-Qaida in the Lands of the Islamic Maghreb; Abu Sayyaf Group; Islamic State of Iraq; Haqqani Network and Lashkar-e-Jhangvi. http://www.start.umd.edu/news/new-data-reveals-al-qaida-linked-groups-among-most-active-terrorist-groups-world

16. Silke, A. (2008). Research on terrorism: A review of the impact of 9/11 and the global War on Terrorism. In H. Chen, E. Reid, J. Sinai, A. Silke, B. Ganor (Eds.), *Terrorism Informatics: Knowledge Management and Data Mining for Homeland Security.* (p. 28). New York: Springer.

17. Silke, A. (2008).

18. Silke, A. (2008).

19. Silke, A. (2008).

20. Silke, A. (2008).

21. An ethical system which is sometimes attributed to the German Philosopher, Immanuel Kant (1724–1804), because of his emphasis on performing a moral act out of a sense of duty and not inclination.

22. A normative ethical theory which is sometimes stated as "the greatest good for the greatest number."

23. Kleinig, J. (n.d.). *Criminal Justice Ethics* Oxford Bibliographies http://www.oxfordbibliographies. com/view/document/obo-9780195396607/obo-9780195396607-0080.xml

24. Kleinig, J. (n.d.).

25. Harman, G. (1996). Moral relativism. In G. Harman and J. Jarvis Thomson (Eds.), *Moral Relativism and Moral Objectivity*. Blackwell: Oxford.

26. See Shin Kim (n.d). *Moral Realism* http://www.iep.utm.edu/moralrea/ for an exposition on these concepts.

27. Schmid, A., & Jongman, A. (1988). *Political Terrorism: A Research Guide to Concepts, Theories, Data Bases and Literature*. Amsterdam: North Holland.

28. Mythen, G., & Walklate, S. (2012). Global terrorism, risk and the state. In Steve Hall and Simon Winlow (Eds.), *New Directions in Criminological Theory* (p. 318). Abingdon, Oxon: Routledge.

29. Weston, N., & Innes, M. (2010). Terrorism. In Fiona Brookman, Mike Maguire, Harriet Pierpoint and Trevor Bennett (Eds.), *Handbook on Crime*. Cullompton, Devon: Willan.

30. Williams, K.S. (2008). Terrorism and state violence. In K.S. Williams (Ed.), *Textbook on Criminology*. Oxford: Oxford University Press.

31. Spree killings are killings which take place in two or more locations without much of a time break between the murders.

32. Innes, M., & Levi, M. (2012). Terrorism and counter-terrorism. In Mike Maguire, Rod Morgan and Robert Reiner (Eds.), *The Oxford Handbook of Criminology* fifth edition (pp. 660–685). Oxford: Oxford University Press.

33. Carrabine, E., Cox, P., Fussey, P., Hobbs, D., South, N., Thiel, D., & Turton, J. (2014). Political violence, terrorism and counter-terrorism. In E. Carrabine et al. (Eds.), *Criminology: A Sociological Introduction* (p. 440). Abingdon, Oxon: Routledge.

34. Cohen, S. (2001). *States of Denial: Knowing About Atrocities and Suffering*. Cambridge: Polity.

35. Innes, M., & Levi, M. (2012). p. 662.

36. Mythen, G., & Walklate, S. (2012).

37. Mythen, G., & Walklate, S. (2012).

38. Mythen, G., & Walklate, S. (2012).

39. Cited in Carrabine, E., Cox, P., Fussey, P., Hobbs, D., South, N., Thiel, D., & Turton, J. (2014).

40. Saikia, J., & Stepanova, E. (2009). Introduction. In J. Saikia & E. Stepanova (Eds.), *Terrorism: Patterns of Internationalization*. New Delhi: Sage.

41. Saikia, J., & Stepanova, E. (2009). p. xvii.

42. Saikia, J., & Stepanova, E. (2009).

43. Saikia, J., & Stepanova, E. (2009).

44. Saikia, J., & Stepanova, E. (2009). p. xxiii

45. Young, R. (2004). Political terrorism as a weapon of the politically powerless. In I. Primoratz (Ed.), *Terrorism: The Philosophical Issues*. Hampshire: Palgrave MacMillan.

46. Bin Laden, O. (2005). The example of Vietnam. In B. Lawrence (Ed.), J. Howarth (Trans.), *Messages to the World: The Statements of Osama Bin Laden* (pp. 139–144). London and New York: Verso. http://plato.stanford.edu/entries/terrorism/

47. Primoratz, I. (Ed.). (2004). *Terrorism: The Philosophical Issues*. Hampshire: Palgrave MacMillan.

48. Fotion, N. (2004). The burdens of terrorism. In I. Primoratz (Ed.), *Terrorism: The Philosophical Issues*. Hampshire: Palgrave MacMillan.

49. Honderich, T. (2003). Our responsibility, and what to do. In *After the Terror*. Edinburgh: Edinburgh University Press.

50. Honderich, T. (2007). *Humanity, Terrorism, Terrorist War: Palestine, 9/11, Iraq, 7/7 . . .* London: Continuum International Publishing Group Ltd.

51. MacKinnon, B., & Fiala, A. (2015). Violence and war. In *Ethics: Theory and Contemporary Issues* 8th edition. Stamford: Cengage Learning.

52. Fotion, N. (2004).

53. Saul, B. (2006). *Two Justifications for Terrorism: A Moral Legal Response* in Foreign Policy in Focus http://fpif.org/two_justifications_for_terrorism_a_moral_legal_response/

54. Primoratz, I. (2011). Terrorism. In *The Stanford Encyclopedia of Philosophy* http://plato.stanford.edu/entries/terrorism/

55. Smilansky, S. (2004). *Terrorism, Justification and Illusion* http://www.ucl.ac.uk/~uctytho/SmilanskyTerrorism.html

56. Held, V. (2008). *How Terrorism Is Wrong: Morality and Political Violence*. Oxford: Oxford University Press.

57. Held, V. (2008). pp. 89–90.

58. Gewirth, A. (1981). Are there any absolute rights? *The Philosophical Quarterly, 31*, 1–16. Cited in http://plato.stanford.edu/entries/terrorism/

59. Bauhn, P. (1989). *Ethical Aspects of Political Terrorism: The Sacrificing of the Innocent*. Lund: Lund University Press. Cited in http://plato.stanford.edu/entries/terrorism/

60. Primoratz, I. (2008). book review of Held, Virginia, 2008, *How Terrorism Is Wrong: Morality and Political Violence*. Oxford: Oxford University Press. In Notre Dame Philosophical Reviews https://ndpr.nd.edu/news/23851-how-terrorism-is-wrong-morality-and-political-violence/

61. Williams, K.S. (2008). p. 572.

62. Williams, K.S. (2008). p. 573.

63. Council of Europe. (1950). *Convention for the Protection of Human Rights and Fundamental Freedoms as amended by Protocols No. 11 and No. 14.*

64. The acronym USA PATRIOT stands for Uniting and Strengthening America by Providing Appropriate Tools Required to Intercept and Obstruct Terrorism

65. Williams, K.S. (2008). p. 570.

66. Gellman, B. (2013). NSA broke privacy rules thousands of times per year, audit finds. *Washington Post* August 15, 2013. http://www.washingtonpost.com/world/national-security/nsa-broke-privacy-rules-thousands-of-times-per-year-audit-finds/2013/08/15/3310e554-05ca-11e3-a07f-49ddc7417125_story.html

67. The Fourth Amendment in Cornell University Law School: Legal Information Institute http://www.law.cornell.edu/wex/fourth_amendment

68. Macnish, K. (n.d.). Surveillance ethics. Internet Encyclopedia of Philosophy http://www.iep.utm.edu/surv-eth/

69. Macnish, K. (n.d.).

70. The Guardian Online. (2012). Former Senior Bush official on torture: 'I think what they did was wrong' Philip Zelikow, top adviser to Condoleezza Rice, talks to the Guardian about his top secret 2006 memo on interrogation http://www.theguardian.com/world/2012/apr/05/bush-official-torture-condoleezza-rice

71. United Nations. (1984, 1987). *Convention against Torture and Other Cruel, Inhuman or Degrading Treatment or Punishment*. p. 1. Retrieved May 7, 2008 from www.ohchr.org/english/law/cat.htm. In Costanzo, M., & Gerrity, E. (2009). The effects and effectiveness of using torture as an

interrogation device: Using research to inform the policy debate. *Social Issues and Policy Review, 3*(1), 181.

72. Costanzo, M., & Gerrity, E. (2009).

73. Costanzo, M., & Gerrity, E. (2009).

74. Ginbar, Y. (2008). *Why Not Torture Terrorists?: Moral, Practical, and Legal Aspects of the "Ticking Bomb" Justification for Torture*. Oxford: Oxford University Press.

75. Posner, R. (2002). The best offense. *The New Republic* September 2 2002, 28. http://www.newrepublic.com/article/the-best-offense

76. Ginbar, Y. (2008). Chpt 12.

77. Ginbar, Y. (2008).

78. Ginbar, Y. (2008). Chpt. 14.

79. Ginbar, Y. (2008).

80. Ginbar, Y. (2008). Chpt. 15.

81. Ginbar, Y. (2008).

82. Ginbar, Y. (2008).

83. Dershowitz, A. (2002). *Why Terrorism Works: Understanding the Threat, Responding to the Challenge*. New Haven: Yale. p. 137.

84. McGreal, C. (2010). Bush on torture: Waterboarding helped prevent attacks on London. *The Guardian* 9 November 2010 http://www.theguardian.com/world/2010/nov/09/bush-torture-waterboarding

85. Thienel, T. (2006). The admissibility of evidence obtained by torture under international law. *The European Journal of International Law, 17*(2), 349–367. http://ejil.oxfordjournals.org/content/17/2/349.full

86. Costanzo, M., & Gerrity, E. (2009).

87. Costanzo, M., & Gerrity, E. (2009).

88. Schiemann, J.W. (2012). Interrogational torture: Or how good guys get bad information with ugly methods. *Political Research Quarterly, 65*, 3–19.

89. Buckley, W.F. *Tortured Thought* in Townhall.com January 31 2002. http://townhall.com/columnists/williamfbuckley/2002/01/31/tortured_thought/page/full

90. Costanzo, M., & Gerrity, E. (2009).

91. Rieckhoff, P. (2006). Do unto your enemy. *The New York Times*. September 25.

92. Conroy, J. (2000). *Unspeakable Acts, Ordinary People*. New York: Knopf. p. 115.

93. Kant, I. (1993). *Grounding for the Metaphysics of Morals*. Translated by James W. Ellington 3rd edition. Indianapolis: Hackett Publishing Company, p. 36.

94. Skelton, A. (2012). William David Ross. *Stanford Encyclopedia of Philosophy*.

95. Kleinig, J. (2005). Ticking bombs and torture warrants. *Deakin Law Review, 10*(2), 614–627. In Cyndi Banks (Ed.) (2009). *Criminal Justice Ethics: Theory and Practice* 2nd Edition. Thousand Oaks, CA: Sage, p. 276.

96. Harel, A, & Sharon, A. (2008). What is really wrong with torture. *Journal of International Criminal Justice, 6*(2), 241–259.

97. Harel, A., & Sharon, A. (2011). Necessity knows no law: On extreme cases and uncodifiable necessities. *University of Toronto Law Journal, 61*(4), 845–865.

98. Harel, A., & Sharon, A. (2011).

99. Harel, A., & Sharon, A. (2008).

100. William J. Haynes II, General Counsel of the Department of Defense to members of the ASIL-CFR Roundtable, 12 December 2002 at http://www.cfr.org/international-law/enemy-combatants/p. 5312.

101. Haynes, W.J. II. (2002).

102. Haynes, W.J. II. (2002).

103. Teson, F.R. (2012). Targeted killing in war and peace: A philosophical analysis. In Claire Finklestein, Jens David Ohlin, and Andrew Altman (Eds.), *Targeted Killings: Law and Morality in an Asymmetrical World*. Oxford: Oxford University Press.

104. See Feldman, N.R. (2002). Choices of law, choices of war. *Journal of Law & Public Policy, 25*, 457–485.

105. Teson, F.R. (2012).

106. Teson, F.R. (2012).

107. Wedgwood, R., & Roth, K. (2004). Combatants or criminals? How Washington should handle terrorists. *Foreign Affairs, 83*(3), 126. http://www.foreignaffairs.com/articles/59902/ruth-wedgwood-kenneth-roth/combatants-or-criminals-how-washington-should-handle-terrorists

108. Center on Law and Security, New York University School of Law. (2011). *Terrorist Trial Report Card: September 11, 2001–September 11, 2011.*

109. Open Society Justice Initiative. (2013). *Globalizing Torture: CIA Secret Detention and Extraordinary Rendition.* New York: Open Society Foundation, p. 5.

110. Open Society Justice Initiative. (2013). p. 6.

111. Teson, F.R. (2012).

112. Teson, F.R. (2012).

113. Teson, F.R. (2012).

114. Teson, F.R. (2012).

115. Teson, F.R. (2012).

116. Teson, F.R. (2012).

117. Khatchadourian, H. (2005). Counter-terrorism: Torture and assassination. In Georg Meggle (Ed.), *Ethics of Terrorism & Counter-Terrorism* (p. 179). Cited in Cyndi Banks (2009) *Criminal Justice Ethics: Theory and Practice* 2nd Edition. Thousand Oaks, CA: Sage, p. 273.

118. Moore, M.S. (2012). Targeted killings and the morality of hard choices. In Claire Finklestein, Jens David Ohlin, and Andrew Altman (Eds.), *Targeted Killings: Law and Morality in an Asymmetrical World*. Oxford: Oxford University Press.

119. Drones are remotely operated unmanned aerial vehicles that can be armed with laser-guided missiles so as to deliver precision strikes.

120. Bergen, P., & Rowland, J. (2014). *Drones Decimating Taliban in Pakistan*, CNN (July 4, 2012), http://edition.cnn.com/2012/07/03/opinion/bergen-drones-taliban-pakistan/index.html

121. *Covert War on Terror*, The Bureau of Investigative Journalism, http://www.thebureauinvestigates.com/category/projects/drones/

122. Pew Research Center. (2012). Pakistani Public Opinion Ever More Critical of U.S.: 74% Call America an Enemy. *Available at* http://www.pewglobal.org/files/2012/06/Pew-Global-Attitudes-Project-Pakistan-Report-FINAL-Wednesday-June-27-2012.pdf

123. Moore, M.S. (2012).

124. Moore, M.S. (2012).

125. KGB *(Komitet gosudarstvennoy bezopasnosti)* translated in English as Committee for State Security. The KGB was the state security police of the former Soviet Union from 1954 to 1991. It was responsible, among other things, for external espionage and internal counter-intelligence.

126. See Hijazi, I.A. (1985). Beiruit captors free 3 Russians after a month. *New York Times*, October 31, A-1; Chi Halevi, C. (1987). A hard united line on the Mideast. *Chicago Tribune*, August 22, 17. Cited in Moore, M.S. (2012).

127. Khatchadourian, H. (2005). p. 178.

APPENDIX I

ETHICAL DILEMMAS IN CRIMINAL JUSTICE

The following ethical dilemmas pertaining to criminal justice are meant to stimulate discussion and debate about the moral question at hand, possible ethical foundations upon which individual decisions can be made, and the importance of considering stakeholders and differing points of view. Where based on factual events, the vignettes are listed with media references about the incidents.

This section is broken down into two parts. Part 1 are brief vignettes that can be used for classroom discussion. Part 2 ethical dilemmas are more in-depth stories of dilemmas that criminal justice practitioners might face while working in the system.

For each question, discussion can involve determining what the central moral issue at hand may be in the case, and what the particular stakeholders who are involved may have at risk when a decision is made.

PART I

1. A military veteran uses a service dog which assists him in navigation, walking, and mental health. While walking the dog on a beachfront boardwalk, the veteran is issued a citation by a police officer who points out that there is a "no animals allowed" policy on the boardwalk. The policy may exist for good reason, but the officer enforces it strictly by issuing a citation for violating the law, and the veteran and his spouse are told to leave the boardwalk (Alba, 2013).

2. A policy by a local fast-food restaurant is to grant free meals to officers in uniform. One officer, while off duty, puts on his uniform and visits the restaurant for the sole purpose of receiving a fee meal that day, even though he is not working. When other officers who are working arrive at the restaurant later in the day, the manager informs them that one officer has already been there to eat earlier in the day—causing the supervisor to realize that the officer in question is in fact off duty. He is confronted at his home by the supervisor who sees evidence that he did in fact put on his uniform and go to the restaurant just to get free food. When pressed for an explanation, the off-duty officer tells the supervisor that he was hungry and did not have enough money to eat.

3. An off-duty police officer is chased by officers from another jurisdiction as she speeds through their town, and when stopped asks why she isn't given a "free pass" because she is a police officer. In angry discussions with the officers who stopped her, the speeding officer states that her husband is a lieutenant with her department, and that she routinely gives officers she stops a "break" for traffic violations. She is arrested for disorderly conduct as she resists getting ticketed (Smith, 2010).

4. A newer police officer who maintains a close relationship with the public is angered by his immediate supervisor's demand that the department hand out more traffic citations, meeting a numerical minimum and causing fears of a "ticket quota." The officer secretly records

conversations with the supervisor which show that the department is in fact instituting a ticket quota. He takes the footage to a news media outlet and exposes the department publicly after he voices concerns to his superiors and they do not act to eliminate the policy. He is later fired by the department and voices publicly that his firing was related to his dissatisfaction with the policy (Miller, 2013).

5. Police officers on patrol in an area known for having high school students loitering and parking after hours see an SUV parked with what appears to be two occupants. Upon making contact, the SUV's occupants are a 17-year-old male and a 15-year-old female, and the officers catch them in the act of kissing in the vehicle with the windows rolled up. The female identifies herself as the daughter of the Chief of Police. She begins crying hysterically and says to the officers, "my dad is going to kill me" and begs for the officers to let her go.

6. At the scene of a traffic stop where both the driver and the passenger (both female) are suspected of having hid contraband or drugs on their bodies, a male police supervisor asks a female officer to perform a cavity search on the scene. The search is performed in view of the in-car camera to document the event, but questions arise as the video is made public as to the appropriateness of the search. The female officer is fired, but reinstated once she divulges that she was ordered to perform the search by her supervisor (Tomlinson, 2013).

7. On Christmas Eve night shift, an officer spends the bulk of the night on-duty, in uniform, at his residence with his family. The residence is located in the officer's patrol zone. The supervising sergeant is notified by other officers who are far from their homes and do not get to see their families. Although he is in uniform, the officer states to his supervisor, "we're not that busy with any calls, and I want to spend time with my two kids before they go to bed, lighten up, it's Christmas." One of the other officers on the shift is known as a proactive officer, and states "we're going to go out there and do some traffic stops, there's a lot of drunks out tonight because of the holidays."

8. A citizen filming a police SWAT standoff with his cameraphone catches the eye of officers who confront him and place the man in handcuffs in temporary custody. The man's pet dog, who is secured in his vehicle feet away from the encounter, gets loose and charges police officers, possibly because he sees his owner in distress. The dog becomes aggressive and is shot and killed by officers on the scene. The department has taken sincere steps toward engaging the community, but the entire incident goes viral after it is filmed by bystanders and posted to YouTube (Mai-Duc, 2014).

9. An officer in a police department, who is single, posts photos of himself on a personals website in uniform in various poses. Although the photos are not inappropriate, there are concerns among other officers about professionalism, and whether his personal safety is at risk. There is no policy in the department against use of the internet and work-related activities, photos, or information. In the past, other officers have posted photos of themselves on Facebook in uniform with their families, and information about where they work.

10. A patrol sergeant and another officer request to meet with the chief of police concerning a female officer who has been taking extended breaks, often for up to an hour, to pick up her child from day-care and take the child to her house in her patrol car. When confronted by her supervisor, the female officer says, "I'm not really doing anything wrong because everyone takes a long lunch break," and says that she cannot get anyone to pick up her child from day-care at certain hours of the day.

11. A local citizen has started a website devoted to photographs of police officers she has taken doing what she feels are inappropriate behaviors, such as sleeping in patrol cars on duty, smoking in their patrol cars and on traffic stops, and texting while driving. The website is a source of embarrassment to the entire city and its officers. Morale in the department is already very low due to budget cuts, many officers have resigned for "better pay somewhere else," and there is difficulty recruiting new officers who want to work in the department.

12. A recently promoted female sergeant has complained to her chief of police that other officers have talked behind her back about her "not being qualified," and that she got promoted "just because she's a woman." One of the officers was previously involved in a relationship with her that ended when they were both applying for the same promotion. When the chief discusses the matter with two officers on her shift, they deny saying anything to her, and say that she is on a "power trip" and that the lingering effects of the relationship are to blame.

REFERENCES AND FURTHER READING

Alba, M. (2013, August 9). Disabled veteran kicked off boardwalk because of service dog. *NBC 40 News*. Retrieved April 3, 2014, from http://www.nbc40.net/story/23096761/disabled-veteran-kicked-off-boardwalk-because-of-service-dog

Mai-Duc, C. (2014, February 14). Man who watched police shoot his dog sues city of Hawthorne. *LA Times*. Retrieved April 21, 2014, from http://articles.latimes.com/2014/feb/14/local/la-me-ln-hawthorne-dog-shooting-lawsuit-20140214

Miller, J.R. (2013, July 29). Former Alabama cop claims he was fired after blowing the whistle on ticket quotas. *Fox News*. Retrieved April 17, 2013, from http://www.foxnews.com/us/2013/07/29/former-alabama-cop-claims-was-fired-after-blowing-whistle-on-ticket-quotas/

Smith, G. (2010, January 14). Tape reveals officer's comments. *Charleston Post & Courier*. Retrieved April 7, 2014, from http://www.postandcourier.com/article/20100114/PC1602/301149902

Tomlinson, C. (2013, August 9). Trooper who conducted cavity search reinstated. *NBCDFW News*. Retrieved April 20, 2014, from http://www.nbcdfw.com/news/local/Trooper-Who-Conducted-Cavity-Search-Reinstated-219055671.html

APPENDIX II

PART II

1. Bribery with a Side of Cancer

Officer Jones is on routine patrol with his partner through the poorer district of his city. There has been an upsurge in drug related gang violence on his beat. Jones and his partner have been instructed to keep an extra eye out for the drug deals that have become more frequent over the past few weeks.

It is nearing 11:00 PM. The streets are, for the most part, dark and quiet. A few flickering streetlamps light the way for the occasional pedestrian. Some of the surrounding apartment buildings have lights lit and every so often a car passes by.

With a few hours left in their shifts and nothing particularly interesting happening, Officer Jones and his partner turn to mundane conversation.

"How's the family?" his partner asks.

"Good, good . . . " Jones says, but trails off. "Jessica's due in for surgery day after tomorrow, the cancer is spreading."

His partner cringes. Jessica is Jones's youngest daughter. "They think the surgery will do any good?"

Jones shrugs. "Don't know. I hope so. Insurance is only willing to cover so much. They're saying that it's a preexisting condition and they're fighting us every step of the way for her coverage, some of her meds especially have to come out of pocket."

His partner is about to reply when he notices something off to the left: two young-looking men in bulky clothing walking toward the unlit rear parking lot of a convenience store. He points it out to Jones, who nods. As his partner steers the patrol car into the convenience store lot, they notice the two suspicious men trade something between themselves. Jones is out of the car and on the first of the suspects before his partner has a chance to throw the car into park.

There is a scuffle and some confusion, but Jones manages to keep hold of his suspect; his partner is forced to chase down the other one.

"Man," his suspect groans, "I can't get another mark on my record. Look man, I've got two gees cash on me, you can have it all if you just let me go."

Jones pauses for a second. Two grand is a lot of money, especially with his daughter's illness eating up so much of the family finances. Out of sight of his partner, it would be so easy to let the guy go and no one would have to know. **What would you do?**

2. Just a Two-Dollar Cuppa

Officer Smith works the graveyard patrol shift in one of the lower-middle-class neighborhoods of his district. It's not the greatest shift in the world, but he works it diligently and he's managed to get used to it. Every day, like clockwork, around two or three in the morning, Officer Smith starts to feel the late hours of his shift. Every day, like clockwork, he stops at one of the late-night fast-food restaurants or convenience stores to get a fresh cup of hot coffee. It's one of the few pleasures Officer Smith takes during the long, often boring, graveyard patrol hours.

Recently, there have been a string of robberies of convenience stores in the city, several of which have been on his patrol route. Officer Smith has noted that many of the store managers and clerks working the graveyard shifts have been getting more and more nervous, a few of them have even been cutting down their store hours.

The night before, while Smith was enjoying a night off, the 7-Eleven that Officer Smith frequented was robbed. Tonight, as Smith drives by on his patrol, he determines that the 7-Eleven is still open. It appears that the staff have cleaned up from the investigation and it is business as usual. He decides to go ahead and check up on how things are, give the store clerks some peace of mind, and get his usual cup of coffee, so he pulls into the empty parking lot.

Inside, the clerk gives him a friendly wave as he goes to prepare his coffee. Officer Smith nods and preps his coffee black with two sugars. He is the only person in the store besides the clerk, so there is no line to pay for his coffee. As Smith pulls out his wallet, the clerk waves him off, "No charge, sir."

Officer Smith frowns, "It's all right, I don't mind paying for my coffee." Officers of the law are not supposed to accept gifts or gratuities on the job. Those things always come with an expectation or a price.

The clerk insisted, "No, no, I insist. Please take it."

Officer Smith frowns, his hand still on wallet, as he thinks for a few seconds about it. It is just one cup of coffee worth maybe a couple of dollars. **What would you do?**

3. **Gotta Pay the Bills**

Money had been always been a little tight for Lieutenant Garcia, her husband, and their three kids. Between bills, two cars, a mortgage, the kids' school costs, and the recent economic crash that had resulted in a pay cut for her husband, money was even tighter than ever.

It was harder for her husband to take additional time at work, so Garcia had been picking up additional shifts and taking overtime whenever she could. She was doing her best to remain within regulations, but every hour counted toward making ends meet, so there were some weeks where she pushed the overtime limit. Of course, Lieutenant Garcia was constantly exhausted, but so far ample amounts of coffee had been keeping her awake.

Or so she thought . . .

While on desk duty in the middle of a triple shift, one of her subordinates caught her after she had nodded off. "You ok, boss?" He asked.

She sat up straighter and shifted some things on her desk, "Of course, I'm fine. Why do you ask?"

The patrol officer gave her a strange look. "You've got bags under your eyes, Lieutenant. Are you getting enough sleep?"

"Yes . . . yes, I'm fine, did you need anything in particular?"

"Yes, actually . . . this duty assignment doesn't make any sense, Lieutenant, you've got some of us listed for patrols on totally separate beats at the same time."

Garcia could feel herself flush, she could remember having a lot of trouble focusing when she wrote that duty assignment. "Thank you for bringing it to my attention. I'll get that fixed right away." Her tone was more dismissive than she intended and she cringed internally. Lack of sleep must have been shortening the fuse on her temper.

"All right, boss," the officer said, still giving her a strange look as he turned to leave.

Garcia sighed and rubbed her eyes, earlier this week she had nearly botched a simple arrest because she had been going through the motions through muscle memory, and earlier in the morning she had been called into the Captain's office because of some reports she had written that didn't make coherent sense—probably because she'd been burning the midnight oil to write them. Yesterday the Captain had to warn her that she was going to go over her overtime allowance for this week if she wasn't careful. Maybe it would be in her best interest to stop taking extra shifts for a while. Except then she and her husband wouldn't be able to make ends meet. **What would you do?**

4. **A Mistaken Case of Violence**

Officer Kim was out on routine patrol duty when his radio went off. It was dispatch asking for a response to a noise complaint and a potential domestic dispute at a residence a few blocks away. Kim radioed in that he would respond and arrived at the residence a few minutes later. He could hear the couple arguing in their backyard.

Officer Kim walked up to the gate and announced himself; the arguing stopped immediately. He took a moment to take in the scene. The couple were standing on their back patio. The man was holding a baby in one arm and had his other arm out, as if warding the woman off. The woman look frustrated and exasperated. Kim unlocked the gate and entered the yard. "How're we doing back here, folks, you were getting a little loud."

The woman was the first to speak, her words came out slurred, "He won't lemme have my baby! He pushed me!"

"You're drunk," her partner said as he tried to calm the crying baby down. The woman screamed and tried to rip the child out of her partner's hands. He turned and the woman started beating on the man's back.

"I'm sorry, sir," the man said to Officer Kim, "We just received some bad news about her grandmother and during dinner tonight I might have let her have a few too many glasses of wine. She's not normally like this, I just don't want her to accidentally drop the baby."

Officer Kim cringed internally, his district had mandatory arrest laws in cases of domestic violence. The situation was made worse by the 911 call received from a neighbor. Kim was inclined to believe the man's story that his partner wasn't usually violent. He certainly couldn't recall any instance where he'd had to respond to a 911 call about this residence before. The woman was clearly drunk and obviously posed a danger to the child, but the man did seem to have the situation under control.

If he arrested the woman it would be a boatload of paperwork and hassle for the family. He was duty bound to make an arrest in this instance, especially since he saw the woman assault her partner, but Kim felt fairly confident that once the woman was able to sleep the alcohol off, things would be fine. **What would you do?**

5. **Sorry, Judge, it Just Suddenly Went Missing**

Joshua Thompson was lead chair in prosecuting the case of the year in his district. A brutal rape, a violent murder, it was everything the press could possible want, and there was a lot of pressure from higher up to land a solid conviction in this case. The police investigation led to one individual and they had made an arrest, but the man refused to confess to the incident. The evidence against the man was largely circumstantial, but the police were convinced that they had their man and Joshua was inclined to agree. They had one eyewitness to a man fleeing the scene of the crime and she had picked the suspect out of a photo lineup. He could made a case against the man and he was reasonably sure he could make a conviction.

There was only one problem . . .

The suspect had produced a receipt from a gas station and convenience store where he had made purchases about forty minutes before the time of the murder. The gas station was about thirty-five minutes away from the murder site if driving at around five to ten miles an hour over the speed limit. The eyewitness saw the man leaving the scene of the crime about ten minutes after the crime took place. It was plausible that the murder could have taken place in the ten-minute time frame between the suspect arriving at the crime scene and the suspect fleeing.

However, it was just as possible, if the defense were to get hold of this evidence, that they could instill enough reasonable doubt into the case that the jury would return a not-guilty verdict. If that were the case, Joshua would suffer a lot of flak from his bosses.

It would be really easy to lose the receipt, the defense wouldn't have to know it ever existed. And it would secure the conviction of a violent criminal. **What would you do?**

6. A Deal with the Devil

Jennifer Moreno is a full-time public defender. Due to the caseloads she'd been experiencing recently she'd found that she couldn't devote all of the time she needed to develop her cases. Her last several cases had resulted in convictions. Some of the defendants certainly deserved to go to prison, but a few of them she'd not been so sure about. Regardless, the series of losses had been disheartening and they did nothing to reduce her caseloads. As it was, on average she was lucky if she got to spend an hour with her clients before court.

She received a phone call from the district attorney's office one morning. One of the prosecutors wanted to meet her for lunch. Moreno presumed he wanted to negotiate a series of plea bargains in her upcoming cases. She cleared out time to meet the prosecutor for lunch.

Her suspicions were confirmed at the restaurant when, as soon as they both had ordered food, the prosecutor immediately began launching into an offer he had created. However, it was an unusual offer. "All right, let's be frank," the prosecutor said, "I know you're looking to move on up in the world and you're being held back by your ability to get results in court." Moreno frowned, but didn't interrupt him. "I'd like to offer you a deal, it's for your benefit, and you'll get some wins in court."

"Yeah, what do you want in return?" Moreno asked.

"Your office has picked up the Luis Garcia case, yes?" The prosecutor didn't wait for Moreno to answer, "I know you're due in the rotation for a new case, and the Garcia one has to be it."

He was right, she'd received the case file that morning. Garcia was being charged with armed robbery and assault, but the case on him was shaky at best, it was one of the few cases she was confident she had a chance at winning. "What are you offering him?"

"Not him. You," the prosecutor responded. Moreno frowned at him. "You get him to plead to thirty years, parole in fifteen, and I'll shoot you a few easy wins on five cases of your choosing." The prosecutor sat back in his seat looking satisfied with his offer.

Moreno's frown deepened. That was actually a very tempting offer. Garcia probably wasn't completely innocent in the armed robbery case so it wasn't like she'd be throwing an innocent man to the wolves. Five good wins could also put her in a good position to move out of the defender's office and into the district attorney's office. **What would you do?**

7. Family Reunion

It is well known that when a judge encounters a case in which he or she has a personally vested interest in some part of the trial, then the judge should be required to recuse themselves from the trial proceedings. Judge O'Reilly knew this, but had never been in a situation in which he had a personal connection to the trial proceedings. That changed one day when he was presiding over a rather routine trial of a young man pulled off the streets for dealing drugs and assisting in perpetuating gang turf wars.

Judge O'Reilly thought the defendant's name seemed familiar when he looked over the file, but Carpenter was a fairly common last name. He thought nothing of it, until he'd entered the court room and took note of the woman who appeared to be the defendant's mother. It took several moments for him to process why he recognized her. She had dyed her hair and gained some weight, but the woman was definitely the same woman he had dated in his early college years. He distinctly remembered, even now, twenty or so years later, because he had gotten her pregnant.

She pushed him away after the birth of the child, a son she had named Justin. Judge O'Reilly hadn't been allowed to see the boy or be involved in his life. But he cared that the child existed, he had even sent his mother monthly checks for a long while, until the checks started coming back marked "return to sender." Judge O'Reilly glanced down at the trial records . . . sure enough the twenty-two-year-old defendant's name was Justin Carpenter.

Judge O'Reilly knew immediately that he should recuse himself from the trial. But the charges levied against the man carried a fairly hefty price. If Justin were convicted he could be sentenced to twenty years or more, and, if Judge O'Reilly recused himself, that is the sentence Justin would likely receive. But if Judge O'Reilly remained on the trial he could make sure that Justin received an easy sentence. He blamed himself to some degree that Justin had ended up in this situation; if he had fought harder to be a part of the boy's life then maybe he could have prevented Justin from ever ending up in court. At the very least, if he remained on the trial then he could do everything in his power to make sure Justin received the help he needed to rehabilitate himself and get out of a life of crime. **What would you do?**

8. Witness Polishing, not Witness Coaching

Julie Rodriguez is the lead chair for the prosecution on a big murder/arson case. The trial is scheduled to begin in two months. Currently, Julie and her team are scheduled to work with the state witnesses to give them an idea of the questions they might be asked on the stand. The team also wants to get an idea of what the individual witnesses' answers might be. Key to the case are two eyewitnesses who saw the defendant at the scene of the crime.

Julie and her team are confident that their case is airtight, but better safe than sorry. In the process of preparing the eyewitnesses, she realizes that the two are having trouble keeping their story straight. They are just confusing little details, like the color of shirt or what type of shoes the defendant was wearing, but these sorts of little details can sometimes completely derail a case. All it takes is a little bit of doubt in the jurors' minds and a defendant can get off completely free.

Coaching a witness to say what you want them to say is illegal. Gauging what a witness is going to say and suggesting appropriate phrasing for answers is not. Julie has complete access to investigative reports and all evidence on file. She can corroborate the witnesses' testimony to the actual files and make sure the witnesses' statements can match the evidence. Surely correcting a few details and making sure the eyewitnesses are able to correctly recall these details on the stand can't be doing anything wrong. The eyewitness testimony is vital to making an airtight case, but their stories have to coincide and make logical sense or it might be enough to instill reasonable doubt into the jurors. **What would you do?**

9. The Case of the Sympathetic Inmate

CO Ruis was on duty monitoring the inmates working in the kitchens. All was normal and as it should be, though a couple of the larger inmates were bullying one of the smaller ones. Ruis knew that this particular inmate had been having trouble recently; he knew of a few instances where this inmate had had his food stolen from him at meal times. Ruis felt a little bad for the kid, but knew he would make the situation worse if he stepped in unnecessarily.

Ruis kept a sharp eye out, in addition to his duty of keeping track of the inmates, he also made sure that the situation for the smaller inmate didn't get too bad. The shift came to an end without a significant incident. Ruis and the other officers working with him rounded up the inmates according to post-shift procedures.

Ruis noticed that the smaller inmate was taking longer than the others to get in line. He moved over to make the inmate move. As he moved over, he saw the inmate slip some food into his pocket. Ruis frowned, but didn't immediately say anything. The inmate noticed Ruis coming toward him and hurriedly moved toward the line.

The officers moved the inmates out of the kitchen and Ruis found himself left with a dilemma. He should report the inmate as protocol required; however, he knew the inmate was probably starving. Ruis didn't know for sure how many meals had been stolen from the inmate, but he knew it was enough to make the man quite hungry. He honestly couldn't blame him for stealing. If Ruis reported him, the inmate would lose his job in the kitchen—which was counting toward good credit. If Ruis didn't report him, he wouldn't be doing his duty. **What would you do?**

10. **Prison of Brotherly Love**

CO Jones had no problems doing his job, he followed every rule and regulation to the letter. He lived a perfectly fine life, having nothing major to worry about beyond the usual stuff that everyone worries about. Recently, however, he'd been having some familial trouble. His younger brother was recently tried and found guilty of a felony in relation to gang activity. Jones's brother was slated to do ten years in the facility that Jones worked in.

At first Jones thought he was going to be reassigned to a different facility. But he was not reassigned. Jones decided that he would just tough it up and do his job; someone above probably knew better than him. He would just have to treat his brother like he would any other inmate.

For the first few months of the sentence everything was fine. Jones was able to pull his brother to the side and lecture him to make sure that his kid brother didn't make it obvious that he and Jones were related.

Somehow, though, a rival gang discovered the relation between Jones and his brother. The gang leader made it clear to Jones that if his demands weren't met, Jones's younger brother was going to suffer fatal consequences. CO Jones could report this to the warden; however, the rival gang leader made it clear that he had influence in other facilities and could kill Jones's brother from just about anywhere. Jones is not sure whether or not to believe him.

He feels stuck between a rock and a hard place. On the one hand he has the duty to report these threats to his immediate supervisor, possibly all the way up to the prison warden. On the other hand, he is concerned for his younger brother's life, and it could just be easier to give in to the rival gang leader's blackmail. **What would you do?**

11. **Emotionally Compromised**

CO Jennifer Warren is one of the few female correctional officers at the local high security prison. She constantly feels her gender in the prison environment. Over the years she has become used to the catcalls and inappropriate comments from the inmates. Most of them disgust her and she has no doubt that many of them belong behind bars. If one were to ask her, she would claim that those two factors have caused her to build up an immunity to the men she keeps behind bars.

Warren knows that some of the other COs she works with are willing to trade favors and privileges for sexual acts with the inmates. She can safely say that not once in her tenure has she ever fallen to that sort of temptation.

She has recently left a steady long-term relationship. Needless to say, she is feeling emotionally compromised. Of course, feeling emotional because of the loss of a relationship is not a good enough reason to take off long-term from her job. One prisoner in particular seems empathetic to her problems. She finds herself talking to him more and more frequently. It helps, too, that this prisoner is particularly attractive. In fact, she is fairly certain that he has an almost cult-like fan following on the outside, primarily due to his looks.

Over time the prisoner starts to grow on her. She finds herself really liking him and beginning to think that maybe he doesn't totally deserve to be behind bars. One day the prisoner comes to her with a proposition: He needs several items smuggled in from the outside and in return he could provide her with certain sexual favors. The proposition is tempting, she even knows how they could get away with it. **What would you do?**

12. **The Needle Would be an Easier Way to Go**

Today was execution day. As dramatic as that sounded, it was a fairly routine procedure for the death-row unit. The tie-down team and those who were involved in the execution knew their roles and had done them so many times that they were almost muscle memory. However, there was a new member on the execution team.

Louis Morgan had witnessed a few executions as part of his training process. Until he had the opportunity to witness an execution he was firm in his conviction that the death penalty was a necessary and important part of the criminal justice system. Now he was still fairly certain he believed in that, but was not sure he could continue to be part of the execution process. It was hard to get to really get to know someone, only to kill them a few hours later.

Morgan was part of the team that was involved in transferring this particular inmate from the prison unit he was housed in to the execution unit. It would be forty-eight hours before the execution. During the transfer phase, Morgan was entrusted with the sleeping pills prescribed to the inmate. He found it kind of morbid that the bottle had more than enough pills to last through the next few weeks, let alone for tonight. The transfer was uneventful.

That night Morgan was tasked with giving the inmate his sleeping pill. As he opened the bottle outside the inmate's cell the inmate suddenly perked up. "Man, could you just . . . give me the whole bottle?"

Morgan was startled by the question, "Pardon?"

"Give me the whole bottle, c'mon man, it would be so easy, just drop the bottle and it'll just be an accident, you won't get in trouble. I don't want to die under the juice tomorrow, man."

Morgan looked down at the bottle. It wouldn't be totally his fault if he accidentally dropped the bottle and the inmate just happened to get to some before he could pick them up. He didn't really want to go through the whole execution process tomorrow. Besides the inmate was going to die anyway. **What would you do?**

13. **Probation Officer Field Visit Dilemma**

After applying for the specialized sex offender caseload position for the past two years, it was finally given to you. Your longtime best friend and family friend who works with you gave you a stellar reference which helped you in getting the desired position. The specific caseload is closely monitored by the court due to the possible threat to public safety by the probationers. It is not uncommon for probation officers to make field visits in pairs due to potential safety concerns. Any violations by these probationers could bring negative media attention and could be a liability issue for the probation department if the probation officers are negligent in monitoring the conditions of probation. It could also mean termination of employment for the officer(s) involved.

One afternoon you and your best friend make a field visit to a probationer's home. While at their home you and your best friend check the premises to ensure that there are no items in the home that are in violation of the conditions of probation. You discover that the probationer is in possession of a laptop computer. After leaving the home, the two of you discuss the violation you discovered. On the day of the office visit, one week later, you are asked to see the probationer due to your best friend being out due to illness. Upon going through the file, you discover that the violation discovered and discussed is not documented anywhere. You discuss the violation with the probationer and he informs you that he was told by his probationer to remove the laptop from the home, and not to worry about the violation, but not to let it happen again. **What do you do?**

14. **New Hire: Welcome to the Jungle!**

You have been working for the probation department for the past few years. Your best friend of more than ten years is also a probation officer working with you in the same unit. The cases assigned to your unit are a specialized caseload with very strict court orders.

It is very well understood by all probation officers that all conditions of probation must be followed precisely. If officers fail to adhere to these strict rules, they risk severe consequences including the possibility of termination.

One afternoon you are asked to see one of your best friend's probationers, due to the friend being absent because of an illness. While reviewing the file to ensure the conditions of probation are met, you discover that the probationer had not been administered a urine test for the past three months. The conditions of probation clearly state that the probationer is to be urine tested on a monthly basis. You know that this is a violation of the court's policies and procedures as well as the conditions of probation; however, you don't want to get your best friend in trouble by exposing her failure to comply with a court order. **What do you do?**

INDEX

CPSIA information can be obtained
at www.ICGtesting.com
Printed in the USA
FSOW03n0058260118
43798FS

9 781465 276063